Also by Michael Waldman

Who Runs Congress?
(fourth edition with Mark Green)

The Big Business Reader
(coeditor with Mark Green)

WHO
ROBBED
AMERICA?

·

WHO ROBBED AMERICA?

A Citizen's Guide to the S&L Scandal

•

MICHAEL WALDMAN

and the staff of

PUBLIC CITIZEN'S CONGRESS WATCH

INTRODUCTION

by Ralph Nader

RANDOM HOUSE
NEW YORK

Library of Congress Cataloging-in-Publication Data
Waldman, Michael.
Who robbed America? : a citizen's guide to the S&L scandal
by Michael Waldman.
p.   cm.
ISBN 0-679-73482-1
1. Savings and loan associations—United States—Corrupt
practices. I. Title.
HG2151.W35   1990   332.3'2'0973—dc20   90-47715

Designed by Robert Bull Design
Manufactured in the United States of America
24689753
First Edition

For my parents

—and for Liz

•

PREFACE

THIS BOOK is about crime in the suites, the consequences of deregulation, and why the American taxpayer is being stuck with a $500 billion bailout of bankrupt savings and loans.

Who Robbed America? is written by Michael Waldman, director of Public Citizen's Congress Watch, with the staff of Public Citizen. It reveals how ideological disdain of government's proper regulatory role—particularly the protection of federal financial guarantees—can undermine its essential functions and invite fraud. And it shows how business campaign contributions and lobbying skews congressional decision making. It explains the importance of public availability of information and oversight by the press to honest administration of government agencies. And it shocks us with the stories of corruption and fraud by business charlatans.

Public Citizen does more than write about the misdeeds of business and failures of government. Since our founding by Ralph Nader in 1971 we have fought for public policies that limit white-collar crime and opposed special-interest groups in the halls of government.

We have lobbied Congress for laws that would strengthen insider trading, punish price-fixing and upgrade the antitrust laws to protect competition in the marketplace.

We have asked Congress not to exempt professionals, such as doctors, lawyers and accountants, from the fraud prohibitions already in federal law. And we have opposed preemptive federal legislation overriding state laws allowing injured citizens to sue manufacturers of defective products for damages.

We have petitioned the Food and Drug Administration to ban unsafe drugs and issued reports on the failure of state medical boards to discipline doctors who engage in questionable practices. We have sued the Occupational Health and Safety Administration for not assuring that most workers have the right to know about dangerous chemicals in their workplace, and the Nuclear Regulatory Commission for permitting nuclear waste in our local garbage dumps.

Because Public Citizen is funded primarily by our members and the sale of publications, we can tell the unvarnished truth. *Who Robbed America?* does just that.

Joan Claybrook, President
Public Citizen

CONTENTS

CONTENTS

Introduction
by Ralph Nader

THIS BOOK is a call to action about the S&L scandal—the most outrageous example of banking corruption and governmental deregulatory complicity in American history.

In my time observing Washington, I have not seen such arrogant disregard from the White House, Congress and corporate world for the interests and rights of the American people. Many citizens know there is a growing gap between the rulers and the ruled. Our leaders are representing a runaway business class that funds them, not the people who elect them.

Without doubt, the most telling symbol of this wheeling and dealing run amok is the S&L scandal. It is the massive bill, handed to the taxpayers, for Reagan-era zealotry for sweeping deregulation and for a supine Congress in hock to the lobbyists and political action committees (PACs). Washington insiders have known about the S&Ls for years. "There's a lot of sleaze there," they'd say, and shake their heads—as they moved on to the next fund-raiser. Remember when our governmental leaders first let us in on the secret: did you notice that they called it the S&L "crisis" and never the *crime* and looting of the savers' monies it was and is?

The sums of money involved boggle the mind, and defy the imagination. The corruption at work is epic. A program designed to safeguard the savings of the middle class and poor was used to subsidize an unprecedented frenzy of speculation and business criminality. And the bottom line is this: those we selected to lead our democracy let it happen, turned their back on us, made us pay for it, and, astonishingly, were re-elected.

•

From the start, the politicians knew they were handling highly volcanic material. That was clear from the nervousness of congressional leaders as they rammed the first stage $157 billion bailout legislation through Congress in 1989. After years of delay, and slavish scraping to the S&L lobby, suddenly not a minute could be "wasted" to scrutinize the president's bailout plan. "We need a 'clean' bill," lawmakers repeatedly stated, as they brushed aside consumer proposals and amendments. Meanwhile, without blinking an eye, they tacked on special-interest amendment after amendment, benefiting the big banks, investment houses and S&Ls that swooped in to take advantage of the S&L crack-up.

The bipartisan wheels were greased. This 550-page bill—eventually designed to cost every man, woman, and child $5000 in principal and interest on bailout bonds—was rushed through the Senate Banking Committee unanimously in one day in April 1989 and through the whole Senate in two days of the following week. There was no chance for citizen groups to obtain or read through this huge bill for its obscure loopholes and giveaways before the vote. Pleas to Senate Majority Leader George Mitchell and Minority Leader Robert Dole to give the people a decent interval to react were brushed aside, lest a couple of weeks generate public protest.

The House Banking Committee took more time. Hovering over committee members were hordes of S&L lobbyists whose industry regularly finances many of the members' campaigns. Attempts by Representatives Charles Schumer, Joseph Kennedy, Bruce Morrison, and Chairman Henry Gonzalez to attach consumer-protection provisions, regulatory reforms, and antiredlining housing amendments were struck down in the banking committee by the industry's congressional minions. Only as the preliminary inklings of citizen outrage began to be felt were significant improvements made while the bill was considered on the floor of the House of Representatives in June 1989.

There was far more resistance in Congress to the $250 million loan guarantee to Lockheed and the $1.5 billion loan guarantee to Chrysler in the 1970s than there was to this $500 billion bailout. Congress went along with President Bush's demand (under threat of vetoing his own bill) to remove the bailout from the federal budget, so as to minimize the impact on the deficit. The bipartisan effort to hide the cost of this calamity continues apace.

•

Two central points have been absent from the S&L debate so far.

First, nothing makes citizens angrier than being required to pay for a crisis they neither benefited from nor caused. The key issue in the bailout—who pays for it—was not even debated and voted on; it was assumed it would be the taxpayer. A proposal was offered by Representatives Kennedy and Morrison that would have cut the cost of the bailout in half (by paying for it quickly, thus saving on interest costs) and would have paid for the consequences of corporate crime through corporate taxes. This amendment was ruled "out of order" in the banking committee. Then the House Rules Committee refused to let the full House vote on this amendment, though with Speaker Tom Foley's approval it allowed a vote on an amendment backed by the S&L lobby that would have weakened regulation of thrifts.

Second, what was striking about the whole process that led to the S&L bailout was the absolute absence of consumer involvement. How many consumers or taxpayers were fully aware of what was happening? The bankers had hundreds of experts and attorneys working the system. How many did consumers have? Only a few stalwart citizen groups.

The lessons of the S&L system breakdown are clear: At each

"cause-point," the opportunity for greed and thievery was exploited, and at each check-point, safeguards that would have stopped the nation's biggest bank robbery, the people were betrayed. Clearly, we need a new breed of citizen watchdog groups, and there is a simple, proven way to launch them. S&Ls, commercial banks, insurance companies and other financial institutions should be required to carry, in their regular statements or billing envelopes, a printed insert inviting their customers to join financial consumer organizations chartered by Congress and representing the public. This idea works. In Illinois, for example, a state Citizen Utility Board communicates with members through an insert in state government mailings. With some 200,000 dues-paying members, Illinois' CUB has saved rate-payers about $3 billion since 1983. If we'd had similar financial consumers associations in all fifty states, they could have saved all of us billions on S&Ls.

Consumers cannot rely on the politicians—elected officials of both parties have their fingerprints on this hot potato. Nor can we rely on the press. Readers of some regional papers, such as the *Dallas Morning-News* and the *San Francisco Chronicle*, knew early what was going on. But with the exception of the corruption probes of Brooks Jackson in the *Wall Street Journal*, the country's major national media virtually ignored the real S&L story until it was too late. They then relied heavily on "official sources" in Washington, plus a few banking industry quotables, to tell the story, ignoring the early alerts, reports, press conferences, and street demonstrations by consumer groups.

In short, we have to organize ourselves much more effectively to open up the process to taxpayer and consumer concerns.

•

Who Robbed America?: A Citizen's Guide to the S&L Scandal, if widely read, could mark a turning point in this crisis.

Only citizens who are informed and motivated in ways that name names, point out who's responsible, and outline solutions will produce the necessary and decisive political force to make changes. This report to the American people was written by Director Michael Waldman and the staff of Public Citizen's Congress Watch. It amounts to a primer for citizen mobilization. If we let the high rollers who have driven the American economy into a wall of debt and insolvency, and their protectors and allies in Washington, get away with this holdup with barely a peep, it will be a historic collapse in our two hundred year attempt to practice democracy.

Use this book as you decide how to cast your vote in this election and elections to come. Let the men and women who ask for your support know that you are fed up, and that you won't support a candidate who wants to stick you with the cost for this bailout. In the 1988 elections, over 98 percent of the members of the House of Representatives who ran were reelected. Since that election has come the S&L bailout, the HUD scandal, the congressional pay grab, nonexistent or phony-baloney campaign finance reform, the resignations under scandal of the Speaker of the House and majority whip, ethics probes of seven percent of the U.S. Senate, ballooning federal deficits, and now a significant economic downturn. Let's make sure that the reelection rate in 1990 is considerably lower than 98 percent.

When the first installment of the bailout was rushed through, the citizens were not powerful. The Bush administration is hoping to rush through another megabillion-dollar installment soon. Let's send Washington a message: *This time we're ready!*

Ralph Nader
Washington, D.C.

ONE

·

WHO ROBBED AMERICA?

•

IT WAS 1986, the height of the S&L boom, and Charles Keating, the owner of Lincoln Savings and Loan, was showing a camera crew the headquarters of his real estate and financial empire.

"How old are you now?" he asked one employee.

"Thirty-one."

"Thirty-one? Okay, you're going to be the first girl that started off as a secretary to make $100,000," Keating said boastfully in front of the camera.

In 1989, Keating's S&L failed, following what a federal judge ruled was a systematic "looting."

The total estimated cost to the taxpayers: $2.5 billion.

•

In 1983, Vernon Savings and Loan of Dallas, Texas, sent its president, Don Dixon, on a "gastronomique fantastique" tour of Europe. He and his wife ate their way through six French cities, and hired a European nobleman as an "adviser."

"You think it's easy eating in three-star restaurants twice a day six days a week?" Dixon protested to a reporter. "By the end of the week, you want to spit it [the food] out."

By the time Vernon S&L was seized by regulators in 1987, some 90 percent of its loans were in default.

Estimated cost to the taxpayers: $1.3 billion.

•

Once, S&Ls invested their money in home mortgages. Miami Florida's CenTrust had a different idea. The spendthrift thrift bought a classic painting, Reubens's *Portrait of a Man as Mars*, for $12 million. CenTrust stored the painting "temporarily" at the mansion of its owner, David Paul, supposedly until its executive offices were finished. When regulators forced the

S&L to sell the painting at an auction in 1989, it sold for $4 million less than the S&L had paid for it. CenTrust failed in 1990.

The estimated cost to the taxpayers: up to $2 billion.

•

It was, young Neil Bush had to admit later, "an incredibly sweet deal."

Bush was referring to a $100,000 "loan" given to him in 1984 by Kenneth Good, a prominent Colorado developer. The loan had a special term: If Bush lost the money, he didn't have to pay it back; if he made a profit with the money, he could keep the extra funds. Bush still hasn't paid back the funds; nor has he declared the $100,000 as income, though now he says he will.

A year after receiving the loan, Bush joined the board of Silverado Banking S&L, which voted to lend huge sums to his benefactor Kenneth Good—only to have him default on $30 million worth of loans.

Total estimated cost to taxpayers of Silverado's failure: up to $1 billion.

•

Who robbed America?

Charles Keating, Don Dixon, David Paul, and, yes, Neil Bush: we might be tempted just to laugh and shake our heads at their flagrant excess and self-enrichment. But it wasn't their money they were gambling with; it was *ours*, because we, as taxpayers, insured the deposits in their banks. The result is an unprecedented government bailout, with an estimated cost of up to $15,000 per taxpayer.

The S&L scandal is the biggest and most expensive financial debacle in American history. The numbers are incomprehensible. After insisting for years that the cost would be much lower, the federal government now admits that the crisis will cost between $300 and $500 billion over the next decade alone. That sum is greater than the Marshall Plan (which rebuilt Europe after World War II), the New York City bailout, the Lockheed bailout, the Chrysler bailout and the Continental-Illinois bailouts *combined,* even when adjusted for inflation. The S&L bailout is beginning to approach the cost of the Korean War.

One mathematician calculated that $500 billion is enough to give every person on earth ten dollars *per finger.* Unfortunately, even this staggering sum may be an underestimate. A team of economists at Stanford University has examined the numbers, and when they add together all the S&Ls expected to fail, and all the interest payments that have to be made paying off the debts, they came up with a new estimated cost: *$1.369 trillion* over forty years.

Citizens are justifiably furious about the S&L debacle. They are appalled at the waste, astounded at the criminality, and astonished by the scope of the corruption. But the details of the scandal are often more confusing than illuminating as they tumble forth. The purpose of this book is to answer some basic questions about this mess.

Who caused the collapse of the S&L industry?

How did it happen?

And *what* can we do about it?

•

The first thing to understand is that this crisis was not merely the product of adverse economic conditions, or an act of nature. Instead, it was the result of greed on an epic scale—what Al Capone called "the legitimate rackets." Bank robbers use guns and physical force. The thrift robbers saw a new method —persuading the government to enact laws that actually *allowed* them to empty the till.

The thrift robbers aren't shadowy figures, operating at the margins of society. Instead, they are some of the powerful and the wealthy, who were so celebrated in the money culture of the 1980s:

- **S&L owners and executives.** A platoon of riverboat gamblers took over many of America's savings and loans and threw the money away—or worse. There was the Beverly Hills thrift that hired nineteen Uzi-toting bodyguards to protect its chief executive officer. And then there was Texas—land of wild parties and wilder land deals. Prosecutors believe that these S&L high-flyers weren't just frivolous, they were fraudulent. At as many as six out of every ten failed S&Ls, insiders engaged in serious misconduct. And now some investigators believe that many failed S&Ls were linked through an elaborate network of fraud, involving ties to organized crime.

- **Ronald Reagan's deregulators.** The probusiness ideologues in the Reagan administration believed that letting the S&Ls gamble with taxpayer money was "the free market at work." When one official begged the White House for more enforcement personnel to combat the pervasive fraud, he was told, "The policy of the administration is to have fewer, not more, [bank] examiners."

- **A "kept" Congress.** Politicians of both parties took millions of dollars in campaign contributions and speech fees from the financial industry, and then voted to deregulate the S&Ls. Shills for the S&Ls included some of the most powerful men in Washington—from former Speaker of the House Jim Wright, who held vital legislation hostage for the benefit of a few cronies in the Texas S&L industry, to the notorious five senators who intervened for Lincoln Savings and Loan and took $1.4 million from Charles Keating. But it's not the Keating Five—its the Keating 535: the entire Congress was on the dole from the financial industry. According to a comprehensive analysis conducted for this book, all financial industry PACs together gave current members of Congress $26.8 million in campaign contributions over the past five years.

- **George Bush.** He wasn't president when the thrifts were looted, but he *is* responsible for much of the bailout cost—by insisting that it be paid for over four decades with bailout bonds instead of financing it now with taxes.
- **"Hired-gun" accountants and lawyers.** These professionals are supposed to abide by professional standards, but instead watched out for their fat fees. At one point, nearly every major accounting firm in the country was being sued by the government for negligence—or worse —in the S&L debacle.
- **Wall Street's "Masters of the Universe."** In the 1980s, Wall Street was where the action was. And aggressive investment bankers enmeshed the S&Ls into elaborate investment schemes more appropriate to Ivan Boesky than to Jimmy Stewart. Wealthy investors put billions of dollars in S&Ls, reaping extra-high interest rates and giving S&L owners taxpayer-insured money to invest. And these thrifts, in turn, poured billions of dollars into junk bonds, corporate mergers, and other financial shenanigans.
- **The press.** Our media watchdogs didn't bark while the rich plundered the S&Ls. They didn't cover it while it was happening, gave minimal coverage as the full extent of the blowout became clear, and still won't listen to anyone other than the official bureaucrats and pundits in Washington.

In short, average citizens have been had . . . by the very people who are supposed to be watching out for our best interests. Their action, or inaction, created the costs that are now mounting for every taxpayer. Our leaders failed us, an abdication as stark as any in American history.

•

How do you lose $500 billion, anyway? As important as knowing *who* robbed America is knowing *how* it was done. Where is all that money? A skeletal explanation will help to make sense of the morass of detail.

Start with the Great Depression. In 1929, the financial system crashed. Thousands of citizens waited on bank lines to withdraw their funds in a panic and lost their jobs because the banking system was unstable. President Franklin Roosevelt's New Deal introduced a new system: consumers' deposits would be insured, and in return banks would have to invest the money prudently. It was a social contract that worked well for forty-five years.

In the early 1980s, the government deregulated the S&Ls. The limits on how S&L bankers could spend other people's money were stripped away, one by one. Where S&Ls were once required to specialize in lending money for home mortgages, now they could fling their funds at anything and everything. The Wild West atmosphere was an open invitation for fraud.

Then the deregulated S&Ls took in billions of dollars in new money from depositors. Wealthy investors put their funds in S&L bank accounts, often in blocks of $100,000. The purpose was to take advantage of deposit insurance. The consequence was to give unscrupulous S&L owners a pool of money to invest. To attract this "hot money," the S&Ls had to pay high interest rates.

To pay these high interest rates, S&Ls began making increasingly risky investments. The S&Ls pumped their money into tantalizing new investments that promised a big payoff, enough to fund the higher interest rates being paid to depositors. Billions of dollars were lent to fund commercial real estate deals, such as office buildings and shopping malls, which have a high risk of failure and of not being able to pay back the loan. Savings and loans also made "direct investments," buying commercial businesses and funding them with taxpayer-insured dollars. Some bought risky junk bonds and other intricate financial instruments, which looked good on paper but which ultimately couldn't pay off. Often, the money was merely being siphoned off to fund pet projects or to ensure that S&L vice presidents could emulate the life-style of the Sultan of Brunei.

As the S&Ls' loans soured, the institutions slid toward insolvency. When a thrift's balance sheet starts showing lots of red ink, bank regulators are supposed to monitor its financial health, to make sure it doesn't edge too close to insolvency. But in the 1980s, lax enforcement and political pressure from S&Ls kept these agencies from fulfilling their mandate. With every day of delay, the cost mounted. That's because an insolvent thrift—one that doesn't really have enough money-making investments to pay its depositors—loses money each time it brings in new deposits.

When the government seizes control of a failed S&L, it must act to guarantee consumers' deposits. That's where the cost to the taxpayer comes in. When economists say "the cost of bailing out Silverado is estimated to be $1 billion," that means that the cost of paying off the depositors, minus whatever funds can be raised by selling off the thrift's assets, is $1 billion. If the property owned by the S&L is not worth very much, and it has a lot of money deposited by consumers, then the costs pile up. These government guarantees apply on all accounts up to $100,000. That means that a widow's $5,000 for retirement is protected, but so is a lawyer's $100,000 investment.

So the money went *from* taxpaying citizens *to* wealthy bankers and developers, and also to affluent depositors who reaped high interest rates and whose deposits were protected. A program designed to secure the nest eggs of middle-class families was transformed into a subsidy for the affluent and corrupt.

•

Millions of dollars in PAC gifts . . . Floating Potomac River fund-raisers, on a yacht owned by a crooked S&L . . . Top

White House aides trying to stymie strong enforcement . . . Chief regulators chosen by the industry they are supposed to oversee: The story of the S&Ls is also a story of the corruption now taken for granted in Washington.

Sadly, the politicians and officials, who are supposed to guard the public treasury, instead handed the keys to the plunderers. The scandal is bipartisan, soiling Republicans and Democrats, executive branch and legislative branch alike. The S&Ls are nothing less than a Watergate scandal for the entire government. There's no need to subpoena secret tapes; just read the *Congressional Record* and the campaign finance disclosure forms.

The reasons varied. Ronald Reagan's belief in deregulation was the core of his economic philosophy. Give the forces of unleashed business free rein, he promised, and the result would be an eruption of productive investment. But deregulation in practice meant looking the other way while private sector forces ran wild. Only two years after Ronald and Nancy Reagan returned to their ranch, the costs of deregulation are coming due. And they are larger than even his harshest critics imagined.

Congress, for its part, responded less to ideology than to the imperatives of campaign financing. The United States is the only western democracy in which legislative elections are entirely funded by private parties, mostly with an interest in legislation. The legalized bribery of PACs, large individual campaign contributions, and speech fees have created a perpetual reelection machine more responsive to contributors than to constituents. The S&L scandal is proof of just how badly Congress has lost touch with the people it is supposed to represent.

George Bush, in turn, has tried to minimize the scandal. As a result, it has grown and grown. Here's how: *Most* of the huge estimated cost of the bailout is comprised of interest payments. When Bush pushed through the first installment of the bailout in early 1989, he insisted that the measure be paid for by borrowing billions of dollars, then paying interest on special bailout bonds for forty years. Bush hoped that by pushing the cost onto our children and grandchildren, no one would notice. Congress went along. Of course, the public *did* notice.

Under Bush's tenure, it is becoming clear that there are really two S&L debacles. The first was the industry's collapse itself. But the second is the botched bailout, and the Bush administration's anemic effort to catch the crooks and recover the funds. To date, federal prosecutions have recovered less than one percent of the lost taxpayer funds conservatively attributable to fraud. And, incredibly, the administration is backing an effort by the accounting industry—deeply implicated in the S&L scandal—to *weaken* the civil racketeering laws.

In short, the savings and loan crisis has exposed deep fissures in the fabric of American democracy.

•

Unlike previous governmental scandals, the S&L mess is having a seismic impact on the entire economy. President Bush, of course, has revoked his "no new taxes" pledge, saying the revenues are needed for the S&L bailout. Borrowing for bailout bonds has helped nudge interest rates higher. That, combined with sharp cutbacks in lending by overextended banks and S&Ls, began to push the United States into a recession—even before Saddam Hussein loosed his terror on the Persian Gulf. As real estate values plummet, even previously healthy financial institutions are sliding toward insolvency. At present, 2,505 savings and loans are left standing, down from 4,732 a little more than a decade ago. And the colossal cost of the bailout may have erased any possible "peace dividend" from the end of the Cold War.

In June 1990 Treasury Secretary Nicholas Brady announced a new, more expensive phase of the crisis. The bailout would need another $70 billion to $130 billion by the end of 1990, or thrift rescues would have to come to a halt. This disclosure led to a burst of sudden public awareness that the problem hadn't been solved, as promised—it was getting worse.

This avalanche of bad news has shaken the American public into anger. "We have more will than wallet," said President Bush when he was inaugurated. Sure enough, when worthy programs are proposed—from education and child care to the environment and repairing roads and bridges—Washington declares that there just isn't enough money. But when it came to cleaning up after the hogs of the S&L industry, it seemed there was barely any discussion.

Similarly, many people feel that if they make a mistake on their taxes, the IRS will be after them; but our chief law enforcers say with a shrug that there's no way to recover the hundreds of billions of dollars in lost S&L funds.

In its final section, this book challenges the conventional assumption that nothing can be done. In fact, a populist agenda of reforms can greatly ease the pinch. *Simply put, average citizens do not have to pay for the S&L bailout.* Why should working Americans willingly fork over $5,000 each to pay for the bailout, when they didn't cause it and didn't benefit from it? A menu of solutions exists that would pay for the bailout more fairly, recover more money from the crooks, and ensure that this fiasco never happens again.

Underlying this citizen's guide is the thesis that the people who brought us the S&L debacle can and should be held accountable. At the end is an appendix—"Taking Names and Kicking Behinds"—that will enable you to find out how your senators and representatives stood on key S&L votes over the past decade. It also reveals, for the first time, the amount of money your representatives received from PACs associated with the financial industry overall. *Who Robbed America?* is a shopper's guide in this political season.

TWO

·

THE GREAT S&L SWINDLE

•

IT'S A LONG WAY from *It's a Wonderful Life* to the swindlers and con artists of today's S&L scandal. What happened?

The story of the S&L scandal is a saga of a worthy industry and a good government program gone haywire. Savings and loans were designed to provide capital for home ownership. To encourage that, and to guarantee the safety of the banking system, the government insured consumers' deposits. But in the late 1970s and early 1980s, officials in Washington deregulated the S&L industry. A remarkable collection of swindlers, con artists, and high rollers took over many thrifts, and proceeded to run them into the ground.

When regulators tried to crack down, in the mid-1980s, powerful political forces blocked them—first Ronald Reagan's free-market aides in the White House, and then thrift allies on Capitol Hill. As the industry's problems grew and grew, a bipartisan conspiracy of silence in Washington prevented timely action. It would have been one thing if these buccaneer bankers were wheeling and dealing with their own money, but they were using taxpayer-insured dollars. The ultimate result: an unprecedented taxpayer bailout.

But let's begin at the beginning.

WHAT IS AN S&L?

What are S&Ls? Why do they exist? And why are taxpayers backing their deposits?

For most of this century the answer was fairly simple: *A savings and loan association is a financial institution that specializes in offering home mortgages.* Thrifts were originally small-scale institutions, usually formed by members of a neighborhood for the purpose of pooling together savings and building residential housing. The first thrift—they were then known as "building and loan associations"—was founded as a neighborhood club in Frankford, Pennsylvania in 1831. By 1900, 5,356 had been established. In the early 1920s, the president of the U.S. League of Savings Institutions said: "[We] are serving just two classes of customers: receiving the savings of thrifty and far-seeing people, and loaning these funds to members who wish to buy a home." That same year, an industry newspaper editorialized that "thrift breeds virility. It strikes at sensuality, self-indulgence, flabbiness. It teaches the heroism of self-denial, temperance, abstemiousness, and simple living. It is the way to success and independence."

To the naked eye, many S&Ls look just like commercial banks. Like banks, S&Ls accept deposits, maintain savings accounts, and make loans. But unlike banks, thrifts historically relied almost entirely on savings deposits, and made primarily long-term loans for home construction and purchase. In contrast with large commercial banks, operating out of skyscrapers in large cities and distant from the concerns of working people, S&Ls were grass-roots banking—a frugal way to save and to provide homeownership for the average citizen. That is why they are known commonly as "thrifts."

In keeping with this community ethos, depositors themselves owned these S&Ls, through a form of ownership known as a "mutual association." This ensured that the thrift would act in the interests of the community, since only hometown citizens with their deposits in the institution owned it.

The enduring image of the S&L comes to us from the classic Frank Capra movie, *It's a Wonderful Life.* In it, George Bailey, played by Jimmy Stewart, stops a depression-era run on his building and loan by appealing to his neighbors' sense of community. "You're thinking of this place all wrong, as if I had the money back in a safe," he tells a group of depositors. "The money's not here. Why, your money's in Joe's house. And in the Kennedy house and Mrs. Maitland's house. And a hundred others. You're lending them the money to build and they're going to pay it back to you as best they can. What are you going to do, foreclose on them?" Warning that the local bank, owned by Mr. Potter, would try to take over the thrift, Bailey concludes, "If Potter gets a hold of this building and loan there will never be another decent house built in this town!"

But then came the Great Depression—and not every thrift had the benefit of Jimmy Stewart's "aw shucks" persuasiveness to stop bank runs. The financial system was inherently unstable. Savings and loans, like other banks, were prone to panics as depositors withdrew their money en masse at the first sign of instability. If a bank or S&L failed, any depositor not lucky enough to get his or her money out lost everything. During the Roaring Twenties speculation reached a fever as bankers sucked in deposits with high interest rates and gambled away the funds on risky or fraudulent investments. Wall Street was consumed by mergers and acquisitions, many of which went bust; bankers made risky loans to land-rich South Americans. In 1929 the bubble burst. During the Great Depression, many S&Ls failed, as nearly one quarter of the nation's home mortgages were in default. Between 1930 and 1935, almost a thousand thrifts crashed, losing nearly $300 million in assets. Because home loans were less risky than the commercial loans made by banks, the depression hit S&Ls somewhat less hard than banks.

The biggest wave of bank and S&L failures came in the early months of 1933, as an anxious nation waited for Franklin Delano Roosevelt to be sworn in as president. By the time of Inauguration Day, bank runs caused a full-fledged panic as people withdrew their funds. When FDR memorably declared that "the only thing we have to fear is fear itself," he was urging calm in the face of bank panics. He immediately closed the nation's commercial banks and S&Ls, and Congress began work on legislation to shore up the financial system.

Thus began the modern system of federal bank regulation, which stopped the cycle of financial boom and crash. *Deposit insurance* was by far the most important reform.

Commercial banks were given deposit insurance first, in 1933. From then on, the deposits of bank customers were guaranteed through the Federal Deposit Insurance Corporation (FDIC). In conjunction with this, banks were heavily regulated, and were restricted from making risky investments (such as playing the stock market). Ironically, President Roosevelt at first resisted deposit insurance, arguing at his first press conference, "We do not wish to make the United States government liable for the mistakes and errors of individual banks, and put a premium on unsound banking in the future." But as prominent historian, Kenneth Davis, later wrote, "Of all New Deal reform legislation, this was the most resoundingly and unqualifiedly successful, measured in terms of its specific purpose." Conservative economist Milton Friedman reports that commercial bank failures numbered in the triple digits from 1921 to 1933, in the double digits from 1934 to 1942, and in the single digits from 1943 to 1960.

Congress extended deposit insurance and federal regulation to the S&Ls in 1934, shortly after the protections were created for commercial banks. The newly created Federal Savings and Loan Insurance Corporation (FSLIC) insured deposits up to $5,000. If a thrift failed, consumers knew that FSLIC would pay them for the amount they had on deposit, as long as it was below the $5,000 ceiling.

Along with deposit insurance came a necessary corollary: *regulation*. In 1934, Congress created the Federal Home Loan Bank Board (FHLBB) to keep the S&Ls safe and sound. The FHLBB coordinated the activities of twelve regional Home Loan Banks, which gave thrifts loans to assure their smooth and efficient operation. Savings and loans could be chartered either by the federal government, or by states, but in either case federal funds backed up their deposits.

The plan amounted to a social contract between the citizenry and the bankers. Banks and S&Ls were given access to a stable, steady supply of money to invest. Small savers, in return for a somewhat lower interest rate than preregulation, knew that their nest eggs were secure. The thrifts and commercial banks paid money annually to help support the federal insurance funds. If everybody did their job right, that fund would be enough to cover any losses in the thrift industry.

The New Deal protections for S&Ls made good social policy sense and good economic sense. Housing has always been the core of the American dream, and S&Ls promoted homeownership for the middle class. Otherwise, why have separate S&Ls? From the Homestead Acts in the 1800s to the GI Bill in the 1940s, the government has sought to give every citizen a chance to own his or her own home. The federal government also took steps to guarantee that S&Ls would use the money from insured deposits on home lending. It prohibited thrifts from offering nonmortgage loans, and set strict limits on how far away from the home office those loans could be made. In return, Congress kept the thrifts free from the ceilings on savings account interest rates that it had imposed on banks, so that S&Ls could attract the deposits necessary to foster homebuilding. It also prohibited them from offering some services—like checking accounts—that banks could offer.

Over the years, S&Ls developed an unusually cozy relationship with the regulators who were supposed to be watching over them. In fact, the S&Ls were put in charge of their own regulation. The twelve Home Loan Banks were actually *owned* by the thrifts themselves, even though they took the form of an arm of the government. In practice, nearly all the board members of these regulatory banks were thrift executives or people with close ties to the S&L industry, with no allegiance or obligation to the taxpayer. Policymakers in Washington considered regulation of the S&Ls to be less important than the "main event" in financial regulation—the commercial banks and securities houses on Wall Street.

Still, for forty years, the system worked. Thrifts made mostly home loans. In 1977, according to economist Dan Brumbaugh, federally insured S&Ls had about 67 percent of their assets in home mortgages. Industry wits joked that S&Ls

operated on the 3-6-3 system: pay interest to depositors at 3 percent, lend at 6 percent and tee off on the golf course by 3 in the afternoon. There were problems, to be sure. During the 1960s, some S&Ls paid extra-high interest rates and made reckless land investments; in 1967, Congress slapped on "Regulation Q," which capped the interest S&Ls could pay, but kept it slightly higher than the interest commercial banks could pay. By doing so, the government was trying to keep S&Ls in line and to guarantee plentiful funds for housing mortgages. As other methods for financing housing grew (such as government-backed loans and mortgage companies), the rationale for a separate S&L industry shrank. Still, 4,732 S&Ls remained in business in 1979, and they financed nearly 80 percent of the home mortgages in the United States.

At the turn of the decade, in 1980, the sleepy S&Ls were primed for policies that would transform them from a mainstay of the housing market into a casino for wild speculation. How this happened is the story of deregulation.

DEREGULATION REMAKES THE S&LS

"All in all, I think we've hit the jackpot," declared President Ronald Reagan as he signed the big S&L deregulation bill on October 15, 1982. Gathered before him on the White House lawn were the administration officials, bankers, lobbyists, and members of Congress who had pushed for the change. The Great Communicator's casino imagery was apt. For the sweeping series of legislative and regulatory changes would allow the S&Ls to gamble away billions of taxpayer dollars.

Washington let go of the S&L reins at a time when deregulation was the watchword in Washington. In the 1960s and early 1970s, Congress enacted new consumer and environmental protections. Then business fought back. Corporate and banking lobbyists of every pinstripe flocked to the capital, all clamoring for deregulation of *their* industry in the name of "fighting red tape" or "getting government off our backs." Underlying all of these changes—in antitrust, environmental protection, food safety—was the idea that the free market, unfettered by government, could cure economic ills. Ronald Reagan, the new president, shared their agenda. "Government isn't the solution," he declared in his 1981 inaugural address. "Government is the problem."

One of the pillars of Reagan's regulatory policy was to cut loose the financial industry. So it wasn't only the S&Ls who were deregulated. Commercial banks were allowed to merge and expand across state lines. Eventually, regulators let many banks open securities offices to trade stock. Antitrust and securities laws went unenforced, letting Wall Street launch a wave of unprecedented corporate mergers and hostile takeovers. In addition, a group of entirely new financial institutions encroached on the traditional territory of the banks and S&Ls. Known as "nonbank banks," they offered a range of financial services without being subject to the protections governing banks and thrifts. A customer at Sears in 1982, for example, could shop for insurance (from Allstate), buy a house (from the largest real estate firm, Coldwell Banker), obtain a credit card (Discover), get a loan (Sears Financial), trade stock (Dean Witter), and even open a savings account (Greenwood Savings). The government did relatively little to regulate these new giants.

Of all the deregulated financial industries, the S&Ls most successfully slipped their harness. Deregulation took place in four steps. First, ownership rules were dramatically altered. Second, caps on interest rates were lifted. Third, deposit insurance was expanded. Finally, S&Ls were allowed to shift away from home mortgage investments.

Deregulation, Stage I: New owners

The seeds of disaster were first planted back in the mid-1970s, before governmentwide deregulation was in vogue. Recall that before deregulation, S&Ls were mostly mutuals—that is, they were *owned by the depositors themselves.* New federal rules instituted in 1974 changed that. Now speculators could transform S&Ls into stock corporations, giving them the same ownership structure as a huge company such as General Motors or AT&T. This would allow S&Ls to raise more money by selling stock to investors. But distant shareholders care much less about the details of a business than do local depositors. The move inevitably helped transform them from institutions interested in developing a local community, into a business concerned only with making a profit. Ominously, this was done in a way that shortchanged consumers and enriched business insiders. Depositors, as "owners" of the S&L, should have been given stock in the newly constituted institutions. Instead, federal bank regulators let S&L operators give depositors merely a first option to buy stock. The bank executives themselves often made a killing as they took advantage of inside knowledge to buy control of their institutions.

Then, in 1982, regulators completed the transformation. Federal rules had required that S&Ls be owned by at least 400 shareholders, with no one person owning more than 25 percent. Now S&Ls could be owned by *just one person.* The rationale was to infuse new capital into the S&L industry. This created an easy route for a real estate developer or some other entrepreneur looking for a cozy relationship with a lender: buy one.

Deregulation, Stage II: Letting interest rates rise

Looking back on the mess that the S&Ls became, some people argue that the industry's problems stemmed from the inflation of the 1970s. Not exactly. In fact, the real trouble began with the government's *reaction* to the inflation of the 1970s: jerking up interest rates in an effort to cool overheated prices. Even after inflation eased in the 1980s, policymakers kept interest rates artificially high, forcing S&Ls to seek ever-greater returns on their investments or lose customers to money market funds.

The high-interest policy was launched by the Federal Reserve Board (known as the Fed). In October 1979, in a surprise announcement, the Fed abruptly hiked interest rates, slamming the brakes on the economy and starting a recession that lasted, with some interruptions, for four years. By 1980, some banks were paying out interest rates of 20 percent. Then came Ronald Reagan's 1981 tax cuts, which ballooned the federal deficit. When the government runs in the red, it gets money by borrowing from private sources, which raises interest rates even further. For the next decade—the 1980s—interest rates stayed high. Even during the 1982–1983 recession, writes conservative commentator Kevin Phillips, "interest rates persisted in the 10–15 percent *nominal* range and a 3–8 percent *real* range, despite falling inflation, because of financial-market and Federal Reserve fears of what a string of $200 billion deficits might mean." In all, real interest rates (that is, the amount that interest rates exceed inflation) were the highest of *this century.*

High interest rates hit the S&Ls with the force of a hammer blow. Since thrifts were limited in the amount of interest they could pay to depositors, customers began shifting their accounts to other financial instruments that paid higher rates, such as money market funds.* At the same time, big banks and other financial institutions were being allowed to create new investment opportunities, such as "Now accounts" (checking accounts that paid interest if the depositor keeps enough money in the account).

So in 1980, Congress enacted legislation phasing out controls on interest rates thrifts and banks could charge. (The bill was known as Depository Institutions Deregulation and Monetary Control Act—DIDMC, or "Diddymac.") In effect, this repealed "Regulation Q," which had been enacted fourteen years before. The S&Ls could now pay higher interest rates, to

---

* The financial term for this is "disintermediation."

reattract the depositors' funds that had been flowing to other investments.

It's worth pausing for a moment to consider the impact of these high interest rates. High interest rates don't affect everyone equally. If you are a "net creditor"—that is, if you have more money invested and paying you interest than you owe to banks or other lenders—high interest rates benefit you. If, on the other hand, you are a "net debtor"—if you owe more, in student loans, house payments, or credit card interest than you have in your bank account—then high interest rates hurt you. Most Americans, by far, are net debtors. That means that the high interest rates charged by S&Ls and other institutions during the 1980s helped those who had money deposited, but hurt those who wanted to borrow money. In short, not everybody benefited from the brave new world of high interest rates.

Deregulation, Stage III: Insuring larger deposits

When Congress took the lid off interest rates in the 1980 deregulation law, it also increased the amount of insurance for each deposit. Up until then, the insurance fund (FSLIC) covered accounts up to $40,000. The Senate version of the legislation raised the cap to $50,000; the House bill did nothing. But late at night, senators and representatives meeting to iron out their differences broke off their session, and retreated to a back room. They emerged with a "compromise": the cap would be raised to $100,000. According to eyewitnesses, lobbyists from the U.S. League of Savings Institutions pressed lawmakers for the change. Within the secret congressional meeting, Representative Fernand St Germain (D–RI), a powerful banking committee member, insisted on the higher level. "I begged, literally begged, Senators Bill Proxmire and Jake Garn to hold the figure down to $75,000, which would have kept it in line with inflation," Irvine Sprague, then the chairman of the fund insuring bank deposits, told the *Washington Post.*

This little-noticed provision ultimately had monumental

consequences for the S&Ls. For better or worse, this change more than doubled the volume of funds potentially at the disposal of the thrifts—and the amount taxpayers would have to pay if the thrifts failed.

Deregulation, Stage IV: Allowing risky investments

After 1980, S&Ls now attracted more depositor money because they could now pay higher interest rates, and because more of the funds were federally insured. But this put a devastating new squeeze on the thrifts. To pay stratospheric interest rates, they needed to reap big profits from their investments. But the fifteen- and thirty-year home mortgages had been made during a period of lower interest rates, and they weren't providing enough money. This was known as the "negative spread": with each dollar the S&Ls took in, they lost money. (In Texas, S&L operators explained this through an "Aggie" joke: An Aggie opened a gas station, bought gas at $1 a gallon, and sold it at 95 cents. "Aren't you losing money with each sale?" he was asked. "Yep, but I hope to make it up in volume.") As the economy worsened, many people defaulted on their home mortgages, further squeezing the thrifts.

As the economy suffered under the 1982 recession, hundreds of S&Ls edged toward bankruptcy as they struggled to pay the new higher interest rates. The industry pressed Congress for further deregulation. Now it wanted Washington to decontrol the types of investments thrifts could make, so S&Ls could earn more money, and faster.

Journalist Ronnie Dugger, writing in the *Texas Observer*, puts it well:

> Probably, the S&Ls should have drawn back in 1980, serviced their mortgages, and bided their time, letting the high-interest deposits go to those who could pay the cost of attracting them. That would have been the conservative, laissez-faire solution. Perhaps, beyond that, the government should have subsidized conservative S&Ls and prospective home-buyers to help them through the interest rate binge which the government, after all,

had authorized. But what Washington did was gamble with the federal credit by inviting the S&Ls to gamble with federally insured deposits.

If the Congress had decided to act then, and shut down insolvent thrifts or give them money to tide them through tough times, it would have cost the government billions of dollars, though not nearly as large a sum as today's bailout does. But instead of acting in 1982, policymakers decided to deregulate the industry.

Under prodding from the thrifts, President Reagan and the Congress decided to enact the most radical banking law in fifty years. The plan, supported by Treasury Secretary Donald Regan and introduced by Republican Senator Jake Garn of Utah, chair of the Senate Banking Committee, and Democratic Representative Fernand St Germain, chair of the House Banking Committee, broadly deregulated federally chartered S&Ls.

Amazing as it may seem now, "Garn–St Germain" attracted the lobbying of competing trade associations, but little substantive debate in Congress. As the Senate voted on the legislation, the bill's sponsors pointed to industry support. "When the process [of writing the bill] started, most of the various trade organizations involved were in vastly different positions, poles apart," said Senator Garn as he began his defense of the bill. He added, "I am pleased that these groups have been willing and able to work together, to give up some of their own self-interest, in order to achieve something for the common good." Nearly all the amendments involved one financial industry pushing for advantage over another. Rebutting one such amendment, Senator Donald Riegle (D–MI) said, "There are important provisions in this bill for the S&L industry, for commercial banks, and for others." Senator John Tower, a powerful member of the banking committee, rose to praise the deregulation of Texas's thrifts, which preceded federal legislation and served as a model. Not a single lawmaker stood up to say, "Wait a minute, here, folks. This is a big gamble we're taking. These investments are risky. What if these S&Ls fail?" Congress instead preferred to listen to the reassurances of S&L and banking lobbyists.

In particular, Garn–St Germain greatly expanded the types of investments federally chartered, federally insured S&Ls could make.

- Federally chartered S&Ls could now have up to 40 percent of their assets in nonresidential real estate loans (such as office towers or shopping malls).
- Instead of shutting down insolvent thrifts, regulators would offer them "net worth certificates" equal to the amount they were insolvent. These certificates were simply pieces of paper, but the government would treat them as if they were money. With a regulatory "abracadabra," sick S&Ls were deemed to be healthy. Many of them would stagger along, only to collapse later in the decade. The act went so far as to *prohibit* the bank board from requiring that institutions receiving a net worth certificate change management or merge with a healthy thrift!
- Thrifts could now lend up to 15 percent of their *entire* capital to one borrower.

The Reagan administration's regulators went even further in a series of new rules issued in 1982 and 1983.

- S&L owners would now have to put up less of their own money. Previously, thrifts, like commercial banks, had to have 3 percent of their net worth in capital. Now, in effect, they would only have to have 1 percent. That means an S&L owner would only have to put up one dollar of his or her own money in order to lend out one hundred dollars.
- Regulators gave S&Ls a variety of accounting tricks to meet even this flimsy standard. Most outrageously, the regulators let the bankers count "goodwill" as capital. Lots of businesses rely on goodwill—a good name in the community,

customer relations, a loyal clientele. But banks should have a certain amount of real money on hand before they begin making loans. In the topsy-turvy world of deregulated banking, some S&Ls were allowed to rely for their capital *entirely* on goodwill, which doesn't actually exist. That meant these S&Ls could lend out millions of dollars even though they had no assets that could be resold to pay off depositors in an emergency.

· Buyers could start an S&L or buy one without actually paying a cent. "Noncash assets," such as land, were now all that was needed. This let real estate developers turn unwanted parcels of property into a spanking new thrift.

· S&Ls would now be allowed to offer 100-percent financing to borrowers. That means a businessperson could get a loan for a precarious project without investing any of his or her own money.

· Previously, loans had to be made in the vicinity of the home office, where loan officers would know the applicant and the feasibility of the project. Now the money could be loaned out anywhere. An S&L in Denver, Colorado, could loan money to developers in Miami, Florida, to build a new shopping mall.

· Thrifts could now be owned by commercial firms (ranging from real estate developers to multinational corporations such as Sears). This broke a long-standing rule of American banking law, which seeks to separate "banking" and "commerce" and keeps lenders from being able to acquire their borrowers.

Deregulation, Stage V: The states pass "me-too" laws

The deregulators in the states made the policymakers in Washington look like fuddy-duddies. Under a quirk of banking law, S&Ls could be chartered and largely regulated by state governments—but have their deposits backed up by federal deposit insurance. States knew that their spree at the gambling table was underwritten by their rich Uncle Sam in Washington. So several states, especially Sunbelt states such as Texas, California, Colorado and Arizona, passed broad deregulation bills both before and after Garn–St Germain was enacted.

Under California's law, which took effect in 1983, S&Ls could invest 100 percent of their net worth—every dollar—in risky commercial real estate loans. Federally chartered thrifts were limited to 40 percent. The California deregulation bill, introduced by Republican Assemblyman Pat Nolan, passed with only one dissenting vote after heavy lobbying by the California League of Savings. According to Stephen Pizzo, Mary Fricker, and Paul Muolo in *Inside Job*, California officials pushed for the change partly because the state banking office was funded by fees from S&Ls, and the thrifts would switch to federal charters if the state didn't deregulate. They add, "A former federal regulator said state politicians were also concerned they would lose contributions if state chartered thrifts switched to federal charters."

Texas's law, like California's, let state-chartered thrifts make unlimited amounts of loans "secured" by office towers, shopping malls, and other nonresidential real estate. (A loan is "secured" when the lender has a legally enforceable right to seize the property.) And while federally chartered institutions could invest 10 percent of their assets in *unsecured* commercial real estate loans, Texas-chartered thrifts could make such loans in unlimited amounts. That meant loans with no collateral.

•

All in all, deregulation completely transformed the laws under which S&Ls would operate. The "race to the bottom" between states and the federal government left taxpayers unprotected against the risks of reckless banking. Seven decades ago, Supreme Court Justice Louis Brandeis warned of the dangers when bankers are allowed to speculate with "other people's money." This "moral hazard"—when the person taking the risks won't have to pay the price for failure—is exacerbated by federal deposit insurance. The S&L bankers could now run wild—while taxpayers guaranteed most of the potential losses. And run wild they did, as we were soon to find out.

THE LOOTING OF THE S&LS

In the 1930s, famed felon Willie Sutton was asked why he robbed banks. "That's where the money is," he supposedly replied. In the 1980s, S&Ls were where the money was—huge pools of cash, largely unregulated and happily ladled out by thrift managers anxious to make exotic new investments. Few guidelines existed, including even the most rudimentary conflict-of-interest rules. "Thrifts," in Jesse Jackson's words, "became spendthrifts."

Not surprisingly, thrifts lurched away from their housing mission. In 1977, S&Ls held in their portfolios nearly half the outstanding residential mortgages in the country, but ten years later they held only 27 percent of the country's residential mortgages. In 1981, FSLIC institutions had 64.7 percent of their assets in home mortgages, but only 38.1 percent in 1986. While in 1981, these S&Ls invested $68.3 billion of their assets in commercial and consumer loans, commercial real estate mortgages, and ownership of other businesses, by 1986 they had $231 billion in those ventures.

As you read about the land deals and the phony investments, the limousines and Learjets, remember: this was all done with taxpayer-insured money. There was little chance that any of the businesses involved would lose their shirts. As thrift executives joked at the time, it was heads the S&Ls win, tails the taxpayers lose.

Where the money came from

The first noticeable change in the industry was its very clientele. Thrifts were once the little people's bank, but now, increasingly, they were attracting deposits from the rich. The new, higher interest rates lured wealthier depositors, who would never before have thought to put their money in an S&L. Now people with cash to invest could put their money into a thrift and receive a high interest rate, without facing any risk of loss. Unlike mutual funds or real estate syndicates, however, this speculative boom was underwritten by the federal government.

A big reason for the influx of wealthy money was a phenomenon called "brokered deposits," which was authorized by regulators for S&Ls starting in 1980. With their newly expanded deposit insurance, thrifts were now offering certificates of deposit (CDs) in $100,000 denominations, known as "jumbo CDs." Big investment banks on Wall Street would assemble bundles of money from well-heeled investors. This "hot money" would then be deposited in whichever S&L offered the highest interest rate, all of it federally insured. At stock brokerages such as Merrill Lynch—where future Treasury Secretary Donald Regan was known as the "father of brokered deposits"—red-suspendered, yellow-tied young men on the make phoned around the country, electronically shifting the funds under their control first to one thrift, then to another. Deposit brokers didn't care much whether the S&L was well run or making wise investments; all that mattered was the interest rate, and the fee that came from successfully placing a deposit.

Here's how it would work. Say a group of ten dentists from the Upper East Side of Manhattan want to invest their money. They call on their investment adviser. They could get a pretty good return through a tax shelter in horse breeding, he tells them. But if they put their money in Jumbo CDs, the interest rates are just as high—and there's *no risk*. So each dentist puts in $500,000, for a total of $5 million. After the dentists leave, the broker begins dialing for dollars. A one-year CD will pay 10 percent at one Arizona thrift, he's told. Too low. Then he calls a small S&L in a shopping center in California: 11 percent. Better. Then a third call, this one to a booming S&L in Dallas. *Bingo!* This one pays 13 percent. True, the thrift didn't have much of a track record, but it was paying well, and besides . . . the money is federally insured. With a flick of a computer keyboard, $1 million in $100,000 accounts are transferred to the S&L. The process is repeated, with four more S&Ls. Then it's off to the squash club for lunch.

Using jumbo CDs, ambitious thrifts in the Southwest and elsewhere sucked in funds from all over the country, especially from wealthy enclaves on the Atlantic and Pacific coasts. With alarming rapidity, the new funds flooding into S&Ls came not from homeowners but from the wealthy. Some of the money, including funds drawn from deposit brokers, were those of insurance companies, municipal pension funds, and unions. Savings and loans that subsequently failed depended more heavily on brokered deposits than did other thrifts. In 1989, Sheshunoff Information Services, Inc., a consulting company based in Texas, found about one hundred floundering thrifts that had at least one fifth of their funds from broker deposits, some much more.

The story of Lincoln Savings and Loan, a controversial thrift based in Irvine, California, shows how anemic institutions bulked up through a diet of hot money. In the first six months after a new owner, Charles Keating, Jr., took over Lincoln, Merrill Lynch put $200 million into the S&L. Later, Dean Witter Reynolds became Lincoln's main source of brokered deposits. Dean Witter channeled $671 million to Lincoln (earning the brokerage firm a fee of 2.86 percent, plus interest). Half the money on deposit at Lincoln came from brokers.

Money magazine advice columnists explicitly spelled out the equation. In 1986, the magazine advised its affluent readers, "Some experts . . . worry that some of today's high-paying Oil Patch banks could be tomorrow's candidates for insolvency if oil prices keep falling. But even if you assume the worst, should you still consider sending your money on for the extra interest? The answer is yes if you stick to federally insured accounts up to $100,000, including the interest income you are earning, and brace yourself for certain minor inconveniences." (Those "inconveniences" refer to the delays when the S&L fails, and taxpayers have to pay for its insolvency.) *Washington Monthly* editor James Bennet, who unearthed the columns, commented "One minor inconvenience for a *Money* reader, one giant disaster for American taxpayers."

With each new dollar deposited in an insolvent S&L, the cost of an eventual bailout rises a dollar. So, as we ponder the question "Where did the money go?" one big answer is: higher interest rates, paid to attract the deposits of wealthy individuals living far from these former neighborhood thrifts.

Where the money went

This new source of money lured a new breed of banker. Throughout the Sunbelt, where land values were rising due to inflating oil prices, S&Ls were taken over by real estate developers and other swashbuckling entrepreneurs. Gray flannel suits were out; cowboy boots and diamond studded belt buckles were in. Before, thrifts were stodgy and set in their ways. Now, lending standards were brushed aside, and there were exciting investments to make.

Nowhere was the change more evident than in Texas. By 1987, half of the thrifts that had failed in Texas were run by people who entered the business after 1979, and 80 percent of them came from the real estate industry. It became clear that for a gung-ho real estate developer, the best way to get a loan was to buy a thrift. Their bravado was fueled by the belief that the Texas economy, surging at the crest of increased oil prices, would never again hit hard times. The S&Ls' statehouse lobbyist defended the fleets of private airplanes owned by thrifts and their executives at Dallas airports. He told *Business Week,* "That's not criminal. That's Texas."

There was Stanley Adams, chief executive officer of Lamar Savings of Austin, Texas. In 1985, he applied to open a branch office . . . *on the moon.* Within two years, his thrift had collapsed in a pile of bad debt and questionable transactions. In early 1990, he ran unsuccessfully for governor of Texas, stating his occupation as "alleged white-collar racketeer."

And there was Don Dixon, whose Vernon Savings and Loan grew in deposits from $82.6 million in 1982 to $1.3 billion in 1986. Much of the money, it turned out, was in loans to a network of corporations all owned or controlled by Vernon. Dixon lived the high life. On his notorious "gastronomique fantastique" tour, he hired a dissolute European nobleman as a "guide" to the ways of the elite. All told, according to federal regulators, Vernon charged at least $12 million in personal perks as business expenses, including five airplanes and a helicopter. Prostitutes were allegedly presented to clients as if they were business cards.

Then there was Edward "Fast Eddie" McBirney, owner of Sunbelt Savings at age twenty-nine, a Texas version of *The Great Gatsby.* Known as "Gunbelt" because of its shoot-from-the-hip lending policies, McBirney's Sunbelt Savings grew from a sleepy $90 million institution to a $3.2 billion financial conglomerate in 4 years. The thrift owned real estate in several states, had a telemarketing firm to peddle loans to other S&Ls, and invested in hundreds of risky office buildings, shopping centers, and a hotel. Millions of dollars were tossed at shady or unexamined real estate deals. Witnesses recall seeing McBirney at parties, waving a blank contract. "Anybody want to borrow $100,000?" he would bellow. "We can make a deal right on the spot." In one particularly whimsical transaction, Sunbelt financed the purchase of more than eighty Rolls-Royces from the Bhagwan Shree Rajneesh, an Indian guru living in Oregon, in the hopes of selling them to Texas millionaires.

"Fast Eddie" was famous for hosting opulent theme parties at his mansion, paid for by Sunbelt (and orchestrated, for a fee, by his wife). At a 1984 Halloween bash, the McBirneys served broiled antelope, lion, and pheasant, accompanied by fog machines and a live performance by the disco group Two Tons of Fun. The next year, the theme was the jungle: guests strolled through the back yard, snacked on water buffalo ribs, and watched a magician make a live elephant vanish. At Christmas, revelers found themselves transported to a Russian winter, with serving staff costumed as serfs and a bear roaming the premises.

If there was one thing Texas developers and thrift owners lusted after more than parties or prostitutes, it was deals, deals, deals. At Jason's restaurant in North Dallas, the manager spread brown butcher paper on the tables so that wheeler dealers wouldn't scribble bargains on the tablecloths. "A rolling loan gathers no loss," they would joke, as they passed obligations from one to the other. "A loan repaid is money lost forever!" With little forethought, S&L executives impulsively bought K-Mart property at Tiffany's prices. At night, the high-flyers would gather at a private nightclub called the Rio Room. Wrote reporter Byron Harris: "One evening a guest, exuberant from a big deal he had signed earlier in the day and impaired by the cocktails he had been drinking since noon, proceeded to the parking lot, where he kicked in the door of a Rolls-Royce, just for fun."

These Wild West transactions were driven by the desire for "front-end fees." These payments—such as a fee to the lender and a percentage of a loan ("points")—were paid to the S&L as soon as the deal was consummated, whether the project flopped or paid off. Also, big loans to developers show up as big assets when a regulator scrutinizes a S&L's financial records. (After all, the thrift's financial records don't indicate, WARNING: THIS PROJECT IS REALLY A DUD.) *And the bigger the assets, the more "successful" the S&L—thus the more lavish the salaries, dividends and perks.* By the time it becomes clear that the deal was a disaster, the banker has been living off the "profit" for years.

Creativity became the name of the game. Here are some of the tricks of the trade:

"Land flips." This was one of the most common, and most pernicious, ways for S&L owners to make a quick profit and fatten their balance sheets. In a land flip, one parcel of land is sold back and forth among business executives, each time for a higher price. Each time the parcel changes hands, the developer shows a "profit"—and the banker gets a fee and "points" for originating the loan. In the end, the land is "worth" much more than when the game started, and shows up on the balance sheet of the S&L as a big winner. The developer, in turn, gets to take out a big loan. Often, the parties in this game of real estate frisbee were actually different parts of the same company.

"I remember one closing we had," recalled one real estate salesperson who pleaded guilty to criminal charges in an S&L probe. "It was in the hall of an office building. The tables were lined all the way down the hall. The investors were lined up in front of the tables. The loan officers would close one sale and pass the papers to the next guy. It looked like kids registering for college. If any investor raised a question, someone would come over and tell them to leave, they were out of the deal."

In fact, the very same day that President Ronald Reagan signed the Garn–St Germain law in 1982, a group of mortgage brokers and developers bought and sold three parcels of land among themselves, over and over again. In all, the day's flips created $12 million in paper profits for the developers, and an eventual $14.4 million loss for a small S&L when the loans couldn't be paid back.

Another deal, described by journalist Byron Harris, is a textbook example of how a network of lending institutions works in concert to escalate the price.

> The property was a collection of more than 1500 acres in South Fort Worth. . . . On November 2, 1983, the acreage sold for $17 million on a note from First City Investments. One day later it sold for $24 million on a note from State Savings of Lubbock. Thirteen months later on a note from Stockton Savings the property sold for $32 million. Finally, on December 26, 1985, the acreage sold for $50 million. It roughly tripled in price in just over two years. The final loan on the parcel was made by . . . Western Savings.

Within a year, the project was in bankruptcy. Western Savings, the loser in the game of financial Russian roulette, was seized by the federal government. According to Congressional testimony by regulators, a Western executive received more than $3 million in salary, bonuses, and dividends while his thrift went into the red.

"Time-bomb loans." That's what regulators call some "Acquisition, Development, and Construction" (ADC) loans, since the loan looks good for years, then blows up. In an ADC loan, a thrift lends a real estate developer 100 percent of the money for a project. That means enough money to buy the land, build the project, pay the S&L the fees owed—and even, in some instances, to pay *interest* to the thrift for years. The S&L gets to count the fees and part of the interest as "net income," even though the money may have come directly from the loan, which in turn came from depositors. This is not in itself illegal. But it is subject to tremendous abuse. An unscrupulous S&L owner can cook the books so that a sick bank can show a steady stream of income from loans, long after its loans have actually defaulted.

Time-bomb loans let high-flying S&Ls pour money into projects that never had a chance of paying off. According to regulators, in November 1984, Sunbelt S&L loaned $49 million to one of its consultants and his partner to convert a huge tract of raw land into a commercial-industrial park to be called "Lake Ridge." Instead of using the money to begin the project, the two bought land, then used some of the land as collateral to secure more funds from another thrift to buy more land. They then borrowed more money from Sunbelt to buy still more land. Five years later, the tract was still undeveloped except for a handful of roads and sewers, and the developers had their pockets full of depositors' money.

"Cash for trash." One of the shiftiest practices takes place when a borrower can't repay the S&L, and the thrift has to repossess the property. The easiest thing is for the S&L to pawn the property off on the next borrower. Say a business executive wants a $10 million loan from an S&L. The banker says: "Fine. I'll give you the loan, but only if you borrow an extra million. Then I'll sell you this here piece of land for a million dollars." The borrower gets the loan; the S&L gets rid of a probably worthless piece of property, and gets to cover up the loss on its books. Regulators searching for clues of insolvency are none the wiser.

A close cousin to "cash for trash" is what's called "trading a dead cow for a dead horse." That's when an S&L has to foreclose on a piece of property because it isn't earning any income. The S&L then sells that "dead cow" to another S&L—in exchange for the first S&L buying a foreclosed piece of property from the second thrift (the "dead horse"). Now both S&Ls have new property, and it may take years before regulators figure out that the investment is defunct.

"Straw" loans. Before deregulation, federal regulations limited the amount of loans a thrift could make to one single borrower. After all, what if that one individual went broke? After deregulation, the restrictions were greatly loosened—but there were still limits. So many S&Ls routinely, if fraudulently, loaned to "straw borrower" who would actually be securing the money for someone else.

•

For a time, as the "Oil Patch" prospered, some of these thrifts thrived too. In Denver, Phoenix, and especially in Dallas, condominiums, office towers, and shopping malls sprouted like desert weeds. The assets of Texas's S&Ls soared from $23.8 billion in 1979 to $83.1 billion in 1986. But at far too many thrifts, underneath the sheen of success was the decay of corruption. Many of these S&Ls began to collapse before the economy in the Southwest began to worsen. When oil prices plummeted starting in 1986, so did land prices. Loans began to sour. The last developer to enter into a "land flip" got stuck with overvalued land—and just as often, the S&L that financed the deal had to foreclose and take over the property.

One by one, the Texas high-flyers crashed. Today, it is estimated that as many as *half* the S&Ls in Texas are insolvent. "Fast Eddie" McBirney resigned from Sunbelt Savings, which was hemorrhaging red ink, in 1986. McBirney was indicted in 1990. By the time Vernon S&L was seized by the government in 1987, *90 percent* of its loans had gone bad. Vernon's chief executive officer, Woody Lemons, was convicted of taking kickbacks, and sentenced to thirty years in jail. "You have no moral values," the judge said. "You are a thief in every sense of the word." Another executive was convicted and sentenced to five years in prison for using Vernon's deposits to pay for female escorts for a former savings industry regulator and for political contributions. Five more executives pleaded guilty to various charges for their S&L misdeeds. In June 1990, Don Dixon was indicted for allegedly using thrift funds for prostitutes and for illegal political contributions. Finally, in July 1990, Stanley Adams—the man who had applied to open a branch office on the moon—was indicted for fraud and conspiracy. The party was over.

Playing the market

Other S&Ls poured money down a different hole: buying up the bonds and other investments newly available during the Roaring Eighties. Many of them, used to the routinized world of home lending, invested foolishly. At least four thrifts failed in 1989 because they gambled on futures markets and lost. In one single day, reports the *Washington Post,* Seapointe S&L of Carlsbad, California lost half of its depositors' money by betting that government bond prices would go down when they went up instead.

Wall Street's sharks took easy advantage of the new investors. One of 1990's bestselling books was *Liar's Poker,* the first-person account of a young investment banker. According to the author, Michael Lewis, after a new tax break was passed in 1981 for S&Ls, thrifts flocked to the investment bank Salomon Brothers to sell it home mortgages (which would be packaged into bonds for resale to investors). Salomon Brothers had a near monopoly on the sales, and picked the pockets of the thrift executives as if they were a bunch of tourists gawking at Wall Street's skyscrapers. On one occasion, a bond trader proposed an outrageously bad bargain to a thrift executive. "That doesn't sound like a very good trade for me," the S&L man said. "It isn't, from an economic point of view," the trader replied, "but look at it this way, if you *don't* do it, you're out of a job." The head of Salomon's mortgage-backed securities department estimated in 1984 that his division had made more money than the rest of Wall Street combined, much of it coming from inept S&L executives.

Some of that money came from a thrift in Ottowa, Kansas, named Franklin Savings and Loan. Franklin was once a traditional thrift with assets of less than $400 million. But in the mid-1980s, its chief executive, Ernest Fleischer, turned it into an MBA's plaything. The thrift plunged into money futures, interest-rate swaps, and even purchased the Wall Street investment firm L. F. Rothschild Holdings, Inc. To fund these trades, Franklin relied mostly on brokered deposits; by the end of 1989, 71 percent of its deposits came from "hot money" or through telephone marketing programs. Eventually, Fleischer's financial genius could not keep up with the high interest rates needed to attract depositors' funds. When federal regulators seized Franklin in February, 1990, the S&L claimed to have $11.4 billion in assets, many of which were sophisticated investments that were not paying off. (In September 1990 a federal court voided the seizure, although the government quickly appealed. Fleischer argues that he hedged his gambles, so the apparent losses aren't really so large.)

Junk bonds. Throughout the 1980s, the mergers and leveraged buyouts of Wall Street were fueled by a new, risky financial instrument: junk bonds. These bonds paid higher interest rate than usual—but only because they were unusually risky, or because their safety was unknown. About 200 of the nation's 3,000 S&Ls used their depositors' funds to buy junk bonds, and about 25 invested more than $100 million apiece in the securities. By 1990, one of the biggest holders of junk bonds in the United States was none other than the federal government, which took over the failed S&Ls that heavily invested in the risky debt.

The bonds were peddled most heavily by the investment firm Drexel Burnham Lambert, home of junk bond impresario Michael Milken. Throughout the mid-1980s, junk bonds were used by corporate raiders to stage takeover bids against Revlon, Beatrice, Pantry Pride, and a host of other megafirms. Companies that were funded by these junk bonds then turned around and bought other companies' junk bonds, in what investigators called a "daisy chain." Milken, who pulled in a salary and bonuses worth $550 million in 1987, orchestrated the trading as if it were his personal feifdom.

Reports the *Washington Post*'s Jerry Knight:

> Government investigators have discovered an elaborate web that connects the bankrupt investment banking firm of Drexel Burnham Lambert, many of Wall Street's best-known corporate raiders and some of the highest flying savings and loans.
>
> Working closely together, those organizations bought each other's bonds, gave each other loans, traded securities back and forth, financed corporate takeovers, participated in real estate deals together and sometimes allegedly helped each other create phony profits and evade regulatory requirements, investigators said.

This round-robin held the junk bond market together. To at least one observer, it all resembled a classic fraud known as a "Ponzi scheme." In a Ponzi scheme, early investors are lured with promises of quick reward; they are then repaid by funds obtained from later investors, and so on. The scam can flourish so long as it keeps attracting new investors. When the scheme collapses, the last investors in are stuck holding a very expensive bag. Benjamin Stein, writing in *Barron's* magazine, notes that the junk bond market functioned the same way: Milken's bonds generated income supposedly because of his investing genius, but actually because previous junk bond beneficiaries bought each new round of bonds. "If Milken were removed or the string of captive buyers were snapped or if markets started getting wise to bonds from Drexel/Milken, all the balls would come crashing down onto the juggler."

But in 1988, the Securities and Exchange Commission charged Drexel Burnham and Milken with securities fraud, and the next year Drexel pleaded guilty to six criminal charges. In March 1989, Milken was indicted on ninety-eight counts of securities fraud and racketeering. (He later pleaded guilty to six charges.) By early 1990, Drexel had declared bankruptcy, the junk bond market collapsed, and junk bonds became just that—junk. One study, by an economist at the Massachusetts Institute of Technology, indicated that half the junk bonds would not be paid back, even before Drexel's collapse. In early 1990, the government owned one third of all the junk bonds in the hands of S&Ls nationwide. In the summer of 1990, the Resolution Trust Corporation, established by Congress to sell-off assets from seized S&Ls, published an inventory of junk bonds for sale to investors, which had been issued by 330 major corporations. And federal regulators have established a special task force to probe for possible improper conduct by Drexel and its friendly S&Ls.

Columbia S&L: Junk bond junkie. Milken used a string of Southern California thrifts as a capital pool for junk bond–financed hostile takeovers. The most ravenous junk bond junkie among thrift executives was Thomas Spiegel, chief executive officer of Columbia Savings and Loan of Beverly Hills. Columbia was by far the biggest investor in junk bonds among thrifts, pouring $3.8 billion into the risky securities—approximately 40 percent of the S&L's assets. The savings and loan helped Drexel stage raids on Revlon and Texaco.

Spiegel and his mentor Milken were involved in a swirl of business deals. Drexel scratched Columbia's back: in an annual series of transactions, Columbia sold some of its junk bonds back to Drexel in late December. That way, on December 31, Columbia could take advantage of federal government tax breaks for thrifts that have most of their assets in home loans. After the new year, Drexel sold the bonds back to Columbia. And Columbia scratched Drexel's back: when Milken couldn't find enough buyers for some of his dicier junk bond offerings, Spiegel would step in and buy an extra $10 or $20 million. Other backs got scratched as well. Regulators charge that one luxury car dealer got a loan from Columbia at special low interest rates; during the negotiations, Spiegel was given the use of a Mercedes Benz 560 SEL and a Bentley. (The loan eventually went bad, costing Columbia over $5 million, according to the government.)

Spiegel's compensation was anything but junk. Milken's protégé was the highest-paid executive in the S&L industry, earning a total of $22 million between 1985 and 1989. In 1988, Columbia lost nearly $600 million, but paid top executives $4 million.

And Columbia spent lavishly on perks for its chief that were, well, out of the ordinary.

- "Spiegel and his family at times had 19 security personnel protecting them," reported the *Los Angeles Times*, "some assigned to 'chase cars' loaded with automatic weapons that would trail Spiegel whenever he rode through the streets of Beverly Hills. An aircraft hangar for the company's jets had an electronic map of the world showing recent terrorist activity. Executives joked that the thrift's name should be changed to *Colombia* Savings and Loan.

- Columbia spent at least $55,000 for approximately one hundred guns, ammunition, and accessories for Spiegel's personal use, according to an administrative action filed by the Treasury Department in 1990. (After Spiegel was ousted, Columbia's new management demanded that he return the guns; he refused to turn over fifty-five of them and reported that forty more were missing.)

- Columbia hired an English butler and a martial arts instructor. And it paid for vacation condominiums used by Spiegel in Jackson Hole, Wyoming, Indian Wells, California and Park City, Utah. For one four-day stay at the Dorchester Hotel in London, the government said, Spiegel and his wife charged the S&L $2,197. That ain't Motel 6.

- "Spiegel," charged the Treasury Department, "was reimbursed by Columbia in the amount of approximately $250,000 for expenditures that did not have any necessary business purpose." The expenditures included $2,000 for a French wine-tasting course, $10,736 for cashmere throws, blankets, and quilts, and $7,840 for Michael Jackson concert tickets. (Spiegel says the tickets were for business associates and business school recruits; the government says they were for friends.)

For years, junk bonds pumped up Columbia's portfolio; *Forbes* named it the best-managed thrift in the country. A real estate magnate named Sam Zell gushed that Spiegel was an example of the wonders of deregulation. "If the entire S&L business had been run by guys like Tom Spiegel, then this country would be a couple of hundred billion bucks richer." Even in early 1989, as the rest of the S&L industry was drooping and Congress prepared for the bailout, the *New York Times* lauded Columbia in an article headlined, "Here Are Solid Savings and Loans."

But as the junk bond market collapsed, so did Columbia's

reputation. Spiegel resigned at the end of 1989. Between October 1989 and February 1990, the thrift reported losing $575 million; in April of 1990, the new management announced that the S&L was insolvent. In July, the Treasury Department sued Spiegel, asserting that he had diverted $19 million of the thrift's funds for his personal benefit, and sought to bar him from the S&L industry forever. As of August 1990, Columbia held on by a thread, seeking to avoid federal takeover and a taxpayer bailout.

Miami Vice: CenTrust. Across the continent from Beverly Hills in Miami, the sixty-story CenTrust Tower dominates the skyline. Designed by the renowned architect I. M. Pei, the strikingly beautiful glass semicircle is an opening shot on the television show *Miami Vice.* Television viewers should cast a jaded eye on the CenTrust tower: for a time, they owned it. For CenTrust is a busted thrift, one that rode junk bonds and currency speculation to the top, but which could ultimately cost taxpayers $1 billion.

David Paul was a small-time businessman, who left New York in a cloud of lawsuits and fraud allegations. Squat in stature, a bundle of nervous energy, Paul was driven to succeed. He arrived in Miami, took over nearly insolvent Dade Savings in 1983 (using his unfinished yacht as collateral), and turned it into largest thrift in the southeast United States, claiming assets of $8.2 billion in 1988. According to the State of Florida, between January 1, 1988, and September 30, 1989, CenTrust paid Paul a total of $4,851,040, and furnished his mansion with $150,000 worth of appliances and other amenities.

CenTrust alarmed regulators when it paid $12 million for a classic painting, *Portrait of a Man as Mars* by the great Flemish master Peter Paul Reubens. As art connoisseurs charged that Paul had overpaid for the work, it was revealed that CenTrust had paid a total of $28 million for paintings, sculpture, and Persian rugs. Paul kept the disputed painting at his mansion, supposedly until CenTrust's executive offices were finished. (One servant recalls seeing Mrs. Paul bundled up in a coat because the house was kept so cold to preserve the art.) Ultimately, regulators forced CenTrust to auction off the collection, at a loss of $4.3 million.

The upstart assiduously wooed Miami's social, political, and journalistic elite. "All it takes is money, my dear," confessed one society matron to the *Washington Post.* "Character has nothing to do with it." Paul gave money to charities and politicians, and he socialized with the publisher of the *Miami Herald.* It barely put a dent on Paul's social cachet when it turned out he had falsely claimed to have a Ph.D. from Harvard and a business degree from Columbia University. Miami's upper crust was too eager to be invited to parties such as the 1988 Grand Chefs affair, when Paul flew six famous French chefs first-class to Miami for a soirée attended by senators and federal judges—and paid for by CenTrust. (Paul eventually repaid the bank; regulators say it was only after they told him to.) He hosted politicians on his yacht *The Grand Cru,* named after top-quality French wine. The boat featured a gold-leaf ceiling, which matched one in CenTrust's offices. One employee told regulators that Paul had ordered her to use thrift funds to buy gold nails for the ship. "That's false," responds Paul. "I've never seen a gold nail in my life."

CenTrust relied heavily on junk bonds, risky real estate deals, and other sophisticated financial instruments for its reported profits. But as at Columbia Savings and Loan, this flimsy foundation collapsed in 1989. In December of that year, the state comptroller sought to remove Paul as head of CenTrust, alleging that he ran the thrift "as if it were his own public piggy bank." After the junk bond market evaporated, and accounting rules were changed under the S&L bailout, CenTrust began bleeding red ink. In February 1990, regulators seized the S&L shortly before it was about to become insolvent.

The CenTrust saga is not over yet. In August 1990, the NBC program *Exposé* ran a segment on Paul that included some startling charges of political influence-peddling. At a time when bank board regulators were questioning Paul's investments and expenditures, Florida Senator Bob Graham hired a longtime CenTrust lawyer as a temporary staff member. The CenTrust lawyer called for a meeting with regulators, at Graham's office. When the bank examiners arrived, they found the staff member—who never disclosed his prior affiliation with Paul—*and* two CenTrust lobbyists. Senator Graham refused to give NBC an interview, but a camera crew caught up with him on a Washington street. He asserted that he had never helped CenTrust. But NBC produced a letter, sent under Graham's signature, complaining that the bank board's Atlanta regional office was "tougher . . . than are the regulators from other states."

Commercial ventures: From ethanol plants to horror movies

Land deals, junk bonds, currency speculation—that wasn't all the spendthrift thrifts spent their money on. Savings and loans, which once existed primarily to help build the Levittowns of America, also poured their funds into horse farms, office towers, country clubs, race tracks, and overbuilt shopping malls. These commercial ventures were highly fickle. After all, whether a new business makes money depends entirely on whether a market exists for the product, how well it is managed, what the competition is doing. Even honest S&Ls were out of their league as they attempted to take advantage of the new commercial possibilities. In addition, throughout much of the decade, S&Ls were allowed to *own* companies themselves, thus assuming all the risk.

· Instead of frugality, the new breed of S&Ls made their loans with frivolity. Consider the sworn testimony of an appraiser at American Savings and Loan of Stockton California. Officials at that thrift *said* they had "looked at" appraisals for loans. What they *meant* was they had looked at the bookshelves that held documents, not the appraisals themselves. The thrift lost so much money that regulators took control in 1988. Estimated cost to the taxpayers: $1 billion.

- The American Diversified Savings Bank of Costa Mesa, California, began in 1983 and grew to $1 billion within two years. It largely put its money into risky investments including restaurants, ethanol plants, and a company that collected manure for a cogeneration plant. In 1988, the bank board shut the thrift down.

- In the search for higher returns, S&Ls went far afield of their housing mission. An investor named William Gibson discovered just how far when he took over a string of S&Ls at the behest of the FHLBB in late 1988. His thrift network had invested in (and now owned), among other things, the Pine Ridge Winery in Napa Valley, California, an aircraft-leasing outfit, and the film distribution firm that holds the rights to *The Texas Chainsaw Massacre.*

- Some S&L executives guessed wrong in land, junk bonds, *and* commercial lending. One financial incompetent was Imperial Savings and Loan, one of California's biggest thrifts. The firm's management bet the firm on speculative investments, and it lost. Imperial was one of the largest buyers of junk bonds among S&Ls, and by the time the government took over in 1990 the value of the bonds was $1.3 *billion.* (The actual market value was much lower, since so many of them turned out to be worth less than their "face" value.) It pumped money into a Chevrolet dealership that went bankrupt, in a cloud of fraud allegations. And it invested millions of dollars in Global Motors, a company that imported Yugo automobiles. The tiny cars didn't sell, and the company went bust. So did the S&L.

Hired guns: Lawyers, accountants, and appraisers

At many crooked S&Ls, highly paid accountants, lawyers, and appraisers helped cook the books. The public and the government rely on these professions to safeguard the nation's financial institutions. But in the 1980s, the allure of huge fees overwhelmed the demands of professional duty.

Accountants have the most to account for. These auditors are supposed to scrutinize the books of an S&L —or any other company, for that matter—and attest that the numbers are accurate. We think of accountants as solitary figures in green eyeshades, poring over ledgers. Actually, the industry is dominated by the Big Six (until recent mergers, the Big Eight), huge financial conglomerates that earn hundreds of millions of dollars each year. The competition for fees from big clients is fierce, and it creates temptations to turn a blind eye to unsavory behavior.

The congressional General Accounting Office (GAO) conducted a study of eleven failed S&Ls in Texas, and the conclusions were withering. At six of the collapses, the certified public accountants (CPAs) were so lax that the investigators referred the firms to the regulatory and professional bodies for possible disciplinary action. The investigators fingered some of the biggest accounting firms in the country, including Arthur Young & Company, Ernst & Whinney, and Deloitte Haskins & Sells.

Winner of the bent-eyeshade award would probably be Arthur Young. For example, the firm audited the books of high-flying Vernon Savings and Loan just months before federal regulators seized the thrift and discovered that 90 percent of the loans were in default. Arthur Young also gave a thumbs-up to the books of Western Savings and Loan, which crashed in a series of land flips. (A government lawsuit against the accountants charges that negligence and breach of contract cost the taxpayers $500 million.) Regulator William Black charges that the CPA firm's Dallas office offered the "K-Mart blue-light special" to thrifts that shopped for friendly auditors.

As of August 1990, the federal government had sued twenty-one CPAs for fraud, negligence, or misconduct in the scandal. Fourteen of the cases involved Big Six firms, including Coopers & Lybrand; Ernst & Young (Ernst & Whinney merged with Arthur Young); Peat Marwick; and Deloitte, Haskins & Sells and Touche Ross & Co. (which have also merged). The latter merged firm faces over $800 million in damages in government lawsuits. The industry's alleged complicity was so widespread that the FDIC—which had a policy of not hiring accountants that had contributed to the crisis—found itself unable to use major accounting firms, with the exception of Price-Waterhouse. Eventually the agency relaxed the ban.

One big reason for the laxity is flimsy self-policing. In 1987, according to the *Arizona Republic,* the American Institute of Certified Public Accountants revoked the membership of only sixteen of its 280,000 members for violating accounting rules. At present, accountants are not required by law to report wrongdoing to regulators. The industry's self-imposed code, adopted in 1989, merely requires that a CPA tell the government if it has dropped a client; it is up to the client to tell the regulators why. Legislation proposed by Representative Ron Wyden would require accounting firms to warn the regulators of criminality. An earlier version of the bill, opposed by accountants, would have required them to report irregularities.

The lawyers who "papered" the deals that led to the S&Ls' demise are also in the dock. Many of them have been sued by the government or investors for negligently advising thrift high-flyers to make speculative loans that lacked collateral and violated federal rules. One Philadelphia law firm—Blank, Rome, Comisky, and McCauley—paid the government $40 million to settle a civil lawsuit arising out of the collapse of Sunrise Savings and Loan of Fort Lauderdale, Florida. During a 1989 criminal trial at which officials of the thrift were convicted of conspiracy, prosecutors described a partner and an associate at the law firm as "unindicted co-conspirators" for their work on sham loans.

Appraisers face reappraisal. This little-known profession is critical to real estate and to a stable banking system. Appraisers look at property to see how much it is really worth. That way, if a borrower can't pay back the loan and the lender has to foreclose and take back the property, it can sell the land off and recoup its losses. On the other hand, if appraisers are willing to say a property is worth whatever the person paying their fee says it is, then bankers can make a loan that could buy a golf course when the property is really a rubble-strewn vacant lot.

The appraisal system was criticized by a task force appointed by Texas Governor Bill Clements to look into the S&L crisis. "The appraisal system in Texas is unregulated," the panel said. "Appraisers can be influenced by the possibility of repeat business and may be motivated to design the results of their appraisals to suit the desires of their clients. Consequently, inaccurate and inflated appraisals could be obtained in connection with lending activities."

Was it fraud or recklessness?

The losses from the S&L binge were, obviously, a result of colossal mismanagement. But it is increasingly clear that the S&L collapse was also due to out-and-out fraud—a white-collar crime wave of unparalleled dimensions.

Law enforcers who have examined the extent of illegality are astonished by its depth and breadth. Attorney General Richard Thornburgh calls it "the biggest white-collar swindle in history." Said FBI Director William S. Sessions, "This is truly a national crisis."

William Seidman is chairman of the FDIC, the agency that now regulates both commercial banks and S&Ls. In 1989, after the first wave of thrift takeovers, Seidman estimated that fraud, insider abuse, or outright criminality were factors at 60 percent of failed S&Ls. More recently, in testimony before the

Senate Judiciary Committee on July 24, 1990, Seidman revised his estimate slightly:

> As a result of our experience over the past few months, we estimate that:
> - Approximately 50 percent plus of [government]-controlled thrifts have had suspected criminal misconduct referred to the Department of Justice;
> - In about 40 percent of [government]-controlled thrifts, insider abuse and misconduct contributed significantly to the thrift's insolvency;
> - About 15 percent of the thrifts appear to have been involved in irregular and possibly fraudulent transactions with other financial institutions.

At first, Seidman reports, the misconduct showed up most regularly in S&Ls based in the Southwest and Southern California. More recently, though, possible fraud is coming to light in Florida and the Northeast.

Evidence of insider abuse and misconduct, Seidman added, "ranges from embezzlement and loan fraud to complex schemes to generate paper accounting profits that allowed cash to flow to thrift owners through subsidiaries or personal holding companies." Land flip schemes created false values and generated excessive profit for appraisers, developers, and thrift insiders. And some S&Ls' junk bond deals may have given insiders profit, while saddling the S&Ls with the risk.

The GAO spent a year studying twenty-six failed S&Ls that comprised the biggest failures between 1985 and 1987. It found fraud or insider abuse at *all twenty-six.* Of the failed thrifts studied by the GAO, every one had inadequate record-keeping and internal controls; all but two did inadequate credit analysis of borrowers; all but three made too many loans to one borrower; and all but four displayed conflicts of interest. At nineteen out of the twenty-six, regulators had asked the Justice Department to investigate possible criminal conduct.

This financial crime wave may have been even more sinister

than it seemed at first. According to one group of journalists who have examined the S&L scandal, many thrifts were taken over by organized-crime-related individuals who may have been acting in concert. Stephen Pizzo, Mary Fricker, and Paul Muolo, in their book *Inside Job*, describe how they found a network of mob-linked figures who moved from one S&L to another. These shady characters practiced a classic mob move: a "bust out" of a financial institution, which drains it of its funds and leaves it insolvent. The authors warn:

> We were driven in our investigation by evidence that much of the looting in progress at many of the savings and loans around the nation was in fact not the work of isolated individuals but instead was the result of some kind of network that was sucking millions of dollars from thrifts through a purposeful and coordinated system of fraud. . . . At nearly every thrift we researched for this book we found clear evidence of either mob, Teamster, or organized crime involvement. Only one conclusion was possible: The mob had played an important role in the nationwide fraternity that looted the savings and loan industry.

Mario Renda, for example, was a financier who built a huge money-broker business in Long Island, New York, channeling funds from union pension funds to S&Ls across the country. His First United Fund was the number one supplier of hot money to thrifts that failed in the early 1980s. The money came with a string attached: the funds had to be loaned out to a borrower, also sent to the S&L by Renda. (In reality, the borrower was a stand-in for a business partner of Renda.) It was an offer that many thrifts *didn't* refuse. After the federal government indicted Renda, he pleaded guilty and received a relatively light sentence. But the authors of *Inside Job* assert that Renda was laundering money for the Lucchese organized crime family in New York. The authors also trace the influence of Herman Beebe, a New Orleans financier allegedly with close ties to organized crime, who was linked to over one hundred banks and S&Ls that failed in the 1980s.

One prominent analyst rejects the fraud thesis. Bert Ely, a widely quoted S&L industry consultant based in Alexandria, Virginia, asserts that fraud played a minimal role in the crisis. Most of those thrifts, he argues, were already really insolvent when the crooks moved in. He blames the regulators for failing to shut down insolvent thrifts, and thus creating a fertile medium for fraud. Maybe. But we don't say there isn't a mugging just because the foot patrolman is off at the donut shop.

•

Falling real estate values played a role in S&L failures. So did the gap between the interest rate paid by S&Ls on deposits, and the profits returned from investments. But remember— *not every S&L has failed.* Many are still healthy, and those tend to be those that focused on home loans and engaged in honest business practices. When times turned rough, more often than not the S&Ls that failed were the ones involved in the riskiest, most suspect activities. In the words of Robert Clarke, former comptroller of the currency, "When the economic tide goes out, you find out who's swimming naked."

THREE

•

WHY NO ONE STOPPED THE LOOTING

●

BY THE MID-1980s the S&Ls were engulfed in a white-collar crime wave. But as S&Ls racked up losses and the potential cost to taxpayers grew, the executive and legislative branches did little to control the damage. Unfortunately, Republicans and Democrats deserve blame for an abandonment of the public trust.

THE REGULATORY COPS: PULLED OFF THE BEAT

As the spasms of fraud and failure convulsed the S&L industry, federal regulators knew early on that something was wrong. But they were understaffed and ill-equipped to keep tabs on the newly deregulated thrift industry.

The biggest problem was interference from a number of deregulation ideologues in the White House. As soon as the Reagan administration took power, the White House's Office of Management and Budget (OMB) was given sweeping authority over policy and hiring at all federal agencies, including the S&L regulatory agency. Reagan's OMB was headed by David Stockman, and was staffed by conservative adherents of less-government-is-better-government. In 1981, Stockman imposed a hiring freeze on all government agencies, including the FHLBB. (Significantly, the FDIC—which regulates banks—was not under OMB's thumb, and could hire enough examiners.) With attrition, the number of bank board examiners actually shrank. Relative to the growing assets of S&Ls, the examiner force was slashed by 65 percent. Many S&Ls were not examined at all between 1984 and 1986, the peak years of fraud.

The S&L regulatory agencies were plagued by ineptitude and poor planning. For example, just as the industry was being deregulated, the Southwest Home Loan Bank's district office was moved from Little Rock, Arkansas, to Dallas; only a dozen or so of the office's experienced staff made the move. Salaries for auditors started at $14,000, and the Dallas Home Loan Bank Board didn't hire an expert on junk bonds and other sophisticated financial instruments until late 1988.

Reagan's first appointee as chair of the bank board, Richard Pratt, believed in rapid deregulation for the S&L industry. According to one candidate for a regulatory job, Pratt began a job interview this way: "Let me ask you one question. Do you fundamentally believe in deregulation?" Before he left the government in 1983 to become head of mortgage-backed securities at Merrill Lynch, Pratt had stripped away decades of S&L regulation.

But soon the evidence of rot was too strong to ignore. For the new FHLBB chairman, Edwin Gray, the epiphany was a videotape sent to him from Texas in March 1984. The tape was shot with a shaky hand by an outraged appraiser hired by the bank board. It showed real estate development projects, all funded by Empire Savings and Loan, along a stretch of interstate near Dallas known as I-30. The panorama was shocking: rotting plywood, half-constructed condominiums, vacant lots. "Notice the incredible waste, the total lack of contractor control," the narrator said. "Evidence of arson is already available. . . . In the distance, numerous projects, virtually 100 percent complete, no occupancy, and the land between the camera and the buildings is being prepared for more development." Shaken, Gray and his colleagues on the bank board voted to seize Empire immediately. Bulldozers moved in and razed many of the useless buildings. This decision began a three year effort, ultimately futile, to crack down on the S&L swindlers while there was still time to save taxpayers money.

Ed Gray was an unlikely hero. A former Southern California thrift public-relations officer, for a time he served as press secretary for presidential candidate Ronald Reagan. He got his regulatory job as the preferred candidate of the S&L lobby. At first, Gray was a dyed-in-the-wool deregulator, devoted to giving businesses a free hand in the marketplace without government regulation. But he had become worried about warning signs he was seeing in the Texas S&L industry. Gray was affable and slow-moving, and easy to underestimate. Behind his back, skeptics called him "Mr. Ed," after television's talking horse. But Gray grew stubborn, indeed obsessive, in his conviction that the thrift industry was on a collision course with catastrophe.

At first, Gray tried to crack down on broker deposits. The same day he viewed the videotape of the I-30 fiasco, Gray traveled to a Capitol Hill hearing, where he lit into the hot money that was allowing thrifts to make reckless investments. Brokered deposits, he said, constituted 85 percent of Empire's deposits. The FHLBB voted to limit deposit insurance to $100,000 per money broker. But a court decision struck down the ban, saying that deposit insurance covers all deposits.

Gray came under fire from the S&Ls for his aggressive efforts to police the industry. One lobbyist angrily told a regulator: "You can't restrict our God-given right to make profits!" In August 1986, Lawrence Taggart, a former California S&L commissioner, complained to White House Chief of Staff Donald Regan that the bank board was squeezing the fast-growing thrifts. "My father and I have been politically active in both the [Governor George]Deukmejian administration in California and the Reagan administration in Washington," he wrote in a letter to Regan. "The actions being done to the industry by the current chief regulator of the Federal Home Loan Bank Board are likely to have an adverse impact on the ability of our party to raise needed campaign funds in the upcoming elections."

White House Chief of Staff Donald Regan began a quiet campaign to have Gray fired. Regan had been an ardent booster of brokered deposits when he ran Merrill Lynch. Now Regan's aides, along with some S&L executives, began leaking damaging stories about Gray to the press. (Gray had been under investigation for allowing the S&L industry to pay his way to conventions, and for using a plane paid for by the local

Home Loan Banks. Ultimately, he was cleared.) Rumors swept Washington that Gray was leaving. But he held on.

Gray tried to hire more regulators. But his superiors at the White House would have none of that. "One of the highest ranking members of OMB told me that I was being disloyal to the administration by even seeking to hire more people because the policy of the administration was to have fewer, not more, examiners," Gray recalled. Finally, in 1987, Gray transferred supervisory responsibility to the local Home Loan Banks, just to get them out of the clutches of the OMB. The White House made a last-ditch offer: it would let the Central Bank Board hire a grand total of thirty-nine new examiners. But Gray pressed on, and began hiring hundreds of enforcers at the local level. At last, the regulators could begin to hire enough supervisors, and pry the lid off the S&L mess.

Ultimately, it became clear that the fraud and waste in the savings industry demanded government intervention. Gray made plans to seize dozens of thrifts in Texas, to replace their management and try and sell them off to new owners. The sooner the agency could act, the better; waiting until later would just give the rogues more time to bilk their S&Ls. But paying off the depositors in these institutions would cost money, lots of it. Bank board economists and some outside observers began to realize, though, that the FSLIC was broke. It had approximately $3 billion on hand, while its outstanding obligations were already $6 billion. At the time, regulators estimated that they would need *$15 billion* to continue cracking down on mismanagement in the industry.

For that, they had to turn to Congress. In 1986, the bank board proposed legislation to provide $15 billion to replenish ("recapitalize") the FSLIC insurance fund. That would cost S&Ls higher fees, and give the regulators the ability to shut down more insolvent thrifts. But Gray found that Congress, beholden to thrift industry lobbying and campaign contributions, was, to put it mildly, unsympathetic.

CONGRESS FOR SALE

The S&L disaster couldn't have happened without a posse of thrift allies on Capitol Hill—lawmakers purchased by campaign contributions, personal gifts, entertainment, and speech fees.

In the 1980s, Congress was a thoroughly corrupted institution. The main reason? An obsessive need for campaign dollars turned our lawmakers into part-time legislators and full-time fund-raisers. By 1988, the average senator had to raise $12,650 each week of his entire six year term to win reelection; the average representative raised $4,000. The vast bulk of those funds came from business—through PACs, through individual contributions from executives, and through the Washington lawyers and lobbyists who are paid to be chummy with Congress. Washington's political culture revolved around such fund-raising, and few eyebrows were raised about transactions that in another context might seem felonious.

In an election year, Capitol Hill is witness to dozens of fund-raising receptions a week, where lobbyists hand incumbents checks and reap access, goodwill, and even votes in return. But the S&Ls had a special line to power on Capitol Hill. Indeed, as we will see, in a brief six month period three of the most powerful members of the House of Representatives—the Speaker, Majority Whip, and chairman of the banking committee—lost their seats in Congress because of the taint from S&L loan gifts, among other controversies.

The S&Ls' power on Capitol Hill had two roots: campaign cash and assiduous lobbying. As deregulation remade the industry in the 1980s, the S&L industry poured cash into Congress. According to the *Wall Street Journal*, 163 PACs sponsored by S&Ls and their trade associations contributed nearly $4.5 million to House and Senate candidates from 1983 to 1988. At the same time that thrifts were losing billions,

S&L PACs gave millions to congressional campaigns. In fact, payments to federal candidates rose 42 percent in the two years before the S&L bailout—in short, at the very moment the industry was slipping into insolvency.

The single most comprehensive study of S&L campaign money has been conducted by Common Cause, the citizen group that promotes government reform. During the decade of the 1980s, Common Cause conservatively estimated in a June 1990 study, S&L interests gave at least $11,669,499, in PAC and individual campaign contributions to congressional candidates and political party committees.* "Current U.S. senators received a total of $3,176,524 from S&L interests during the 1980s," the study reported. California Senator Pete Wilson, for example, received $243,334 from S&Ls during the 1980s. (He is now running for governor of California.) Senator Don Riegle, chairman of the banking committee, got $200,900. And Texas Senator Lloyd Bentsen, the Democratic nominee for vice president in 1988, got $154,207.

TOP SENATE RECIPIENTS OF S&L PAC AND INDIVIDUAL CONTRIBUTIONS DURING THE 1980s

1.	Pete Wilson (R–CA)	$243,334
2.	Don Riegle (D–MI)	200,900
3.	Lloyd Bentsen (D–TX)	154,207
4.	Alan Cranston (D–CA)	143,700
5.	Alfonse D'Amato (R–NY)	88,235
6.	Phil Gramm (R–TX)	86,098
7.	Dennis DeConcini (D–AZ)	84,200
8.	John McCain (R–AZ)	80,393
9.	Jake Garn (R–UT)	77,600
10.	Robert Dole (R–KS)	72,450

---

* Even these large sums are an underestimate, because Common Cause was able to count only those donors who identify themselves as being connected with a savings and loan on disclosure forms.

WHO ROBBED AMERICA?

TOP HOUSE RECIPIENTS OF S&L PAC AND INDIVIDUAL CONTRIBUTIONS DURING THE 1980s

1.	William Lowery (R–CA/41)	$85,088
2.	David Dreier (R–CA/33)	75,150
3.	Mel Levine (D–CA/27)	69,250
4.	Richard Lehman (D–CA/18)	68,090
5.	Norman Shumway (R–CA/14)	67,425
6.	Esteban Torres (D–CA/34)	60,950
7.	Carroll Hubbard (D–KY/1)	52,652
8.	Frank Annunzio (D–IL/11)	51,620
9.	Stephen Neal (D–NC/5)	47,100
10.	Howard Berman (D–CA/26)	45,950

Source: Common Cause *It's a Wonderful Life*, June 1990

Under federal election laws, individuals are supposed to be limited to giving $1,000 to a candidate in a primary and $1,000 more in a general election. But loose campaign finance laws allow huge gifts. While some families go bowling, billionaire S&L owner Carl Lindner's idea of a family outing is a trip to a political fund-raiser. The Lindner family—brothers Carl, Richard, and Robert and their spouses and children—managed to make $828,920 in political contributions during the 1980s. Republican party committees got $639,020 (and Democratic committees got a paltry $3,000). Current U.S. senators got $68,500, including $17,000 to Robert Dole and $14,500 to Mitch McConnell, the chief foe of campaign finance reform; House members got $59,400. Eighteen challengers or former members of Congress got an additional $62,000.

Campaign funds from the S&Ls themselves only tell part of the story. For starters, several other financial industries, as well as industries intertwined with the thrifts, also gave huge sums to win friends on Capitol Hill. According to Citizen Action, a national public interest group, financial industry PACs as a whole gave $13.8 million in PAC contributions in 1987–88 alone; individuals from that industry gave another $10.2 million. The insurance industry gave $9.3 million, and real estate gave $8.9 million. On occasion, the industries had different legislative priorities, but they all pushed relevant lawmakers in one direction: more deregulation.

As the congressional panels charged with writing legislation governing the financial industry, the House and Senate Banking Committees attracted money from the banking industry like a magnet attracts metal filings. A new study conducted for this book shows why these were considered "cash-and-carry committees." Financial industry PACs as a whole gave current Senate committee members $3,836,598 between 1985 and 1990, and gave current House Banking Committee members $5,193,258. (For a similar analysis of the entire Congress, see Appendixes 2 and 3.)

Political contributions go into a lawmaker's treasury; speech fees, paid by trade associations and lobby groups, can go into a lawmaker's pocket. These so-called honoraria may add up to a substantial special-interest salary. The practice comes so close to legalized bribery that it was dubbed "dishonoraria" by Representative Andy Jacobs (D–IN) and is widely condemned by the public. In 1989, the House banned these fees as part of its 40-percent pay raise; senators can still legally take the fees as income up to 27 percent of their public salary. Not surprisingly, the cash-rich financial industry was the leading provider of honoraria. According to a study by Public Citizen's Congress Watch, *Who Pays the Piper?*, the financial industry gave U.S. Senators $1,390,396 in honoraria between 1984 and 1987. We are faced with the prospect of a Congress employed partly by taxpayers and partly by private interests.

TOP TEN SENATE RECIPIENTS OF FINANCIAL INDUSTRY HONORARIA, 1984–1987

Name	Total	Years	Average
1. Jake Garn (R-UT)*	$63,090	4	$15,773
2. Don Riegle (D-MI)*	$53,500	4	$13,375

3.	Alfonse D'Amato (R-NY)*	$52,000	4	$13,000
4.	John Chafee (R-NY)***	$51,425	4	$12,856
5.	Ernest Hollings (R-SC)	$47,000	4	$11,750
6.	William Roth (R-DE)**	$45,000	4	$11,250
7.	Charles Grassley (R-IA)	$44,000	4	$11,000
8.	Timothy Wirth (D-CO)*	$18,000	1	$18,000
9.	David Karnes (D-NE)*	$15,500	1	$15,500
10.	Thomas Daschle (D-SD)**	$14,500	1	$14,500

*Member of the Senate Banking Committee
**Member of the Senate Finance Committee (which writes tax laws)
***Member of both Senate Banking and Senate Finance Committees

Years refers to the number of years covered by the study that the individual served in the U.S. Senate.

Source: Michael McCauley, Peter Meryash and Edward Zaharevitz, *Who Pays the Piper?: An Analysis of Honoraria Given to U.S. Senators from 1984–1987* (Public Citizen's Congress Watch, April 1989)

Campaign contributions and "dishonoraria" aren't always enough to guarantee desired legislative results. That requires skilled and well-coordinated lobbying, and the S&Ls boasted one of the powerhouse lobby groups in Washington: the U.S. League of Savings Institutions. The league was so successful in its lobbying and so close to both regulators and members of Congress that many citizens erroneously thought it had quasi-official status.

Founded in 1892, the league initially cared little about the activities of the federal government. But when the government began insuring bank deposits in the 1930s, the league quickly developed a keen interest in Washington, and helped draft the legislation governing thrifts. Regulators were mostly drawn from the industry, and then only with the blessing of the trade association. According to former FSLIC director Peter Stearns, "The Bank Board doesn't regulate anything unless the U.S. League and the top S&Ls agree." The league's PAC doled out $1.3 million to congressional candidates from 1983 to 1988, giving heavily to Banking Committee members. Writes Kathleen Day in the *New Republic*, "Thrift executives, lobbyists, lawmakers, and regulators were locked into a relationship so cozy that it was hard to tell (and it still is) where the industry ends and the government begins."

The lobbying was especially effective with lawmakers who knew local thrift executives from the Elks Club or Kiwanis, and who still thought of the industry as a collection of earnest home-builders. Senator David Pryor (D–AK) explained why: "You've got to remember that each community has a savings and loan; some have two; some have four, and each of them has seven or eight board members. They own the Chevy dealership and the shoe store. And when we saw these people, we said, gosh, these are the people who are building the homes for people, these are the people who represent a dream that has worked in this country." Even when the S&Ls were pulling back from home lending, their allies in Congress mistily defended the industry as the bastion of the American dream.

With cash and connections, the S&Ls won the support of some of the most powerful officials in the country. At every turn, as S&L regulators finally sought to bring some law and order to the industry, they ran into a brick wall of opposition from some of the most powerful members of Congress. Congresspersons carry water for their big contributors every day. But this display of politics as usual wound up costing taxpayers billions—and some lawmakers their seats. Here follows a Hall of Shame for some of the most egregious S&L shills.

Showdown: Jim Wright and the S&Ls vs. the Taxpayers

Bushy eyebrows dancing, cornball metaphors flying, Jim Wright dominated Congress during his two years as Speaker of the House. But for all his skill, nothing Wright did had as much impact as when he held a critically important S&L reregulation bill hostage as punishment for a government crackdown on his friends in the Texas thrift industry. He was joined by hundreds of his colleagues, who voted with the

S&Ls to ward off strong enforcement in May 1987. It was one of the most costly examples of special-interest influence ever.

First, some background. The Speaker of the House is the most powerful person in Congress, so when he intervenes with regulators on behalf of constituents it should be done with utmost care. But when it came to his homestate thrifts, Wright chose to play the bully. When regulators, desperate to preserve taxpayer money, began moving to close down mismanaged Texas thrifts, Wright—then the House majority leader—convened a meeting with them in September 1986 and accused them of "Gestapo-like tactics." After another meeting, this one with 150 Dallas bankers and developers angry over federal "harassment," he asked a Fort Worth real estate developer to prepare a "report" on the regulators' conduct.

Moreover, he waged a personal vendetta against the bank examiners themselves. One of the regulators pressing Wright's allies was Joe Selby, about the toughest financial cop in the country. Selby moved from Washington to help run the Dallas Home Loan Bank office in 1986. Soon thereafter, according to bank board chief Gray, Wright demanded that Selby be fired. Selby, Wright asserted, was steering agency business to a "ring of homosexual lawyers" in Dallas. All subsequent investigations found the assertions to be groundless.

Wright's efforts on behalf of the Texas high-flyers extended beyond smears against regulators; on their behalf, he blocked speedy action to clean up the thrift industry. In 1986, the administration asked for $15 billion to replenish the FSLIC fund and begin to clean up the corrupt Texas thrifts. The bill passed the House Banking Committee without serious opposition, and was set to be voted on by the House.

Enter Jim Wright. One Wright ally, a developer named Craig Hall, faced the collapse of his real estate empire in 1986 when he had trouble making payments on more than $1 billion in mortgages to some twenty S&Ls, and he wanted regulators to let him keep his operations afloat for a little while longer. The regulators were hanging tough—until they received word that

Wright had "put a hold" on the bill to replenish the S&L insurance fund, thus blocking it from moving ahead until they gave in to Hall's demands. Anguished bank board officials swallowed hard, and replaced the regulator who was dealing with Hall. A week later, Wright let the "recapitalization" bill pass the House. But it was too late in the congressional session to finalize the measure. Lawmakers would have to begin again in the one hundredth Congress in 1987.

Then Wright called regulators about another Texas thrift operator, Thomas Gaubert, a major Democratic party fund-raiser. Gaubert, barred from the thrift industry, wanted back in the business. Wright asked Bank Board Chairman Ed Gray to meet with the Texan, in clear violation of bank board rules. "I have been in government long enough to know that you don't have to ask the question explicitly to know what the message is, and I knew what the message was," Gray told House ethics investigators. Desperate to move the "recapitalization" bill in the upcoming Congress, Gray met with Gaubert, and even hired an outside lawyer to investigate the S&L executive's accusations of harassment. On nearly all points, the outside examiner sided with the regulators against Gaubert.

In early 1987, the U.S. League of Savings Institutions launched a lobbying drive bitterly opposing the $15 billion plan. Less money was needed, the thrifts argued—and if the regulators got the full amount, they would only shut down insolvent S&Ls, members of the lobby group feared.

The S&Ls had another reason for not wanting the full $15 billion: *they would have to pay for it* through increased fees. After all, the FSLIC insurance fund was supposed to be filled with contributions from the thrifts themselves. Gray says that industry leaders told him privately that they wanted to wait for the problem to get big enough so that the industry wouldn't be able to pay for it. Then the taxpayers would have to step in. Of course, that's just what happened.

Instead, the S&Ls proposed their own alternative bill that

would give only $5 billion to the regulators. Moreover, the S&L lobby insisted on "forbearance" provisions that would force regulators to refrain from shutting down insolvent thrifts. "Soundly operated institutions, if given some time, can recover from the temporary effects of economic adversity," asserted Joe C. Morris, the chairman of the league. These loopholes amounted to an order from Congress to the regulators: stop doing your job. Wright, St Germain, and House Majority Whip Tony Coelho all threw their weight behind the S&Ls, seeking to deny the regulators the funds they needed. Regulators desperately pressed for more funds. Even the antiregulation Reagan administration supported the full amount.

The showdown came in the spring of 1987. At first, the $15 billion plan passed a key subcommittee, pushed by a junior committee member, Representative Thomas Carper (D–Del). A week later came the key vote in the House Banking Committee, where Representative Steve Neal (D–NC) pushed the S&Ls' plan to slash the funds for the regulators. Speaker Wright made a dramatic and unusual appearance before a private caucus of the committee's Democrats to push for the S&L lobby's bill. Some lawmakers who had voted with Carper now switched; Representative Doug Barnard (D–Ga), for example, abstained. The vote was tense: at first, it was a tie. Then St. Germain used a "proxy" vote given to him by an absent member, Delegate Walter Fauntroy of the District of Columbia. The S&L-backed $5 billion plan won. (The accompanying chart shows where the banking committee members stood.)

1987 HOUSE BANKING COMMITTEE VOTE ON THE NEAL AMENDMENT TO REDUCE RECAPITALIZATION FROM $15 BILLION TO $5 BILLION

YEAS (25)	S&L Interests Contributions 1981–1986	NAYS (24)	S&L Interests Contributions 1981–1986
Fernand St Germain (D–RI)	$144,400	Chalmers Wylie (R–OH)	$22,850
David Dreier (R–CA)	49,300	Stewart McKinney (R–CT)	21,075
Norman Shumway (R–CA)	39,100	Steve Bartlett (R–TX)	20,098
Richard Lehman (D–CA)	37,650	George Wortley (R–NY)	16,100
Frank Annunzio (D–IL)	30,920	Barney Frank (D–MA)	15,150
Esteban Torres (D–CA)	26,950	Marge Roukema (R–NJ)	15,095
Stephen Neal (D–NC)	23,300	Stan Parris (R–VA)	12,750
Bill McCollum (R–FL)	19,125	John LaFalce (D–NY)	12,300
Mary Rose Oakar (D–OH)	17,700	Thomas Ridge (R–PA)	10,000
Carroll Hubbard (D–KY)	16,100	Jim Saxton (R–NJ)	9,415
Walter Fauntroy (D–DC)	12,685	Al McCandless (R–CA)	8,100
Bruce Vento (D–MN)	12,050	Jim Bunning (R–KY)	6,000
Bill Nelson (D–FL)	12,000	Gerald Kleczka (D–WI)	5,700
Thomas Manton (D–NY)	11,500	Thomas Carper (D–DE)	5,150
Robert Garcia (D–NY)	10,975	John Hiler (R–IN)	5,000
Paul Kanjorski (D–PA)	10,750	Buddy Roemer (D–LA)*	5,000
Ben Erdreich (D–AL)	10,700	Alex McMillan (R–NC)	4,500
Bruce Morrison (D–CT)	6,440	Joseph Kennedy (D–MA)	4,300
Thomas McMillen (D–MD)	5,325	Doug Bereuter (R–NE)	4,150
Charles Schumer (D–NY)	4,850	Toby Roth (R–WI)	3,960
Marcy Kaptur (D–OH)	4,300	Patrick Swindall (R–GA)	2,400
David Price (D–NC)	1,750	Jim Leach (R–IA)*	1,080
Elizabeth Patterson (D–SC)	600	Henry Gonzalez (D–TX)	450
Floyd Flake (D–NY)	0	Patricia Saiki (R–HI)	100
Kweise Mfume (D–MD)	0		
TOTAL YEAS	$508,470	TOTAL NAYS	$210,723

Note: Representative Doug Barnard (D–GA), who voted for the higher $15 billion bailout figure the day before in subcommittee, passed and therefore did not vote on the Neal amendment supported by the S&L industry to reduce the $15 billion bailout to $5 billion. The Neal amendment, which carried by one vote, would have failed on a tie vote if Barnard had voted the same way he had the day before. Barnard received $27,350 from S&L interests during the period 1981 through 1986.

*Representatives Leach and Roemer did not accept PAC contributions; figures included contributions from individuals only

Source: Common Cause

Did the S&L shills among congressional leaders have an impact? "I'll let today's vote and the broken arms speak for themselves," a disheartened Carper said after the vote. Other attempts to save the situation fared no better. The approved bill included the "forbearance" provisions, authored by Representative Steve Bartlett of Texas, that ordered regulators to keep insolvent S&Ls open. And when Representative Jim Leach, a thoughtful Republican from Iowa who consistently fought against reckless deregulation, proposed to limit risky investments by S&Ls, the measure lost 30–7.

The legislation moved out of the banking committee, and onto the House floor. One new element entered the picture: down in Texas, on March 27, 1987, regulators seized Don Dixon's Vernon Savings and Loan, producing embarrassing revelations about the Speaker. In a surprise reversal, Wright and St. Germain suddenly announced they were switching their support to the $15 billion plan.

Most bills that are backed by congressional leaders *and* the administration would easily pass. But not when it was opposed by the free-spending S&L lobby. Few interest groups can apply the personal touch to lobbying 435 members of Congress, but the S&Ls—seemingly, pillars of the community in nearly every congressional district—jetted dozens of executives into Washington to visit lawmakers. And despite Wright's public support for the $15 billion plan, by all accounts he barely lifted a finger to help it pass. Democratic Whip Tony Coelho spoke against the plan, as did Republican Whip (now U.S. Senator) Trent Lott of Mississippi. By 258 to 153 margin, the House voted to deny the regulators the full funding they needed. Instead, the weaker $5 billion plan passed on May 5, 1987.

The debate accurately foreshadowed the huge taxpayer bailout to come. "One argument is that if we do not provide the bigger dollar figure, then somehow the taxpayers are going to have to pick up the bill," complained Representative Neal, who backed the S&L industry's plan. "That is a red herring."

Rebutted Representative Carper, "We effectively put FSLIC right back on the brink of insolvency if all we do is authorize $5 billion."

In all, it was a major victory by the S&Ls over the taxpayers —one of the most blatant and shameful instances of Congress favoring a powerful industry over the needs of the public. Remarked S&L foe Representative Charles Schumer (D–NY), "the thrifts have a lot of clout, and they lobbied us very heavily. They did a full-court press, and very effectively."

At the same time, in the spring of 1987, the Senate passed a $7.5 billion plan. As the two houses met in a conference committee to iron out differences through the spring and summer, however, it became clear that the S&L situation was worsening and more money would be needed. But the lawmakers could only find enough support for raising the amount to $10.8 billion. On August 10, President Reagan signed the final legislation. Within a year and a half, it would become clear that Congress had woefully underestimated the problem—and had sided with the people who were causing it.

Epilogue. Wright's ham-fisted intervention eventually came to light, and prompted filing of complaints with the House Ethics Committee, first by Republican Representative Newt Gingrich and then by Common Cause. As the ethics panel's outside lawyers probed Wright's finances, they discovered a closetful of sleaze, including a self-published book that was "sold" in lieu of legal speech fees. (For example, the Teamsters PAC, not otherwise known for its literary interests, bought 2,000 copies.) The outside counsel's report to the committee was explosive: it found that Wright had broken numerous ethics rules in his advocacy for the Texas thrifts. But when the Speaker's congressional colleagues on the ethics committee voted, they endorsed the charges involving personal financial chicanery—but not those charges condemning intervention on behalf of individual S&Ls: "[W]hile it may well be that Representative Wright was intemperate in his dealings with representatives of the Federal Home Loan Bank

Board, the Committee is not persuaded that there is reason to believe that he exercised undue influence in dealing with that agency,'' the panel ruled. In this instance, at least, those living in a glass House chose not to throw stones.

The process moved forward—and the Republicans announced they would seek to force a vote on the S&L charges on the House floor. Soon the pressure became too great. On May 31, an emotional Wright went before his colleagues in the House chamber, and resigned.

Fernand St Germain and Jake Garn: The chairmen

Through the crucial years of the early and mid-1980s, the House and Senate Banking Committees were chaired by two staunch allies of the thrift industry—Representative Fernand St Germain (D–RI), and Senator Jake Garn (R–Utah). We've already seen one piece of their handiwork: the Garn–St Germain Act deregulating S&L investments.

The two men presided over committees that were notorious within Congress for being balkanized into factions of the financial industry. Some members spoke out for big banks; others for small banks; others for insurance companies, securities houses, credit unions—all depending on where their cash was coming from. It became all too easy for lawmakers to see their role as that of mediating between competing trade associations. (A few years ago, a top committee counsel was meeting with consumer advocates. One participant commented that the incoming chairman was close to the securities industry. ''Yes, that's true. But if you look closely at his campaign finance reports, I think you'll see he is getting money from banks, too.'' So getting money from both sides is statesmanship? ''I guess so,'' the staffer shrugged.)

But few financial sectors had more powerful friends than the thrifts. Chairman St Germain—known as ''Saint G''—was the moving force behind the increase of deposit insurance coverage to $40,000 to $100,000. And he tried to keep bad news about the thrift debacle from becoming too public. On one occasion, on June 9, 1987, crusading regulator Bill Black was preparing to deliver testimony before the House Banking Committee on fraud in the S&L industry. His prepared text, which pulled no punches, was delivered to the committee staff. "For the unscrupulous [real estate] developer, owning a thrift was a dream come true—a virtual printing press to provide money to develop his real estate." An angry St Germain canceled the hearing minutes before it was to begin.

St Germain styled himself a proconsumer legislator, pushing through limits on the amount of time banks could hold onto depositors' checks without cashing them. In part, his devotion to the thrifts grew out of his opposition to some deregulation of the big commercial banks. But over the years, his independence became compromised, wilting under a torrent of financial industry favors, contributions, and business deals.

A patron at the District of Columbia's Prime Rib restaurant on a typical weekday night in the mid-1980s might notice two jowly, red-faced middle aged men nursing cocktails and hailing the waitresses. One of these men was Saint G. The other was James "Snake" Freeman, a lobbyist for the U.S. League of Savings Institutions. And when the time came to pay, night after night, Freeman pulled out the league's credit card. All told, St Germain took hundreds of meals from the league and ran up bar and restaurant tabs tolling up to $20,000 per year.

Beginning in 1985, the chairman constantly faced accusations of corruption over his dealings with S&Ls. The House Ethics Committee, made up of lawmakers from both parties, is charged with deciding whether a member of Congress has broken House rules. For fourteen months, the House Ethics Committee investigated St Germain's business dealings, including partnerships with the chief executive officer of Florida Federal Savings and Loan in Tampa, which also let him use its jet. St Germain also received $1.3 million in loans from a Rhode Island bank to buy a string of International House of Pancakes restaurants. The committee found that he understated his net worth by $1 million on financial disclosure forms he had to file with the government. But the panel declined to punish him.

Then, just three months later, the Justice Department opened an investigation of the S&L lobby's gifts to the lawmaker. In 1988, prosecutors decided not to seek an indictment. But in a secret letter to the House Ethics Committee, the Justice Department said it found "substantial evidence of serious and sustained misconduct." After a lawsuit brought by the Public Citizen Litigation Group and the *Washington Post* had brought the charge to light a week before the November election, the fourteen-term congressional veteran was defeated.

Six months later, St Germain was back on Capitol Hill: this time, as a paid lobbyist for the S&L industry.

In Republican Jake Garn, chairman of the Senate Banking Committee from 1981 to 1987, the S&Ls had a friend nearly as constant as St Germain, if not as overt. Garn is one of the Congress's leading champions of financial deregulation. Much of his time was spent pushing to give commercial banks expanded investment powers—the same toxic combination of deposit insurance and speculation that caused the S&Ls to collapse.

Today's politicians devise endlessly innovative ways to wring cash from the interests that lobby them. One such method is the Jake Garn Institute of Finance at the University of Utah. The Garn Institute raised more than $2.5 million from the S&L industry, including contributors such as Charles Keating of Lincoln Savings and Loan and David Paul of Cen-Trust. It is, after all, an easy—and tax deductible—way to curry favor with a powerful lawmaker. For their payment, institute donors get to hobnob with regulators and policymakers at retreats in Key Largo, Florida, and elsewhere. The contributor list, included in the institute's official literature, was a who's who of the S&L industry. Still, Garn told *Wall Street Journal* reporter Paulette Thomas that he didn't know who the contributors were. "I don't sit down and read that stuff," he said.

Garn was also one of the Senate's leading recipients of "honoraria." In 1981, Garn made—and kept—$48,000 in honoraria, much of the money coming from speeches to banking groups such as the U.S. League, Citibank, and the American Bankers Association.

But Garn's protégé and alter ego on savings industry matters was his banking committee chief of staff, M. Danny Wall. He first began working for Garn in the Salt Lake City government, and his wife was the senator's secretary. Any good lobbyist knows that the staff assistants, as much as the members of Congress themselves, call the shots; a technical change in a bill, crafted at a legislative assistant's cubbyhole, can be worth millions of dollars to a private interest. In the "permissive" ethical climate of Capitol Hill, it is common for corporations and trade associations to provide free trips and lodging at faraway retreats for congressional staff assistants. But even in that environment, M. Danny Wall stood out. Over the course of three years, he took a total of *ninety-five* trips paid for by private interests, more than any other Hill staffer. In 1985 alone, there were thirty trips, including jaunts to New Orleans (National Association of Consumer Credit), San Antonio (Independent Bankers Association), Dallas (a First Texas Savings event), and San Francisco (Dean Witter Reynolds).

Wall was a city planner by trade, relatively unfamiliar with the S&L industry, and he routinely looked to thrift lobbyists for guidance. "Everything that Danny Wall knew about banking, he learned over a fancy lunch from a banking lobbyist," joked one former committee staffer. Wall described himself as merely a "lab assistant" at the drafting of the Garn–St Germain deregulation law; the mad scientist was Richard Hohlt, lobbyist for the U.S. League of Savings Institutions. Hohlt, a blustery political operative reportedly close to Republican National Committee chief Lee Atwater, spoke to Wall dozens of times a week as they pushed the bill to passage. The two became close friends; Wall even programmed the first speed-dial button on his telephone to reach Hohlt.

As Ed Gray's term as chief regulator was about to expire in 1987, Hohlt mounted an intense campaign to get Wall the job. Senator Garn personally contacted President Reagan, and secured the appointment for his "surrogate son." In July 1987, Wall was installed as the new chairman of the FHLBB, the chief thrift regulatory agency. Once again, the thrift industry had engineered the choice of its overseer.

S&L shills: A cast of hundreds

In addition to Garn, St Germain, and Wright, the S&Ls had help from other influential lawmakers:

Tony Coelho: The next LBJ—The year was 1940. A young man, newly elected to Congress, took over the moribund Democratic Congressional Campaign Committee (DCCC) and turned it into a money machine for cash-strapped Democrats. His name was Lyndon Johnson, and he went on to become president of the United States.

Forty years later, another ambitious young politician sought to travel the same path to power. Tony Coelho, a junior congressman from lush northern California, used his money-raising skill to propel him to the heights of party leadership while still a junior member. But Coelho's deft fund-raising was to be his downfall.

LBJ had tapped a gusher of newly rich Texas oilmen. Coelho, faced with the job of saving a financially comatose congressional Democratic party, turned to the new breed of cowboy bankers in the S&L industry. To the post of treasurer of the DCCC, Coelho named Thomas Gaubert, head of the Independent American Savings Association of Irving, Texas. Gaubert arranged for the DCCC to hold fund-raising receptions on the 112-foot yacht *High Spirits.* Docked on the Potomac, the $2.6 million boat—a sister vessel of the one-time presidential ship *Sequoia*—played host to scintillating evenings in which congressmen and lobbyists mingled under the moonlight. The yacht didn't belong to Gaubert; it belonged to the infamous Vernon Savings and Loan, owned by Don Dixon. And the DCCC failed to reimburse Vernon for the yacht. Later, faced with embarrassing revelations, the party committee reimbursed the S&L $48,451.

Gaubert also helped out his new friends in a key congressional race. He organized the East Texas First PAC, which spent nearly $100,000 to help a single candidate in a special election in 1985. Such huge expenditures are legal only if they are done independent of the official campaign, but according to journalist Brooks Jackson, Gaubert consulted with Coelho's party committee. (Also, some of the money appeared to have been raised illegally from Don Dixon's Sunbelt Savings and Loan.) Three executives of one institution, Commodore Savings and Loan, were convicted of illegally channeling thrift funds to East Texas First PAC. At the trial, one banker testified that the funds were raised in exchange for an explicit promise from Speaker Jim Wright to keep an unnamed bill bottled up in committee.

Ultimately, Coelho was undone not by the money that sloshed through the DCCC's pipes, but apparently by dipping into the S&L cash stream himself. In 1987, Coelho left the DCCC and was elected party whip, the number-three Democrat in the House. Basking in his new policy role, he even coauthored a campaign finance reform measure. But in the spring of 1989, the financial records of Drexel Burnham Lambert revealed that a $100,000 junk bond had been purchased by "Coelho for Congress." Not true, said Coelho, the bond was his; it had been arranged for him by "a friend from Southern California." The "friend" turned out to be none other than Columbia Savings and Loan owner Thomas Spiegel, one of the most flamboyant S&L high-flyers. And where did a congressman get the money to plunge into junk bonds? Half the money had been loaned by Columbia, a loan that was never reported by Coelho. In the face of a growing clamor over legislative ethics, and to forestall further disclosures, Coelho resigned his seat just two weeks after Jim Wright announced his departure—another casualty of Congress's connivance with the S&Ls.

Alfonse D'Amato: "Senator Shakedown." That's what the *New Republic* dubbed New York's junior senator, well known for his relentless hustling for campaign money. Named chairman of the Securities Subcommittee of the Banking Committee in his first term in the Senate, D'Amato operated with the same attentiveness to quid pro quos that he learned in the Nassau County Republican political machine. (There, the party raised funds through a "one-percent" system, in which county employees gave one percent of their salaries to the GOP, according to a jury verdict at a trial in which a letter from D'Amato was key evidence.) D'Amato styled himself a tribune for the suburban middle class, but in Washington he devoted himself to the interests of Wall Street. He was also known as one of the Senate's most aggressive fund-raisers. One witness reported that D'Amato even put the arm on mourners at the funeral of Jacob Javits, the man he had defeated for reelection.

D'Amato was a favored beneficiary of thrift and investment bank largesse. Even though he hails from New York, hardly a bastion of S&L high-flyers, D'Amato received $88,235 from thrift executives and PACs in the 1980s. At least some of this cash came D'Amato's way not for something he did, but for something he didn't do. For many S&Ls—and for the investment banks that funded their speculation—nothing was more important than junk bonds. These bonds pay the investor a high interest rate because they are inherently risky, and S&Ls both bought and sold the bonds with abandon. But public concern over corporate takeovers led to pressure to restrict junk bonds. The *Wall Street Journal* reports that in 1985,

> just one week before holding a hearing on a proposal to limit purchases of junk bonds by federally regulated thrift institutions, Sen. D'Amato was guest of honor at a $1,000-a-plate

dinner arranged by Drexel Burnham Lambert, Inc., the No. 1 underwriter of the high-yield, high-risk securities. The proposal, opposed by Drexel, was dropped from legislation that the Senator introduced.

The dinner was held at the chic Chasen's restaurant in Beverly Hills, and six Columbia Savings and Loan executives were among the guests. Five days after D'Amato introduced the bill —minus the S&L and junk bond restrictions—he received an additional $18,000 from Drexel executives. By September 1986, Drexel's PAC and executives had given D'Amato $70,750.

Drexel, of course, pleaded guilty to six counts of securities fraud arising out of its sale of junk bonds, and ultimately declared bankruptcy. Michael Milken, head of the firm's junk bond department (and mastermind of the merger wave of the mid-1980s), was indicted and subsequently pleaded guilty to securities fraud. D'Amato, for his part, is the subject of an ongoing Senate Ethics Committee investigation for his role in the Department of Housing and Urban Development (HUD) scandal.

Frank Annunzio: The congressman from the U.S. League. In broad pinstripes, 1940s-style padded shoulders, and wide tie, Frank Annunzio of Chicago looks like he would be more comfortable in a summer-stock production than on the congressional stage. But the long-time congressman was a believer in the home-lending thrift industry of days gone by. Whenever any other legislator challenged the thrift industry, he responded with parental protectiveness. One reason: the U.S. League is headquartered in downtown Chicago, and the group's former president, William O'Connell, was an Annunzio constituent. Another reason: Annunzio, his sons-in-law, and his top aide together received hundreds of thousands of dollars from the industry in personal funds, perks, and campaign gifts. For example, the league hired one son-in-law as a staff assistant; another son-in-law was retained by the league as a consultant, and served as Annunzio's 1990 campaign manager. According to Chicago's Pulitzer-Lerner newspapers, Annunzio's chief assistant, Curtis Prins, took three free trips to England courtesy of a New Jersey savings bank.

Annunzio voted the straight U.S. League ticket. When regulators in 1985 finally began to restrict the amount of an S&L's money that could be used to own projects (as opposed to lending for them), Annunzio fought back. He introduced a resolution opposing the action; eventually, 220 of his colleagues signed on. And during the S&L bailout, he used his position as chair of the Financial Institutions Subcommittee to try and weaken capital standards for thrifts.

Denny Smith: Self-service as "constituent service." Denny Smith of Oregon managed to be a partial cause of one S&L failure and an advocate for a second failed S&L—and a possible courtroom defendant in the collapse of a third S&L if litigation is brought. And he managed all this while serving as the Republican representative from Oregon's fifth congressional district.

In the most bizarre case, Smith tried to bully regulators to ensure that he would not be sued in the collapse of a thrift. In 1987, American Federal Savings and Loan of Oregon teetered on the brink of insolvency. Regulators for the Seattle office of the FHLBB found another, healthier thrift that agreed to merge with American Federal, and papers were drawn up. At that point, only one member of the American Federal board of directors balked: Denny Smith. He would not consent to the merger unless the bank board agreed to grant the thrift's board of directors immunity from any lawsuits that might arise if the new thrift failed. The highly unusual demand prompted a return letter from the president of the Seattle bank board promising to recommend against any such civil prosecution.

Smith says his service on the board of directors of a federally regulated and insured institution doesn't pose a conflict of interest, since he kept the two roles separate—as though regulators would fail to notice that the board member they were negotiating with was a congressman. "As a member of Congress, he shouldn't have been on the board of a federally insured institution to begin with," said former bank board chairman Ed Gray. "But then he tried to pull rank."

Previously, Smith had tried to get Gray fired, in a dispute involving yet another S&L. On July 17, 1986, the Oregon lawmaker wrote the chief regulator to advocate civil immunity for S&L boards of directors, beginning with one in his own district, State Federal Savings and Loan. The bank board had filed a lawsuit against twenty-three directors of State Federal, and Smith expressed concern about "the use of tax dollars in the litigation of this case." In the same letter, he admitted that "as fate would have it," friends and financial contributors ranked among the twenty-three defendants, a circumstance which he portrayed as coincidental.

Smith eventually wrote at least six letters on behalf of State Federal to bank board regulators. After the third such letter, a bank board attorney wrote back, beginning his letter by noting that "it is inappropriate for us to be discussing the details and merits of a case that is pending in court." Eventually, seven individuals connected to State Federal were criminally convicted in federal court. A U.S. Attorney later dubbed it "one of the worst economic crimes" in Northwest history.

Smith inadvertently helped wreck a third thrift, Citizens Savings and Loan Association of Salem. In 1982, Smith co-owned an industrial park that had few tenants and was in deep economic distress. Citizens S&L took the park off his hands. As payment to Smith, the thrift gave him 132,000 shares of its stock. All told, the deal cost the S&L $1.4 million and helped contribute to its failure in 1988, according to federal regulators. "If the regulators didn't like it, they should have stopped it," argues Smith. "It's all part of the big picture: they allowed these kinds of things to go on."

American, State, and Citizens S&Ls eventually failed, at a total estimated cost to taxpayers of over $400 million. This sum accounted for 70 percent of the cost to taxpayers of failed Oregon S&Ls. Smith maintains that his conscience is clear. "If I had to do it all over again, I would do it all over again," Smith declared in July 1990. "Except maybe I would be more aggressive to protect my people against regulators."

Such blatantly self-serving actions and attitudes are clear grounds for a complaint with the House Ethics Committee. House Democrats, petrified of the charges that could be leveled against some of their number, failed to file a charge until September 1990.

1988: THE STALL

In 1987 and 1988, hundreds of S&Ls across the country began losing money. It had all the earmarks of a full-fledged banking crisis, except that the economy was otherwise doing well. All those bad loans made to chiselers and dreamers were coming due—and going bad. With increasing desperation, S&Ls juggled their loans and doctored their balance sheets to keep afloat. And they kept making loans on real estate projects that were never going to pay off.

As the situation worsened, Washington pretended there was nothing wrong. A bipartisan conspiracy of silence kept the scandal off the front pages and out of the presidential race. Meanwhile, regulators made secret deals with financial speculators and politically connected insiders in an effort to quietly dispose of failed S&Ls.

"M. Danny Isuzu"

At the Federal Home Loan Bank Board, the fix was in. Ed Gray was gone, his term having expired in June 1987. His replacement was M. Danny Wall, the chief of staff for the Senate Banking Committee when it enacted deregulation, and the candidate backed by the U.S. League of Savings Institutions.

The regulators' adversarial approach to S&Ls was now replaced by shared goals and interests. Bill Black, the crusading regulator who had stood up to Congress, had transferred to the San Francisco office. Joe Selby, the tough enforcer who was leading the crackdown in Texas, was fired in 1988. The first indication of the tone of the new regime came on the day Wall took his oath of office. According to journalist Michael Binstein, Wall's family and friends were gathered, waiting for the ceremony to begin, when S&L lobbyist Richard Hohlt called. A bank board secretary told him Wall was with his family, about to be sworn in. "I don't give a goddamn who in the hell he's talking to," Hohlt snapped. "I want him right now." To the dismay of bank board staffers, Wall took the call.

Wall was acutely political, ever attuned to the sensitivities and needs of his Republican Party sponsors—and his subordinates followed his lead. One branch of the bank board gave the Florida Republican party eighteen months free rent in a building it had seized from a failed S&L. In 1988, the bank board and other S&L agencies donated $11,000 to the Jake Garn Institute at the University of Utah, at a time when FSLIC was insolvent. Wall's response when asked about the gift: "What's the point? So?"

Wall so routinely denied the obvious that his employees gave him a nasty nickname: "M. Danny Isuzu," after the TV auto pitchman. Even S&L executives were struck by what they saw as their chief regulator's optimism: as a gag, they gave a comb to the bald Mr. Wall. Wall repeatedly appeared before Congress to proclaim that the S&Ls would not need a taxpayer bailout. On May 26, 1988, he told the Senate Banking Committee that FSLIC "possesses adequate resources in the near term to deal with problem institutions in the thrift industry," an assertion he repeated before congressional panels in September and in October during the presidential campaign year. "We are within striking distance of having dealt with all of the problems with the resources available," he added.

WHO ROBBED AMERICA?

The Secret Bailout

Robert M. Bass, the reclusive Texas billionaire . . . Ronald Perelman, who gained control of Revlon in a hostile takeover . . . Former Treasury Secretary William Simon . . . A meeting at a Wall Street men's club? Not exactly. These were some of the financial wizards who got sweetheart deals and huge government subsidies to buy thrifts during Ronald Reagan's last days in office.

While Wall and other Reagan administration officials were swearing that no new taxpayer money would be needed to shut down sick thrifts, they were secretly spending huge sums of public funds to do just that. In 1988, when the FHLBB began taking action, it seized and sold off a total of 220 thrifts. In a frantic effort to find buyers for the S&Ls by the end of 1988, Wall's staff was outnegotiated by some of the best dealmakers on Wall Street. A House Banking Committee investigation found that investors received $78 in assets and government subsidies for every $1 they invested for the right to buy an S&L. The fiasco culminated in a costly binge of government giveaways in the days leading up to New Year's Eve, as 75 thrifts were sold in one month.

What was going on? Traditionally, when an S&L (or bank) is declared insolvent, the government will seize the institution, and, if necessary, back up depositors' funds with dollars; eventually, it may be sold to a private buyer, or it may be shut down. All of that drains money from the insurance fund, however, and if FSLIC shut down all the insolvent thrifts it would once again be broke. The Reagan administration didn't want to admit that, however. So Wall and other regulators tried a different method. They would find a buyer, usually another S&L, to take over a sick thrift. If need be, they would entice the buyer with huge tax breaks and other subsidies. These funds would not show up on the government's books as a payout from the insurance fund. But they were often *more* expensive than a traditional crackdown.

In 1988, the bank board's gimmick was known as the "Southwest Plan." Starting in February of that year, the bank board began assembling insolvent Texas S&Ls into packages and selling them to investors or to "healthy" thrifts. Some eighty-seven insolvent S&Ls were reshuffled in fifteen "assisted transactions," at a total cost estimated by the House Banking Committee of $66.9 billion over ten years. Adding to the confusion, the tax breaks expired on December 31, 1989. By nearly all accounts, the transactions—with all decisions being made by a handful of senior officials—were a fiasco.

For starters, the deals were worked out and consummated in secret. Congress and the public were blocked from learning the details of the sales. Bids were never solicited; instead, interested investors quietly discussed terms with FSLIC and bank board officials. Other financial regulators were outraged. "I've never seen a group that does deals and never publishes a piece of paper about it," chief commercial bank regulator William Seidman told a reporter. Congress never authorized such huge government payouts, as required by the Constitution. The regulators consummated the deals in late-night binges, like college students cramming for finals. Five were announced on New Year's Eve itself, as the clock ticked the tax breaks away.

Incredibly, the bank board did not consider the cost of tax breaks given to the buyers in its calculations of whether to finalize a deal. The 1988 tax breaks cost the government an estimated $8.5 billion. According to the GAO, in fully one third of the transactions, it would have been cheaper to simply shut the S&L down and sell off its assets. These huge "tax expenditures" were made without congressional authorization, and despite the opposition of the incoming Bush administration.

Many of the deals also included a "yield maintenance agreement." In plain English, the federal government guaranteed the profitability of all of the money-losing assets taken over by the new operator, at a declining rate, for up to ten years. And

Wall gave the S&L buyers "notes" that could be redeemed later by the government, at a time when the insurance fund had more money. Until then, the government has to pay interest on the notes.

And many of the contracts contained a secret clause. The new owners were quietly given "pocket charters"—newly issued, inactive licenses to operate S&Ls. If a future regulator tries to go back on one of the midnight deals, the acquirer can activate the license and transfer all the profitable assets to the new institution. The government would get stuck with all the money-losers. Incredibly, these secret contract clauses were not revealed until 1990.

In making these sales, the government didn't ask bidders if they were going to put the S&Ls back into making home mortgages or other community-development lending. The sole goal was to get the property off the government's books—to protect Ronald Reagan's budget deficit estimates and to minimize the crisis. An opportunity to steer the thrifts back toward their intended purpose was lost. Instead, a whole new breed of high-flyers took over.

The slick financiers who took advantage of these deals were closer in temperament to Charles Keating than to Jimmy Stewart. Many of them were Washington or Republican party insiders—or they hired insiders to clear the way. And as befits some of the shrewdest investors of the age, they took the government to the cleaners. When the statistics for S&L profitability were released at the end of 1989, it became clear that the big financiers had made a killing.

Ronald Perelman, for example, is estimated to be the fifth richest person in the United States; his fortune is estimated to be $2.75 billion. In a 1988 "assisted" deal, he took over five giant Texas S&Ls and created First Gibraltar Bank of Houston. Perelman put in $160 million of his own money. In the first year, First Gibraltar gave Perelman a $104 million profit, plus a $170 million federal tax break—in other words, a 170 percent return on his investment. Not surprisingly, Perelman has shown little interest in putting Gibraltar's money into home mortgages, especially in poor neighborhoods. According to a study released by the community group ACORN, in 1989 First Gibraltar made eleven cents worth of home loans in minority communities for every *thousand* dollars of federal subsidy.

The Robert M. Bass Group spent $400 million in 1988 to acquire American Savings Bank of Los Angeles, the nation's ninth-largest savings institution. Within one year, the thrift earned $214.2 million, mostly due to federal subsidies. (The same year he was buying a thrift, Bass gave George Bush's presidential campaign $100,000 in "soft money.")

Within a few months, the Bush administration had imposed a moratorium on the deals. Some members of Congress, led by Senator Howard Metzenbaum (D–Ohio) and House Banking Committee Chairman Henry B. Gonzalez (D–Tex) have campaigned to reopen the deals. In the bailout legislation passed in 1989, an FDIC study of the Southwest Plan was mandated. But it is going to be very difficult for the taxpayers to go back on the deals altogether—especially considering the secret clauses in the contracts. In the end, the cheapest way out may be to buy back the S&Ls from the investors.

Mr. Fail Succeeds in Washington

The most startling story to come out of this fire-sale frenzy is that of James M. Fail.

In 1976, Fail was indicted in Alabama for securities fraud; in a plea bargain, he agreed never to do business in the state again, and his company pleaded guilty to a felony. Fast forward to 1989: In a December deal with Danny Wall's bank board, Fail purchased a string of fifteen failed S&Ls from the government, merging them to create "Bluebonnet." To do so, he plunked down a grand total of $1,000 of his own money, plus funds from his insurance empire, and received $1.8 billion in federal assistance. As the story unfolded in the summer of 1990, Senator Metzenbaum said angrily, "In all my years in public office, I have never seen such an abandonment of public responsibility as the S&L deals in 1988, and the Bluebonnet deal is an abomination, the worst case we have found."

Fail moved on from his company's white-collar crime conviction to operate insurance companies in several states. In 1987, he bought a failed commercial bank, winning approval from the FDIC for the bid. He neglected to mention his own indictment and refused to fill out the usual forms the agency required. FDIC Chairman William Seidman now says simply, "We didn't stick strictly to the rules; he slipped through. We were duped." Fail paid the government $500,000 for a bank whose market price was $2 to $6 million.

When it became clear in 1988 that the Southwest Plan offered new vistas of money-making at Uncle Sam's expense, Fail put together a bid for Texas S&Ls. In addition to $1,000 of his own money, Fail borrowed $70 million more, some of it from the insurance companies under his control. His bid was late, and a competing bid was considered the front-runner. But Fail knew that one key to insider politics in Washington is connections, and in lobbyist J. Robert Thompson he had connections galore.

Thompson had been legislative director to then Vice President George Bush. Now a professional lobbyist and consultant, he admittedly was no expert in banking regulation. Instead, as he told Metzenbaum's subcommittee in written testimony, "With a decade's experience working in the executive branch and with members of Congress, and my subsequent time as a lobbyist, I have portrayed myself as someone who understands the processes by which decisions are made and public policy is achieved." The seasoned Washington insider recognized the potential for profit in the chaotic S&L bailout. As an unsigned memo on Thompson and Co. stationery advised the reader, presumably a potential client, "serious inefficiencies likely to result in the first six months of this new program [the Bush bailout] will present very good opportunities."

The lobbyist went to work for Fail on his S&L bid, as he had on the bank purchase two years before. Thompson was suitably well connected. "Dear Danny," began one letter to Wall, which requested that the bank board name someone to be liaison with Fail's group. (Scrawled by an unknown hand, a note in the margin says, "Can this be done?") On one occasion, Thompson was given access to part of a draft of an internal bank board report on Fail's legal troubles; he helped the government's lawyers draft their response. Evidently, Thompson was very well compensated for his efforts, compared with most Washington lobbyists. Thompson claimed that Fail had promised him two percent of the profits from the deal. In addition, he received a $500,000 loan from Fail's bank. Until the Senate subcommittee asked, Thompson never paid Fail any interest on the loan.

Fail and Thompson made their bid in early December, with little time left before the S&L tax breaks expired. But Fail's proposal moved through the bureaucracy easily.

A rival plan, which would have cost the government less money, was the leading contender at the time. Wall and his deputy assert that the other plan fell apart because it was legally too complicated to process in the short time remaining. But the *New York Times* reported that the head of FSLIC told his staff to work out a deal with Fail the very same day that the agency's lawyers were beginning their analysis of the competing bid.

To save time, the regional Home Loan Banks conducted background checks for the central regulatory board. On December 22, the head of the Dallas bank sent his superiors a letter mentioning Fail's indictment, but not his company's conviction; it expressed no opinion on whether Fail was eligible to buy the S&Ls. Later that same day, the Dallas regulator sent another letter. The two missives were identical, except that the second letter now stated that Fail was indeed eligible. The regulator says he doesn't remember why he changed the letter.

Fail succeeded at the political gamesmanship needed to win

in Washington. The bank board sold him the fifteen S&Ls, and threw in $1.8 billion in benefits. In the next year, Bluebonnet made a grand total of *four* new loans. But it was the most profitable thrift among those sold off in 1988, earning Fail a 62 percent return on his investment. It turned out that he may have violated state insurance rules when he financed the bid with policyholders' money, but no matter. Bluebonnet's profitability was almost entirely due to the government subsidies provided by the Southwest Plan.

In the summer of 1990, Metzenbaum's Senate Subcommittee on Antitrust and Business Practices launched an incendiary series of hearings on the Bluebonnet deal. Metzenbaum hopes to use the issue to jimmy open further shenanigans of the entire Southwest plan.

Election Day, 1988

The S&L crisis played almost no role in the presidential campaign of 1988. George Bush, of course, never mentioned it. Michael Dukakis made one abortive attempt to raise the issue, endorsing a study that warned the brewing crisis would cost $70 billion. Republicans attacked back; M. Danny Wall called Dukakis's numbers "rubbish." The hapless Dukakis quickly dropped the subject.

When George Bush was elected, the S&L crisis may have been preoccupying experts in Washington, but Danny Wall and other regulators had done what they apparently set out to do: they kept the lid on until the ballots were cast. It was the one element of S&L regulation that can be called an unqualified success. But soon enough, the issue would explode—and taxpayers would realize that their leaders had presided over a governmental catastrophe without precedent.

FOUR

THE LINCOLN SAVINGS AND LOAN SCANDAL

•

RAMONA MILLER-JACOBS could not believe her eyes. She had invested the settlement from an automobile crash, which left her teenage daughter paralyzed for life, in bonds sold by her local thrift, Lincoln Savings and Loan. A deeply religious, hardworking phone company employee, Ramona understood that her investment was secure. Now, in April 1989, family friends told her that Lincoln Savings was in "some sort of trouble" and she headed for the S&L's Burbank branch.

"To my amazement, the facility was filled wall to wall with people and there was a long line of people outside waiting to get into the branch," she recalled later. Unable to get any answers in the mob of panicked bondholders, she went home. In the end, it turned out, some 23,000 customers, two thirds of them senior citizens, claimed they had been duped into putting their funds into bonds that they had been led to believe were insured. They weren't. When Lincoln failed, the bonds became virtually worthless.

Thus unfolded perhaps the saddest chapter of the S&L drama: the collapse of Lincoln Savings and Loan. At a $2.5 billion possible cost to the taxpayer, it is the single most expensive thrift failure to date, and a breathtaking example of the pervasive corruption at work in the scandal. The debacle, says House Banking Committee Chairman Henry B. Gonzalez, is nothing less than a "mini-Watergate."

At the center of the Lincoln saga is the flamboyant figure of Charles Keating, a Phoenix real estate developer. Beanpole-thin, a champion swimmer, Keating was a leading anti-pornography crusader, traveling the country denouncing smut throughout the 1950s and 1960s. In 1980, he even briefly served as campaign manager for the ill-starred presidential campaign of John Connally, which spent $12 million in the 1980 Republican primaries but won only one delegate. But there was a darker side to Keating's drive. He had already been accused of fraud by the government: in 1979 he settled charges brought by the Securities and Exchange Commission, which alleged that he had milked a bank for funds in his home state of Ohio. Now Keating wanted to buy an S&L (paying for the purchase with junk bonds sold by Drexel Burnham Lambert), and the regulators let him.

In 1984, the real estate developer purchased Lincoln, a traditional Irvine, California, thrift that specialized in home loans. Soon that traditional emphasis was gone. "Lincoln, over one 18-month period, made a dozen home loans, in the middle of the counties that were the fastest growing home building counties in America," Representative Jim Leach reported later. "Half of these loans were to insiders."

Instead of mortgages, Lincoln plunged into a frenzy of speculative investment. Lincoln bought and sold junk bonds, helping fund corporate takeovers. It bought and sold huge tracts of undeveloped land. And it spent $150 million on constructing the Phoenician Hotel, a marble and gold pleasure dome rising out of the Arizona desert. Brochures for the Phoenician bragged that the hotel was "A Masterpiece—of Relaxation," but a masterpiece of wishful thinking is more accurate. To make a profit, government regulators later estimated, the Phoenician would have to be 70-percent occupied . . . at an average room rate of $500 a night!

Soon Lincoln was drained of money, providing a stream of cash for American Continental Corp., Keating's real estate company. According to the government, the thrift became enmeshed in an intricate series of fraudulent land and tax deals. In transaction after transaction, Lincoln would loan a buyer money to buy land from Keating at an inflated price—thus giving a "profit" to the S&L. Lincoln then gave these funds to Keating's real estate company for "tax payments" on the "profits." But the tax payments were never made. Instead, Keating's company pumped the funds into development and construction projects. A federal judge ruled that this amounted to the systematic "looting" of Lincoln.

Still, Keating's devotion to "family values" never flagged. He named as Lincoln board chairman his son Charles Keating III, a twenty-eight-year-old college dropout, for total compensation worth $860,000. Keating paid himself $1.9 million. In all, about ten Keating relatives received $34 million from the S&L and its parent company.

Alarmed by the rowdy investments at Lincoln, regulators began closing in. Ed Gray, the head S&L regulator, became worried about S&Ls like Lincoln that were plunging so recklessly into nonhousing investment. Along with other members of the bank board, in 1984 Gray put forward a new rule limiting the amount of "direct investments" S&Ls could make.

Keating struck back, using White House clout, top-flight accountants and lawyers, and, ultimately, congressional intervention.

White House Chief of Staff Donald Regan chose a candidate for a vacant seat on the bank board: Keating's lawyer, Lee Henkel, who had received a $250,000 personal loan from Lincoln. As soon as he joined the board, Henkel proposed a rule that on closer examination would have exempted from the direct investment rule only two S&Ls—one of which, naturally, was Lincoln. His colleagues on the regulatory board were shocked by the nakedness of Henkel's favoritism. A Senate investigation was launched, and Henkel resigned after only five months.

Keating's extravagance bought him an arsenal of hired guns. Prestigious law firms counted Lincoln as among their biggest clients. Arthur Young, one of the nation's biggest accounting firms, for years attested that Lincoln's books were above reproach. Shortly thereafter, the accountant who prepared the audit, Jack Atchison, took a new job—with Keating, for *$954,000 per year.* To another regulator, the financier bragged that he had spent $50 million in his battles with regulators. He hired Alan Greenspan, soon to be appointed Chairman of the Federal Reserve Board, to issue an economic report certifying Lincoln's soundness. (Greenspan's letter said that Lincoln was as sound as seventeen other "thriving" thrifts. Within three years, sixteen of them would be bankrupt.) Arizona officials were startled when Keating brought in former president Gerald Ford to a meeting where Keating was trying to get a zoning change. And he even attempted to buy regulator Ed Gray, offering him a lucrative job to get him off the bank board.

Despite this cache of purchased clout, the evidence was too overwhelming to ignore. In the spring of 1987, bank examiners decided that Lincoln was insolvent and would have to be seized by the government. Keating's final weapon of choice was raw political power.

All told, Keating, his family, and his associates gave $1.4 million to the campaigns and causes of five U.S. senators. When the scandal eventually exploded into public view, the lawmakers became known as the "Keating Five":

- *Alan Cranston.* The senior Senator from California, known as a crusading liberal who was once sued by Adolph Hitler, became a key Keating champion on the Senate Banking Committee. Keating and his associates gave Cranston's campaign, the California Democratic party, and voter registration groups affiliated with the Senator, a total of $982,000.
- *Dennis DeConcini.* Keating steered $48,000 to the campaign of the procorporate Arizona Democrat. But a real estate firm controlled by Ron Ober, DeConcini's campaign manager, got loans of over $30 *million* from Lincoln.
- *Don Riegle.* The number-two Democrat on the Senate Banking Committee (now its chair) visited Keating's headquarters in Phoenix, even touring his properties by helicopter. Keating, in turn, threw Riegle a $76,000 fund-raiser—the senator's single biggest source of campaign cash. During the 1988 election, when the controversy began to percolate, an embarrassed Riegle returned the money.
- *John McCain.* A former Vietnam POW, McCain wears his honor on his sleeve. But despite his professed misgivings,

McCain was drawn into Keating's orbit: the Lincoln crowd gave McCain's campaign $112,000. McCain's wife and father-in-law were investors with Keating in an Arizona shopping mall. And both the senator and his spouse took three trips to Keating's mansion in the Bahamas—trips McCain failed to disclose on his senate financial disclosure forms. He repaid Keating when the trips were revealed.

· *John Glenn.* It's a long fall from "The Right Stuff" to the muck of the S&L scandal. But Keating gave $200,000 to the former astronaut's Ohio political action fund—money that didn't have to be reported under federal law due to a loophole—plus $34,000 in other gifts.

In politics, if not in real estate, Keating's investments paid off. In early April, 1987, Gray was summoned to a secret meeting in DeConcini's office; there he found Senators DeConcini, McCain, Cranston, and Glenn. Arguing on behalf of "our friend at Lincoln," DeConcini offered a deal: Lincoln would make more home loans if Gray would drop the direct investment rule and leave Lincoln alone. A week later, the bank examiners themselves were flown in from San Francisco for a second meeting, this time with the full Keating Five. Regulator Bill Black took virtually verbatim notes.

"These people saved a failing thrift," Riegle erroneously asserted.

"Charge them or get off their backs," demanded Glenn.

DeConcini, the meeting's convener, pointed to a letter sent to Capitol Hill by Lincoln's auditors. "Why would [the accounting firm] Arthur Young say these things? They have to guard their credibility too. They put the firm's neck out with this letter," said DeConcini. "They have a client," replied regulator Michael Patriarca. "You believe they'd prostitute themselves for a client?" the senator demanded. Replied Patriarca: "Absolutely. It happens all the time."

"This is a ticking time bomb," one of the bank examiners

told the senators. They warned the lawmakers that a "criminal referral" would be sent to the Justice Department.

"Both meetings," Gray later charged, "were exercises in naked political power on behalf of a major political contributor."

Within weeks, the investigation of Keating was put on hold. To this day, the public hasn't been told the full story. But some clues can be found in a May 1988 letter to Keating from one of his attorneys, Margery Waxman of the law firm Sidley and Austin:

> You have the [Bank] Board right where you want them and you should be able to reach an agreement tomorrow which will completely satisfy you.
> As you know, I have put pressure on Wall to work toward meeting your demands and he has so instructed his staff. They all know the Wednesday meeting is crucial to their future. If they mess up this time, it is all over.

Sure enough, the new Bank Board chairman, M. Danny Wall, who met with Keating several times during his tenure, transferred the case away from the San Francisco office that had proved so bothersome to Keating. Lincoln stayed open another two years.

Finally, in April 1989, regulators looked at Lincoln again and finally decided to seize the S&L. And what they uncovered, they believed, was a web of fraud and deceit with few parallels in the history of finance. A new accounting firm hired by the government opened the books and declared, "Seldom in our experience as accountants have we encountered a more egregious example of the misapplication of generally accepted accounting principles. . . . Lincoln was manufacturing profits by giving its money away." In September 1989, federal regulators filed a $1.1 billion fraud lawsuit, alleging a pattern of racketeering. After a complaint from Common Cause, the Senate Ethics Committee launched an investigation of the Keating Five to determine if their help for "our friend" crossed the line from constituent service to contributor service. (To the end, Cranston and DeConcini lobbied for Lincoln, arguing that the thrift should be sold to a private buyer rather than seized by the government.) And the House Banking Committee, prodded by its chairman Henry B. Gonzalez, held a series of riveting hearings that focused public attention on the scandal. At the end, M. Danny Wall resigned.

Perhaps the most disturbing scam that came to light in 1989 was the massive swindle of thousands of senior citizens allegedly perpetrated by Keating and Lincoln. Some 23,000 customers, mostly old or poor, were sold junk bonds in Keating's real estate company through high-pressure tactics out of Lincoln's branch offices. Many of the consumers say they were led to believe that the bonds were insured by the government. Keating's employees were given simple sales instructions. The "weak, meek and ignorant are always good targets," one memo stated. And the sample customer name in sales force training materials was:

> Name: Edna Gert Snidlip
> Address: 1 Geriatric Way
> City: Retiredville, CA 92627

When the company went bankrupt, the bonds became worthless.

Many of the victims lost their life savings. In tearful congressional testimony, Shirley Lampel, who had lost her entire retirement nest egg, said, "It is a whole new definition of the bank robbery. It used to be that the guy put on a mask and a gun and he said, 'This is a stick-up.' Now, you go in there and *they* say, 'Gotcha!'" The bondholders' only hope is a civil racketeering lawsuit against Keating, his lawyers, and his accountants.

Keating, for his part, remained unrepentant, and for a year drew a $500,000 salary as head of a bankrupt bank. Now he's back on the speaking circuit, just as in his antipornography days, this time talking about the S&L crisis and the terrible injustice that has been done to him.

It was not to last. On September 17, 1990, Keating was indicted in Los Angeles for alleged securities fraud involving the bond scam. Accused along with him were three other Lincoln S&L executives. At the arraignment, the judge surprised even prosecutors by requiring a $5 million bail. Keating said that he was unable to come up with the required funds and was taken in handcuffs off to Los Angeles County jail. His mug shot adorned the front pages of newspapers across the country.

Others may look at the Lincoln case and see a paradigm of greed and influence-peddling run amok. Not Keating. "One question, among the many others raised in recent weeks, had to do with whether my financial support in any way influenced several political figures to take up my cause," he told a press conference in 1989. "I want to say in the most forceful way I can: I certainly hope so."

FIVE

·

THE BUSH
BAILOUT

•

BLINK TWICE, and you missed it. In early 1989, after years of stalling and indecision, an S&L bailout was suddenly enacted. Two and a half weeks after his inauguration, George Bush unveiled a bailout that was rubber-stamped, with few substantial changes, by Congress six months later.

Few citizens focused on the legislation, and public outrage only barely began to build as the proposal moved to passage. There's a reason for this public inattention: *the White House officials and Capitol Hill leaders whose fingerprints were all over the disaster wanted it that way.* The legislation, weak to begin with, was swarmed by special-interest lobbyists intent on weakening it further. Newspapers and television failed to cover the scandal until the very end of the legislative process. The biggest bailout in history was enacted with a small fraction of the public debate accorded to prohibiting flag burning or the funding of allegedly obscene art. As a consequence, the plan sticks the cost to average taxpayers, does little to inject accountability into financial regulation, and sets up a bureaucracy that appears destined to fail.

THE S&L BAILOUT LAW: THE BASICS

Formally known as the Financial Institutions Reform, Recovery and Enforcement Act of 1989, Bush's plan was quickly dubbed "FIRREA" for short. To his credit, Bush did at least own up to the seriousness of the crisis, in marked contrast to his predecessor. Nonetheless, the plan sticks the bill for the bailout with the wrong people—and doesn't make the crooks pay for their crimes. Its highlights:

Paying for the bailout. The bailout raises fifty billion dollars over three years through the sale of bonds, to be paid back over forty years. This money will be used to pay for the federal takeover of hundreds of insolvent S&Ls and to reimburse insured depositors' accounts. Because the funds come from bonds, which pay interest to purchasers, more than half the cost of the bailout will consist of these interest payments.

Regulation. The bailout bill repealed many of the deregulation provisions that had helped cause the crisis. For example:

- It limited the types of investments S&Ls could make, and restricted the purchase of junk bonds by federally insured thrifts.
- It barred states from allowing state chartered thrifts to undertake activities that federally chartered institutions could not.
- Most important, the Bush plan sought to repeal S&L executives' ability to gamble with taxpayers' money. This was done by increasing the capital requirements for S&Ls—the rules that tell a financial institution how much money it must have on hand before it can make loans.

The plan, however, does virtually nothing about the regulatory process—nothing to ensure that S&L regulators, or others, don't become "captives" of the industry they are supposed to oversee.

Restructuring the system. The plan abolishes the Federal Home Loan Bank Board and the Federal Savings and Loan Insurance Corporation. Depositor funds are now insured by a branch of the Federal Deposit Insurance Corporation, which previously had insured only commercial banks. The job of oversight was transferred to a new Office of Thrift Supervision at the Treasury Department. The assets owned by failed thrifts were transferred to a new, huge government corporation: the Resolution Trust Corporation.

Housing. Over the strong objections of President Bush, Democrats in Congress insisted that the bailout bill include provisions to bolster the goal of affordable housing. These housing provisions included:

- Requiring federal regulators to release to the public data on S&L and other financial institutions' investments in local communities. Also, the Home Loan Bank system would analyze an S&L's community lending record when giving the S&L loans and other benefits.
- Strengthening the laws against "redlining" (that is, discriminating against a lender based on race).
- Requiring the new S&L bailout agency to give first preference to low income housing when disposing of properties.

HOW IT PASSED

As in the army, the motto in Congress is usually "hurry up and wait." Not this time. In the Senate, rapid-fire hearings in February were marked by a parade of industry witnesses. Meanwhile, Donald Riegle, the chairman of the Banking Committee and a Keating Five member, refused point-blank to let Ralph Nader testify.*

The committee debated exactly one day on the 550-page bill. And on April 12, 1989, the Senate committee unanimously passed the bailout.

A scant six days later, the legislation was rushed to the Senate floor. Copies of the bill were not even made available to senators until three days before the debate. Democratic and Republican leaders locked arms to block any changes or improvements. Most lawmakers who had amendments to offer gave up. Nader had one particularly frustrating encounter in a

---

* Riegle's top banking committee aide, Kevin Gottlieb, had left government service in 1987. During that 18-month sabbatical, he earned $85,000 as a consultant to the American Bankers Association, another $725,000 as head of a billboard trade association, and $105,000 as Riegle's campaign manager. When these payments were publicized during the Lincoln S&L scandal, Gottlieb resigned.

reception room outside the Senate floor. The consumer advocate asked Senator Paul Sarbanes (D–Md), a thoughtful liberal
on the committee, if he would help support a consumer
amendment. Sarbanes refused: "If we open the bill up to
changes, it will only get worse," he shrugged. "The banks will
move in with their amendments."

Only Senator Howard Metzenbaum threatened to upset the
bipartisan rush to enact the legislation. The cantankerous sep-
tuagenarian relishes his role as the Senate's scourge of special-
interest boondoggles. Now Metzenbaum brandished a package
of seven amendments, and he was going to insist on a vote on
each of them. Senate leaders pulled him into a side room, and
negotiated a deal; some of his improvements would be included. But no senators would be called on to vote on the
controversial matters.

Bill Bradley of New Jersey was one of the few senators to
rise to oppose the bailout. "To date, only twenty-three people
have been convicted," he said. "Guilty S&L executives have
been given extremely light sentences, which have often been
suspended The American people are rightfully incensed by
this. They want to know why they should pay for S&L mismanagement and corruption when the people responsible are
hanging onto their limos, their mansions, their planes? Surely,
we should recover what we can from the crooks before we
reach into the taxpayer's pocket."

The S&L bailout bill passed the Senate by a vote of 91–8 on
April 18, 1989. It then moved to the House of Representatives
—where the full impact of S&L industry lobbying was felt.

After deceiving Congress and the public for so many years,
the S&L lobby had reason to tread warily. At the beginning of
the bailout, the industry displayed an inept political touch.
Who did the U.S. League of Savings Institutions blame for the
crisis? The regulators, for not being *tough enough!* "Our overseers were asleep at the wheel," Theo H. Pitt, Jr., chairman of
the league, complained to its Honolulu convention in 1988.

The league even published a study blaming deregulation for the conflagration.

But the S&L lobby soon returned to Capitol Hill, at first tentatively, then with gusto. After a few preliminary victories in the Senate, the thrifts swarmed the House of Representatives as it considered Bush's legislation. The pile-up reached its height during the sessions of the House Banking Committee. Previous financial panics saw lines of depositors nervously awaiting the opening of bank windows. Bank crises in the age of modern telecommunications and federally insured deposits instead saw lines of lobbyists stretched down the halls of the Rayburn House Office Building, talking on their cellular phones. Indeed, the queue for entry into the banking committee's hearing room began the night before, as law firms and trade associations hired bicycle messengers to stand all night and reserve spots. The handful of consumer and community advocates lobbying for reforms were rarely able to squeeze into the room—a marked disadvantage when the only way you can see how a representative voted is to read his or her lips. For a time, citizen groups planned a sleep-in of tenant activists to stay up all night and pack the committee room.

From morning to night, the Rayburn House Office Building hallways outside the committee room were jammed with anxious lobbyists. Pandemonium would ensue whenever a committee staff member emerged, as lawyers shouted the staffer's name and gestured for attention—creating a scene not unlike the Chicago futures pits, except that the commodity was influence, not pork bellies. Large thrifts, small S&Ls, commercial banks, securities houses, and financial "supermarkets" surged and eddied across the committee. Most of the House Banking Committee's resolve withered under the industry onslaught.

On the fourth day of deliberation, Reverend Walter Fauntroy, the District of Columbia's delegate to Congress and a member of the committee, began the final session. "I think it's appropriate at this time to say a prayer," he said. "Help each of us to rise above our narrow self-interest." Incredulous, the assembled legislators bowed their heads. But piety was apparently no match for politics, for within minutes, the Banking Committee began its day's work: discretely inserting exemptions from the bill's requirements to benefit specific thrifts back home.

One amendment, offered by Representative Doug Barnard (D–Ga), exempted Sears, now an established financial giant, from the legislation's provisions barring S&Ls from doing business with affiliated companies. (His explanation of the amendment never mentioned the retailing chain.) Another amendment allowed the infamous Columbia Savings and Loan, which was to become one of the biggest thrift busts, to continue investing nearly all its funds in junk bonds. No one remembers who offered it, the *New York Times* reported at the time, and no one has stepped forward to claim credit.

The *Wall Street Journal* described the influence bazaar:

> Carroll Hubbard Jr. (D–Ky) made the day for mortgage bankers by getting an amendment extending federal insurance to the risky escrow accounts of mortgages sold by thrifts. At the request of the mobile home industry, Bill Nelson (D–Fl) joined Rep. Hubbard to require federal regulators to make allowances for bad loans for "low and moderate income housing"—defined to include mobile homes. Peter Hoagland (D–Neb) has an amendment that would exempt four specific limited partnerships (including Merrill Lynch and Paine Webber) from liability if the thrifts they take over flop.

Representative Nelson also offered an amendment to benefit the Citizens Federal Savings Bank of Miami, at the request of then Rules Committee Chairman Claude Pepper. A colleague asked, "Is this the provision we need to get through the rules committee?" Yes, Nelson replied, it was. The amendment quickly passed without opposition.

It could have been much worse. Fortunately for taxpayers, a few courageous Representatives stood up to the lobbyists. In the sorry saga of the S&Ls, these few heros stand out:

- *Henry Gonzalez.* Most important by far was the new chairman of the House Banking Committee. Fernand St Germain lost his 1988 reelection bid. His unlikely successor—safe in his chairmanship only because of the seniority system—was seventy-two-year-old Henry B. Gonzalez of San Antonio. Gonzalez was a crusty populist, a foe of big financial institutions best known for his long-winded speeches on the House floor condemning high interest rates and the policies of the Federal Reserve. His hero was Wright Patman, an earlier Texas populist who headed the banking committee for decades. Gonzalez had voted against the deregulation of the S&Ls, and received only $1,570 from S&L PACs in the previous six years. Now Gonzalez sat atop the pyramid. At first, his control of the committee seemed tenuous. By the end, he won widespread admiration for his willingness to stand up for principle.

- *Representative Charles Schumer.* When this New York Democrat talks, the Brooklyn accent is as thick as Coney Island air. But the Harvard-educated Schumer was a highly savvy political player on the House Banking Committee who had earlier steered several proconsumer bills to passage. During committee deliberations, he worked long hours swatting down S&L amendments, and this Democrat found himself in the unusual position of working closely with Republican White House aides who wanted a strong bill. He also led the charge to create citizen-run Financial Consumers Associations, pressing on despite little support from his colleagues.

- *Jim Leach.* This Iowa Republican could step out of a Norman Rockwell painting of small-town virtue. One of the leaders in the fight for campaign finance reform, he opposed S&L deregulation throughout the 1980s, offering futile amendments to limit risky investments. In 1989, he suddenly found himself in the crest of a wave of public opinion.

- *Joe Kennedy.* Exuberantly physical, impatient, and earnest, the heir to the Kennedy dynasty charges throughout the halls of Congress like a man with a mission. Kennedy is rare among members of Congress: he is confident enough to push his way past the "we've always done it that way" mentality that governs the House, and many other organizations. Working closely with grass-roots housing groups, Kennedy fashioned housing provisions that failed in the Banking Committee but succeeded on the House floor.

As the bill moved through Congress, and especially through the House, the media finally began to cover the story. Public outrage slowly began to build, turning the lawmakers temporarily away from the S&L lobby. Unlike the clubbish Senate, the House of Representatives is a moody institution. Crowd psychology often governs, as it would in any group of 435 people. By the time the legislation reached the House floor, a full-fledged stampede against the S&Ls was underway. While the underlying flaws of the bill were not redressed, the S&Ls were handed several surprise defeats. And in that rarest of moments, Representative Jim Leach offered an amendment on the floor of the House to strike nearly all the provisions benefiting specific institutions from the bill—and won.

The House passed the bailout bill on June 15, 1989, by a surprisingly wide margin, 320–97. The two houses met for a month to resolve their differences, and the final product was passed on August 5. President Bush signed the measure on August 10.

WHO PAYS? YOU DO.

The worst feature of the Bush bailout is its central element: its cost, who pays for it, and how.

The bailout bill raised $50 billion. Some of these funds came from insurance premiums paid by S&Ls, others from the sale of assets belonging to S&Ls seized by regulators—but most came from the taxpayers. Over time, administration officials asserted, the total cost would be $157 billion. But this was nonsense. Bush's wildly inaccurate numbers simply assumed that interest rates will average 4.7 percent for the forty-year life of the plan. Never mind that interest rates were then over 9 percent, or that this projected average has not been accurate for years. By failing to ask for enough money, the Bush administration simply continued a practice previously perfected by the Reagan administration—"lowballing" the estimate of the problem in the hopes of minimizing political damage. Future funds will undoubtedly come from taxpayers, and delaying will only increase the price tag.

Debate in Congress did not focus on the fundamental question of whether the bailout should be paid for through borrowing well into the future. Nor did it focus on the question of whether the middle class should pay for the folly and crimes of the rich.

Instead, the limited congressional discussion focused on one of the most deceptive elements of the Bush plan: whether the costs of the bailout should be "on budget," or hidden "off budget." The cheapest and easiest way to pay for the bailout would be for the federal government to fund it directly, earmarking the cost on the federal budget like any other spending program. But that would mean the bailout would swell the official budget deficit, forcing President Bush and Congress to deal with its magnitude. In addition, the Gramm-Rudman budget cutting law would require the bailout to compete with other spending programs.

Instead of squarely facing these issues, the bailout plan is a jerry-built contraption of quasi-governmental corporations and deferred payments. Since the bailout corporation is not a government agency, the investment market considers its bonds to be inherently riskier than those sold by the treasury. Investors demanded a higher interest rate to buy its bonds. Estimates vary, but Federal Reserve Chairman Alan Greenspan has predicted that off-budget financing will add billions of dollars to the bailout. (Think of these as the first public-sector junk bonds—high risk, high yield.) Moreover, stretching out the payment over four decades adds further billions to the cost through compound interest. These payments on bailout debt will be borne by taxpayers until the year 2029. In all, the government is paying more for the sole purpose of pretending it is spending less.

Paying for the bailout through a quasi-governmental corporation also meant a windfall for Wall Street. The bailout's funding arm must peddle its bonds to private buyers as if it were a corporation rather than a government agency, paying huge fees and commissions to private investment bankers. Journalists and congressional sources reported that securities lobbyists were intimately involved both in crafting the "off-budget" proposal and in ensuring that it remained intact. In Treasury Secretary Nicholas Brady, Wall Street found a sympathetic ear; before joining the cabinet, Brady was an investment banker with the firm of Dillon, Read. In addition, investment bankers wanted to preserve the fiction that Gramm-Rudman was holding down the federal budget deficit.

In the Senate, Bob Graham of Florida and banking committee Chairman Riegle fought to cut the interest costs by having the federal government itself sell the bonds. Their amendment lost, 48–50. In the House, as the legislation moved through the process, an attempt was made to inject some budgetary honesty. A plan that would have cut the cost by paying for the bailout through a tax on the rich and financial interests was introduced by two junior representatives—Kennedy of Massachusetts, and Bruce Morrison of Connecticut, a former poverty lawyer. The proposal was shunted aside by a parliamentary ruling. When the two lawmakers tried to have it brought up as an amendment on the floor, the powerful House Rules Committee—which decides the format for debate on each bill—said no.

Instead, the House voted to pay for the bailout through long-term bonds, but to put the cost on budget. A victory for honesty in government? Not exactly: the vote also exempted the bailout costs from the Gramm-Rudman budget cutting law, which means it didn't affect other spending and taxing priorities. A proposal introduced by Representative John LaFalce that would have included the bailout in the federal budget *without* excluding it from Gramm-Rudman failed, by a vote of 171–259.

But President Bush was adamant that the cost of the bailout not be put on budget. Ultimately, he threatened to veto the entire bailout bill if the cost were included. Congressional Democrats buckled and agreed to keep future costs of the $50 billion bailout off the government's ledger sheets. (Only money for 1989, which was nearly over, would be counted.) It was, at the height of the effort to "fix" the problem, a classic repetition of the pattern we have seen before: top government officials more concerned about minimizing political damage than solving the broken policy. Financial markets weren't fooled. Only the political blame market was fooled—and then, only temporarily.

DANNY WALL HANGS ON

Incredibly, the decision about whether to put the bailout on budget came in a deal that let chief regulator M. Danny Wall keep his job. That agreement, apparently, was part of a desperate effort to keep the lid on the Lincoln Savings and Loan scandal.

The bank board was naturally a juicy target for reform, and the Bush plan saw the board overhauled and brought within the Treasury Department, its chairman dismissible by the president. But Senator Jake Garn insisted that Bush retain Wall—the senator's protégé—on the job. Bush agreed. The bailout proposal included a provision that the sitting head of the bank board would become the director of the new Office of Thrift Supervision in the Treasury Department—without any Senate confirmation hearings. The bailout bill also blocked the president from dismissing Wall until 1991. An amendment to require that Wall face Senate confirmation, offered on the Senate floor by Florida's Bob Graham, brought a rebuke from Jake Garn. "I would like to have *more* Dan Walls in Washington, D.C.," Garn said angrily. "Boy, why not do an FBI report on this man. It would be so dull, so boring, nobody would want to read it." By a vote of 61–38, the Senate voted to keep the self-described "son of the Senate" on the job without a probe of his conduct.

House Banking Committee chairman Gonzalez, on the other hand, wanted Wall out. "The present bank board—particularly its chairman, Danny Wall—seems incapable of presenting a straightforward story to the American public," he told the *Washington Post*. "The Congress and the public don't need sugar-coated news releases distorting the numbers. We need hard numbers—the truth." The House bill required that the head of the new regulatory agency be confirmed by Congress, as would any other key federal appointee.

The difference would have to be resolved in the conference committee that reconciled the two versions of the bill. So would the dispute over financing—whether to put the measure on budget, as the House wanted, or off budget, as the Senate wanted. In a surprise ending, Danny Wall held on—because he wasn't the only person who didn't want to endure a grueling confirmation hearing. Senator Alan Cranston of California, one of the Keating Five, knew that a hearing on Danny Wall would turn into a hearing on Lincoln Savings and Loan. As *Congressional Quarterly* reported at the time, "Cranston's ties to Keating would almost certainly have been an issue in a confirmation battle."

Cranston was one of the few Democrats who sided with the Republicans in seeking to put the finance plan off budget. Through six hours of tense meetings, Cranston held firm. Then, suddenly, he switched, and sided with the House's position. The House, in turn, agreed to let Danny Wall keep his job. Without that switch, Gonzalez said, Cranston would not have budged. "That's my understanding from the leadership, from the senators, and from Senator Cranston," he said. (Cranston, for his part, has heatedly denied that there was any deal.)

In the end, Gonzalez outsmarted both Cranston and Wall. President Bush's signature was barely dry on the bailout bill before Gonzalez announced that *his* committee would be holding hearings . . . on Lincoln Savings and Loan. The hearings stretched out over months in the fall of 1989. Remarkably, Gonzalez showed he was willing to skewer fellow Democrats as well as Republicans. Cranston trooped across Capitol Hill to ask Gonzalez if he could testify. "Every witness receives a formal subpoena," Gonzalez frostily told him; eventually no senators were subpoenaed. Broadcasts by the cable network C-SPAN made Gonzalez a minor folk hero throughout America.

As the hearings revealed the ineptitude and iniquity at the heart of the Lincoln story, pressure grew for Wall to quit. After all, critics reckoned, letting Wall keep his job as chief regulator of S&Ls was like allowing Joseph Hazelwood to keep his job as captain of the Exxon Valdez. On December 8, 1989, following demonstrations and calls for his resignation from taxpayer groups, Wall angrily announced his resignation. Gonzalez, he said, had "resorted to corruption of the truth and abandonment of our historical devotion to fair play and due process."

Ironically, the last-ditch stand by Cranston and Garn to save Wall's job nearly ditched the bailout itself. Early in 1990, a federal court ruled that many of the actions taken by bailout officials were invalid because Wall, as head of the OTS, had not been confirmed by the Senate as the U.S. Constitution requires. The bailout was temporarily put on hold while the Congress quickly confirmed a successor for Wall.

REREGULATION

In its best feature, the Bush plan applied stringent regulatory principles to S&Ls. Most important was its strengthening of capital standards. Thrifts have to have 3 percent of their assets in tangible capital (the same rule as for banks)—not intangible mumbo jumbo such as "goodwill." By June 1991, banks *and* S&Ls will have to reach 6 percent. Many S&Ls balked at this, since it might put them out of business.

In the Senate, the thrift lobby hammered the banking committee into gutting Bush's capital standards provision. When the legislation came to the Senate floor, Ohio's Howard Metzenbaum insisted that thrifts be restricted in their ability to count goodwill as capital. "I think goodwill is not worth doodly-doo, and I wanted to eliminate it," he said. In a deal struck off the Senate floor, Metzenbaum agreed to a standard requiring $1.50 of tangible capital per $100 of assets.

The U.S. League of Savings Institutions focused its fire on the House. A subcommittee chaired by S&L ally Frank Annunzio swiftly dug into the Bush bill, gouging out dozens of special provisions and weakening many regulations. "It really, really guts this bill," mourned one congressman. The stricter standards were inserted back in the bill in a vote of the full banking committee.

The hum of S&L lobbying became a roar as the bill neared a floor vote. Despite public outrage, representatives were still unabashed about lining up to plead for exemptions for hometown S&Ls and to weaken the rules. Over fifty proposed amendments, introduced at the behest of hometown thrifts, weakened the capital standards. James Quillen, a powerful Republican from Tennessee, led the drive to gut the rule restricting goodwill, at the behest of Heritage Federal Savings and Loan. Eyebrows were raised when it was revealed that Quillen had $200,000 on account at Heritage Federal. (He also owned

$700,000 worth of shares in another S&L.) "It's ridiculous to say I have a conflict," said Quillen.

Newspapers and magazines denounced the S&L lobby. THE HOUSE'S S&L SCANDAL, charged *Newsweek*. A PUSH TO DILUTE REFORM, said the *Washington Post*. A thrift owned by Warren Buffett, the widely respected Omaha investor, quit the U.S. League in protest over its position on the bailout bill. As debate dragged on, voters finally began to feel the pain in their pocketbooks. And what they saw made them angry. Phil Donahue broadcast a show on the bailout, featuring Representative Joe Kennedy and representatives of the grass-roots group ACORN. After the program aired, the Capitol Hill switchboard was flooded with calls. Nervous congressional staff passed around a videotape of the Donahue show and cringed as citizens voiced their outrage at having to pay for the crimes of the high-flyers, committed with the complicity of the politicians.

In the end, the mood of the House swung toward a new, unaccustomed stance: being *tough* on the S&Ls. Three hundred and twenty-six representatives voted to keep the stronger restrictions on S&L investments; only ninety-four voted against. "There's a populist wind blowing on the House floor tonight," crowed Representative Chuck Schumer.

•

SIX

THE RTC: DÉJÀ VU ALL OVER AGAIN?

•

TAXPAYERS ARE spending hundreds of billions of dollars on the S&L cleanup; they have a right to expect a few things, at bare minimum. There are two main ways to minimize taxpayer cost. First, the government should get the best possible price for assets of failed S&Ls. And second, law enforcers should do everything they can to punish those who looted the S&Ls, and recover as much money as possible for the public.

Unfortunately, the first year of the bailout has been an administrative mess and a policy disaster. The Bush administration has made many of the same mistakes that its predecessors did during the S&L industry's slide into insolvency. Most alarming, the regulators have begun to sell off the S&Ls and their assets at bargain-basement prices to big banks and other financiers, some of the very predators who got sweetheart deals in 1988. (Remember that the ultimate cost of the bailout in large part depends on how much the RTC can recoup from selling these S&Ls and their assets.) At the same time, the Bush administration's "war" on S&L fraud has been anemic at best, irresponsible at worst.

Yogi Berra said it best: "It's *déjà vu* all over again."

THE RESOLUTION TRUST CORPORATION

The largest corporation in the United States, measured in terms of assets, isn't General Motors or Exxon. The biggest real estate holder isn't Donald Trump or Harry Helmsley. Headquartered in an eleven-story government building in Washington, D.C., is the nation's newest economic powerhouse: the Resolution Trust Corporation. Seemingly overnight, the RTC—with assets worth over $200 billion and over 3,000 employees—has become one of the major economic forces in the United States.

The RTC was established as part of the 1989 S&L bailout legislation. Its sole purpose, during its short seven-year life, is to manage and dispose of assets from failed S&Ls. The agency's asset portfolio has included virtually every sort of commercial enterprise, including shopping malls, fast-food restaurants, high-risk junk bonds, a small town in Florida, 40 percent of the land in Colorado Springs, Colorado, and 389 acres of forest in Nags Head, North Carolina. As of February 1990, the RTC controlled almost 70 percent of thrift assets in Arizona. It even owned part of the Dallas Cowboys. (Commented the *Wall Street Journal*, "Now they're really America's team.") Referring to the crazy quilt of properties now under the control of the RTC, Donald Crocker, president of a real estate management company, said: "This is the toxic waste of the S&L industry. They don't want you to know they produce it, much less where they dump it."

To be sure, managing this morass is one Maalox moment after another. Unfortunately, the RTC so far has been slow to act and confused of purpose. The agency has dawdled in setting up shop and relies on outside contractors and experts instead of building a stable staff. One of the few explicit commands in the maddeningly vague bailout legislation was a requirement that the RTC make special efforts to encourage low-income housing; this the agency has markedly failed to do. And the bidders and buyers of the assets couldn't care less.

What the RTC actually does

The OTS, the new regulator of the S&L industry, determines if an S&L is insolvent. OTS officials then come to the S&L, usually on a Friday, and close the institution for the weekend. By Monday, OTS has placed the S&L in "conservatorship" by replacing the management. It then turns the S&L over to the RTC. This could be thought of as an attempt to pump life back into the thrift, to see if it can eventually be sold off as a complete S&L. Generally, when an S&L is sold, the RTC retains all of the "nonperforming assets" (that is, loans that are in default), and sells it as a "clean institution." The RTC itself must then manage and sell all of the bad assets.

If the S&L in "conservatorship" is still performing poorly, the RTC then puts the institution in "receivership." Essentially, it dismantles the institution, pays off the depositors, and sells the individual assets. Alternately, the RTC may choose to sell the deposits of the failed institution to a healthy S&L or bank at a premium and retain the assets.

As of August 1990, the RTC has taken over 477 institutions with $210.9 billion in assets, and has resolved (sold the S&L or paid off the depositors) 229 institutions. The RTC has spent $59.6 billion so far. Yet RTC Chairman William Seidman has said it will run out of money before the end of 1990. And, Timothy Ryan, director of the OTS, reports that fewer than half of the nation's 2,505 S&Ls are healthy.

Designed to fail: The stumbling start of the RTC

The new federal agency has a structure so tangled that it is virtually designed to fail. The admirable goal was to ensure accountability to the executive and legislative branches of government. Unfortunately, the bailout has been bogged down in administrative infighting, resignations, and disorganization, not to mention the fiendishly complex task of managing and disposing of assets.

The bailout structure is a Rube Goldberg machine. A government analyst sketched out the relationships between the agencies involved in managing the S&L bailout. The chart looks more like a computer chip than an operational flow chart. Callers to the RTC cannot get a simple question answered without having to be transferred to four or five different people. Often they will get no answer at all, or will be given two different answers. Frederick Alt, former RTC Oversight Board senior vice president for finance, said: "It isn't set up to succeed. It's set up to have no one make a move without five people asking why."

The admirable goal was to hold the executive branch accountable for its management of the S&L bailout. But the resulting hodgepodge is so cumbersome that no one seems accountable to anyone.

The *RTC Oversight Board,* made up of the secretary of the Treasury (who chairs the Board), the secretary of the Department of Housing and Urban Development (HUD), the chairman of the Federal Reserve Board, and two independent members selected by the president and confirmed by the president, serves as the policymaking board. The Oversight Board has its own chief executive. Under the bailout legislation, the Oversight Board is responsible for holding the RTC accountable. Its members, meanwhile, have other things to do, such as running major federal agencies. They seldom meet together, and make decisions by having their aides shuffle documents around Washington until all board members have signed off. The torpor was worsened by President Bush's failure to name his two appointees until *March 1990,* fully eight months after the bailout law went into effect.

The *Federal Deposit Insurance Corporation* serves as the primary manager of the RTC's day-to-day operations (thus putting William Seidman, the head of the FDIC, in charge of the day-to-day operations of the RTC as well). The chair of the FDIC serves as the chair of the RTC, and the FDIC's board of directors doubles as the board of directors of the RTC. The chief executive officer of the RTC reports to the RTC board; the chair of the RTC board, in turn, reports to the Oversight Board.

The RTC divides the U.S. into six regions. Each of the six *RTC regional offices* is advised by a five-member board of community leaders (so far, mostly white businessmen). These feed into a national advisory board, made up of the six chairs of the regional boards plus a national chair, who advise the Oversight Board.

Chaos at the top. Another factor contributing to the chaos and confusion was a wave of resignations, including many in top management at the RTC, the Oversight Board,

FUNCTIONAL

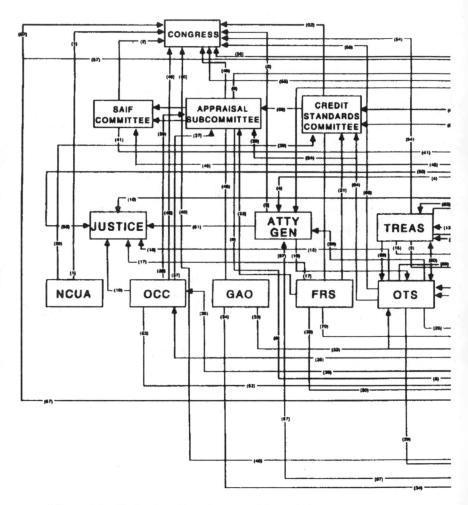

* Placement of entities above is not intended to connote relative heirarchy.

FIRREA
INTERRELATIONSHIPS

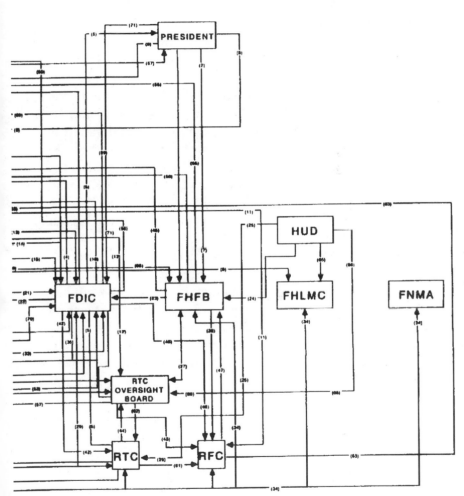

and the OTS (which oversees the entire S&L industry). The first year of the bailout was marked by important jobs going unfilled for months at a time, a key regulatory appointment receiving on-the-job training in financial issues, and the easing out of the most outspoken and independent regulator.

We already have seen how OTS Director M. Danny Wall clung to his post until March 1989, when he was forced out by public pressure growing out of the House Banking Committee's probe into the Lincoln Savings and Loan scandal. He was succeeded by a temporary replacement. Then came a federal judge's ruling, in a suit brought by an Illinois S&L, that actions taken by the OTS since its creation were illegal since Wall, the head of the office, had never been confirmed by the Senate. Even though an appeals court postponed the impact of the judge's ruling, the decision effectively froze the RTC and OTS in their tracks. The ruling finally forced the administration and the Senate to act quickly or risk sending the bailout efforts into complete shambles.

President Bush hurriedly nominated Timothy Ryan, a Washington, D.C., lawyer who was desperately short on experience but long on political connections. Ryan, who had worked for the Labor Department, was virtually unknown to the thrift industry, the Congress, and financial regulation generally. His most important qualification was loyalty: he was the general counsel for the Reagan-Bush transition team in 1980. Ryan began studying S&L bailout issues only a few weeks before he was appointed.

At his confirmation hearing, Ryan admitted that he had no experience working with financial institutions, and had no opinion on the future of the S&L industry, the adequacy of thrift capital standards, and the federal deposit insurance system, among other issues. Ryan told the committee, "To be quite frank with the entire panel, I was surprised when I received the call, just as those of you who are on the panel here, you've looked at my background." He added, "I don't know who else was in the pool quite frankly. And, as I said before, I didn't select myself for this."

"I have been asked the question during the past three weeks whether I have any view on should there be a thrift industry," Ryan said at one point. "And, I do not have a view on that right now." Chairman Riegle interrupted. "Wait a minute. Did I hear that right, that you don't have a view as to whether or not there should be a thrift industry?" "I have no view as to whether the thrift industry should move forward or not move forward, Senator," Ryan responded.

Ryan also raised congressional hackles by correctly asserting that Congress and deregulation shared part of the blame. To cap off the farcical nature of the hearing, Charles Keating showed up and demanded to testify. When the committee refused, he distributed a statement denouncing the Ryan nomination and strongly implying that he should be put in charge of the thrift rescue.

In the end, the banking committee confirmed Ryan by a vote of 11–10. It looked as though the vote on the Senate floor would be close, but it wasn't. The administration "pulled out all the stops to push this nomination through," observed Senator Riegle, "and succeeded." Rumors were rife that the White House won some senators' votes only by cutting deals on pork-barrel projects.

Meanwhile, Daniel Kearney, president and CEO of the RTC Oversight Board, resigned in early 1990 after serving only five months. As his reasons for leaving he cited excessive interference by the Treasury Department, bureaucratic infighting, and the fact that key RTC posts remained unfilled. After Kearney quit, Frederick Alt, the top aide at the RTC, also resigned, after serving only two months.

Most recently, William Seidman, the chair of the RTC and the FDIC, and the regulator most outspoken about the true cost of the crisis, has been pressured by the administration to leave his post before his five-year term is up. According to press accounts, both Chief of Staff John Sununu and Treasury

Secretary Nicholas Brady, bristling at Seidman's independent style, are pushing for his early departure.

Secrecy in the bailout

In several critical respects, the RTC operates without the normal accountability mechanisms that are supposed to prevent scandal and ensure that taxpayer dollars are well spent. **One fault line arises from the RTC's ability, in effect, to print its own money, without congressional approval.** The RTC has the authority to borrow money to tide it over while it attempts to sell the assets of the failed thrifts. This money is called "working capital." For the purposes of working capital, the law allows the RTC to borrow up to 85 percent of the value of the assets it holds.

When borrowing this money, however, the RTC assumes the funds will be paid back in full. Say, for example, the RTC holds a piece of property it values at $1,000. The RTC can borrow $850 on the assumption that it can sell that piece of property for $1,000 and then repay the $850 loan. But this arrangement includes two hidden hits to the taxpayer, which will lead to huge additional costs if they are not remedied.

The first hidden cost results because in its first year the RTC has lost approximately 40 percent on sale of assets. Thus, after borrowing $850 against a piece of property valued at $1,000, the property was actually sold for $600. Therefore, the RTC is $250 short when it pays back the loan it took for "working capital." The RTC estimates that over seven years it will be forced to borrow $87 billion for working capital. At a 40-percent loss rate, $21.75 billion will be added to the overall cost of the bailout to taxpayers.

The second hidden cost is the interest cost on borrowing money for working capital, since the RTC must repay not only the principal but interest as well. According to the RTC's estimate, 8.5 percent interest on $87 billion adds up to $28 billion. Thus, another $28 billion in interest costs will be added to the price tag of the bailout.

Some members of Congress are alarmed about these costs, and about the RTC's ability to borrow based on the inflated calculus of S&L assets without accountability to Congress. (After all, many thrifts are in trouble precisely because their assets are not worth what they say they are.) One proposal would require "market value appraisals" of the property the RTC holds. This method would prevent the RTC from borrowing more money than it can actually sell a piece of property for. Others have suggested allowing the RTC to borrow only 25 percent of the value of the property it holds. However, since it is the RTC that determines the value of the property, this alternative would build in incentives for the agency to value its assets too high. Complicating this alternative, and the RTC's work in general, is the fact that the appraisal industry is in disarray.

A second fault line comes from the fact that the RTC has become a consultant's bonanza. The HUD scandal, which exploded last year, grew out of a reliance on outside contractors to handle billions of dollars worth of government business. Unfortunately, the RTC is primed to be plundered in the same way as HUD. The RTC's mandate is filled with mixed signals. The bailout law commands the agency to dispose of its assets as quickly as possible . . . but at the best price. In order to meet these potentially contradictory goals, the 3,000 RTC employees, far too few to effectively manage the hundreds of billions of dollars of assets at stake, have turned to the sort of private real estate developers, consultants, lawyers, accountants, and appraisers who were involved in both the HUD and S&L scandals. The sharks are indeed sniffing blood. In the words emblazoned on a letter from a consulting service sent to thousands of lawyers, YOU CAN MAKE MONEY FROM THE S&L BAILOUT. One RTC advertisement placed in the *Wall Street Journal*, offering contracting opportunities, brought 2,000 inquiries. RTC officials reported that more than 24,000 individuals and firms have registered to bid on agency contracts and new registrations come in at a rate of

1,000 to 1,200 a week. In August 1990, the RTC awarded its first major contract to a real estate management firm in Virginia to manage and sell $2.4 billion in assets. Chairman Seidman's goal for 1990 is to hire outside managers to handle *$30 billion* worth of assets.

At first, the agency tried to bar anyone who helped cause a thrift collapse from being involved in the overall rescue operation. But it found that disqualified nearly all the major accounting firms in the country. Soon the rules were loosened.

This reliance on outside contractors means that nearly all of the agency's important work takes place out of the public eye. Since private firms conduct the RTC's most critical task, the management and sale of S&L assets, documents relating to these transactions are not generally available to the public. For this reason, among others, the GAO, in January 1990, listed the RTC as the number one possible locus of fraud in the federal government. Within the RTC "the management and disposal of approximately $200 to $300 billion of thrift assets will pose unprecedented management problems," warned the comptroller general. "A sale of this magnitude is unparalleled in history. The desire and potential to acquire these assets at bargain basement prices will make [the RTC] highly susceptible to fraud, waste, and abuse."

Selling off America: More sweetheart deals

To date, the most troubling aspect of the RTC's performance is the way it has treated the sale of S&Ls and their assets—with a helter-skelter desire to get rid of them, regardless of the ultimate cost to taxpayers. As a consequence, the industry that was intended to provide home mortgages for the middle class is now being sold off piecemeal to a Wall Street elite, with little consideration given to the impact on local economies, industry concentration, or the goal of providing credit for housing.

To unload its assets, the RTC has "sweetened the pot" enough to inspire insulin shock. In its first public meeting, the

RTC Oversight Board announced that if a buyer of a sick thrift, on reflection, didn't want particular assets, it could simply given them back to the government. During this "due diligence" period, the agency is allowed to guarantee that the new owner won't lose any money on these assets. But this, asserted the agency, wasn't sweet enough. In February 1990, the RTC asked its overseers to extend the time period in which buyers can pick and choose among the assets to *one year.* The Oversight Board, which is supposed to impose some accountability on the RTC, approved. Then, just two months later, RTC Chairman William Seidman announced that bidders would get *eighteen months* to decide which assets to keep and which to return. The arrangement is a classic example of "lemon socialism"—government gets stuck with the lemons, while the private sector walks off with the money-makers. "Uncle Sam is ending up with all the junk, all the crud," complained Henry Gonzalez.

These subsidies have gone to a handful of financial powerhouses. In the first months of RTC's operation, just two huge banks bought about half of all deposits and assets transferred. North Carolina National Bank (NCNB), the nation's eighth-largest commercial bank, and Banc One of Ohio, the nation's fastest-growing bank, purchased two thirds of the first fifty insolvent S&Ls the RTC put on the market. Nearly all the thrifts were in Texas.

In October 1989, for example, NCNB bought University Federal Savings and Loan of Houston. It paid the RTC $129 million; it got $3.8 billion in consumers' deposits, $750 million of the S&L's assets, $3.8 billion in government subsidies. RTC policy allows the buyer extra time after the purchase of an S&L to see which assets are profitable and decide which assets it wants to keep. So, within a month, NCNB returned to the government $380 million of assets—more than half the assets it had originally agreed to buy. The RTC is stuck with the bad assets. In another transaction, in March 1990, the

RTC *paid* NCNB $700,000 to take off its hands $104 million in deposits from a defunct S&L.

To entice big banks into buying more thrift assets, the RTC has tried to override long-standing state laws that limit bank size. In May 1990, the agency adopted a rule that lets banks buy S&Ls and then operate them as bank branches, even when branching is forbidden by state law. This overrides the law in at least ten states. In the summer of 1990, a federal court ruled that the RTC could not so cavalierly preempt state rules. The decision was subsequently overruled and may ultimately be decided by the Supreme Court.

Now the RTC is loosening its rules further to encourage even more rapid sales. Most important, it instituted a new pricing policy, one familiar to any customer of Boston's "Filene's Basement." Basically, as a piece of property stays on the market, its price drops in regular intervals. This strategy may backfire, causing buyers to buy slower, not faster. Generally, if you know the price of something is going to be marked down if you just wait a few months, you'll wait. Also, this strategy could lead to a chain reaction that drives down the price of other comparable property. Plunging property values, in turn, would drag down other S&Ls and banks.

Any smart shopper knows that one way to get a great bargain is to go to an estate auction. Now the RTC plans to unload huge stretches of property in a worldwide auction, scheduled for late 1990. With so much property being dumped on the market at once, with such urgency on the part of the seller, buyers can expect to make a killing.

In sum, Uncle Sam is selling off its property in the way virtually guaranteed to get the worst value for the taxpayer. Why the rush? As William Greider, writing in the *American Prospect*, explains:

> In order to raise cash so that it can close down more of the several hundred insolvent S&Ls, the RTC has a strong incentive to unload these properties as fast as possible. Otherwise,

when it runs out of working capital, the RTC has to return to Congress for more money, an awkward political moment that all sides wish to defer as long as possible. But most of the real assets the government now owns exist in already depressed markets, most notably Texas. Selling these properties rapidly means accepting fire-sale prices far below their book value as well as further depressing the local real estate markets. Why buy an office building from a private developer when the federal government is selling them cheap?

The Texas real estate market, now thoroughly depressed, can only improve. Oil prices, which had plunged in the late 1980s, were beginning to increase even before Saddam Hussein stormed into Kuwait and ignited a world crisis. That means that any sale made now will turn into a windfall for the buyer. Ten years from now, taxpayers will look back and realize that our government agents handed over hundreds of billions of dollars in property for a song.

Affordable housing

One of the few silver linings in the bailout law was the affordable-housing program, steered to passage by Representatives Henry Gonzalez, Joe Kennedy, and Barney Frank. Under this program, residential property that is valued below $67,500 for a single-family home and between $28,032 and $58,392 for multifamily units is offered first to low- and moderate-income buyers, or to nonprofit groups, for ninety days. If no offers are made and accepted within those three months, the property then goes on sale to the general public, including private investors who are under no obligation to maintain these properties as affordable housing.

But while the RTC has stumbled over itself in a rush to sweeten the deal for developers, the affordable-housing program has been undermined. All told, some 10,000 properties could be eligible for inclusion in the affordable housing program. But since the bailout began, only two hundred units have been sold. Poor people aren't able to take advantage of the program unless they know their way around the federal bureaucracy, have a real estate agent, or closely read the business section of the newspaper.

One reason for the bottleneck is that while developers are given a discount, those who can least afford it are charged full price. Under its rules, the RTC offers poor and working-class people and nonprofit institutions the property *at appraised market value*. Only after ninety days, when the "reserved" sign is taken off the property, does the price begin to drop. "For low-income buyers, the selling price will be kept high for ninety days," notes Brian Maney, research director of ACORN, a national housing group. "Afterwards they may mark it down for wealthy developers." And, the RTC has no plans to offer financial help to poor people to buy houses—in contrast to the millions of dollars in subsidies provided the banks and private investors who seek to take control of commercial real estate.

Another reason the affordable housing program is sputtering is people don't know about it, and aren't able to make use of it. To get the word out, and to assist buyers, the law requires that the RTC appoint a clearinghouse for each region. Under the law, these clearinghouses must be either a state housing finance agency, the Office of Community Investment within the Federal Housing Finance Board, or a national non-profit group. But who did the RTC choose to serve as clearinghouse in Texas, ground zero of the bailout? The Federal Home Loan Bank of Dallas—in other words, the very S&L executives who leapt at the first chance to invest in office towers, not affordable housing.

Other attempts to jump-start the affordable-housing program have been little more promising. On May 23, Treasury Secretary Nicholas Brady testified that the RTC's experimental program with the Texas Housing Agency would serve as a model for future programs. Eight days later, the *Austin American-Statesman* reported that the pilot program was a fiasco. The RTC "are extremely bureaucratic. They need to get their act together," complained Tish Gonzalez, the state housing agency's executive administrator. Ms. Gonzalez said that the agency had planned to issue $140 million in bonds to help poor people buy foreclosed homes from the RTC, but that the sale had to be postponed when the RTC didn't produce a list of the properties. When the Texas agency wanted to start a clearinghouse, the RTC was willing to pay for one phone line and one staff person to handle the calls from the 3.5 million eligible households. "It's one of the most asinine things I could hear them saying," Gonzalez said. "They don't realize the grasp of the problems in Texas. They don't have a clear handle of the properties they own. They don't know what condition they are in."

THE BUSH ADMINISTRATION'S ANEMIC WAR ON S&L FRAUD

On June 21, 1990, the Justice Department auditorium was filled to capacity, packed with the U.S. attorneys from ninety-three field offices flown in from around the country at government expense. As the U.S. Marine Band played "God Bless America," President Bush took the stage. In a rousing stump speech, Bush declared war on S&L fraud. "We will not rest until the cheats and the chiselers and the charlatans spend a large chunk of their lives behind the bars of a federal prison," Bush told the cheering prosecutors. And he announced a program of enforcement measures to go after financial fraud.

There was only one problem. The "new" initiatives were recycled. Bush had announced many of the same efforts previously, some as much as six months before, and they hadn't been put into effect. And his own administration until then had refused to accept the funds Congress authorized to wage a full-scale crackdown. In all, the Justice Department has abjectly failed to bring law and order to the financial industry, and to recover as much of the stolen money as possible.

At the Justice Department, a growing backlog of unaddressed S&L cases gathers dust. As of February 1990, the department was actively pursuing only 891 cases of S&L fraud, while 6,993 referrals and complaints regarding S&Ls went unaddressed. (These figures do not include cases involving losses of less than $100,000.) Even the most notorious S&L kingpins go unindicted for years. "Fast Eddie" McBirney left Sunbelt Savings and Loan and Don Dixon's Vernon Savings and Loan was seized in 1986 and 1987 respectively, but the two were not indicted until 1990. Even when prosecutors do achieve convictions, the defendants have so far been given relatively light sentences. The average term meted out to crooks convicted of S&L fraud was 1.9 years in 1989. In contrast, people convicted of bank robbery were sentenced to an average of 9.4 years in prison, nearly five times as long.

So far, federal prosecution of S&L criminals has recouped less than 1 percent of the losses to the taxpayers conservatively attributable to fraud in these thrift institutions taken over by the government. Since 1988, federal prosecutors won criminal convictions against 232 institutions and individuals who were ordered to pay penalties and restitution of less than $100 million. That sum amounts to 0.5 percent of the estimated $21.6 billion of losses due to fraud under the most conservative estimate. Recoveries through civil lawsuits by the FDIC over the last three years do not add much to this total. From 1988 through March 15, 1990, the FDIC ordered only about $200 million in restitution as a result of S&L cases. Adding together Justice Department and FDIC enforcement, the amount ordered recovered is still less than 2 percent of the losses due to fraud.

Moreover, this figure is only the amount of restitution that has been *ordered;* much less has actually been paid back. In the area around Dallas, Texas, courts ordered $2.5 million in restitution in 1990, but only *$50* had been collected by August. (That amount came from garnishing the prison wages of a convicted S&L executive.) In 1989, courts ordered $3.1 million in restitution, but convicted S&L criminals only paid $2,700.

One of the problems has been money laundering. A Baltimore, Maryland, thrift executive has been indicted for looting Community Savings of Maryland and then allegedly laundering $8 million through Swiss banks. In their lawsuit, the Lincoln S&L bondholders allege that Charles Keating is hiding more than $100 million in bank accounts in Switzerland, Panama, and the Bahamas. "For the same reason that international drug money laundering was for so long ignored, thrift money laundering has been ignored as well," notes Senator John Kerry (D–Mass). "The crime occurs in many jurisdictions, at high speed and under the guise of legitimate business." The Treasury Department has the authority to freeze the assets of individuals who are sued in S&L fraud cases before conviction. But for the first eight months of the bailout, the department refused to use this authority.

A reason for this anemic enforcement has been lack of money to hire prosecutors and investigators. Incredibly, Congress had to force-feed needed funds to the administration. In the 1989 S&L bailout law, Congress authorized $75 million per year for three years to be spent by the Justice Department for S&L enforcement. But when it came time to ask for funds, the Bush administration asked for and received only $50 million. (Finally, in 1990, the Justice Department buckled and agreed to ask for more money.)

By refusing to spend the full amount allocated for enforcement by Congress, the administration shortchanged S&L probes. The FBI asked for 425 additional agents to investigate S&L crimes; the Justice Department allocated less than half. And the attorney general's office allocated only 118 of the 231 U.S. attorneys requested by the department's field offices for financial institution fraud and embezzlement cases. Field offices in Missouri, Virginia, Mississippi, western Pennsylvania, Puerto Rico, and Tennessee all asked for increased personnel, and got none. The Arkansas office, struggling to deal with twelve failed thrifts, wrangled just two new attorneys and agents.

The U.S. attorney for the East Texas region testified before the House Government Operations Committee about the impact of the budget pinch. Robert Wortham told the panel in March 1990 that while fourteen thrifts had failed or been placed under government supervision in his district, he only had manpower to investigate four of them—and two of those would have to stay inactive until reinforcements arrived. "We have many unaddressed failures, many unaddressed institutions that have been taken over, and the reason they are unaddressed is there is no one to go out and do the work."

Toward late 1990, the Justice Department gave hopeful signs that it is finally grappling with the seriousness of the crime wave. It has created a special counsel for financial institution fraud, set up a twenty-seven-city task force, and compiled a priority list of S&L fraud cases to pursue. It remains to be seen if this reshuffling produces more indictments and convictions, and not just new organization charts at the department.

SEVEN

·

NEIL BUSH
AND SILVERADO

•

BY THE TIME it failed in 1988, Silverado Banking, Savings & Loan, had grown from a modest $75 million traditional home-lending institution into the third largest thrift in Colorado. Neil Bush adorned its board of directors, but regulators privately dubbed the thrift "Desperado." How it expanded—so that its collapse will likely cost taxpayers $1 billion—is a tale of politics and influence, with scant regard for propriety.

Silverado was closely linked to Colorado's biggest home builder, Larry Mizel—a top Republican fund-raiser, who garnered more than $1 million for the Reagan/Bush ticket in 1984. His company, MDC Holdings, grew into a real estate powerhouse in part by raising $700 million from junk bonds through Drexel Burnham Lambert, as well as through millions of dollars in loans from Silverado.

In the mid-1980s, MDC and Silverado focused their political savvy on a major goal: building a new airport in suburban Denver. To that end, MDC and its executives donated at least $34,000 to the city's mayor, Frederico Pena, who once opposed the project but who switched once elected. Mizel's company allegedly doled out thousands of dollars more to politicians illegally. MDC would coerce its subcontractors to give to Pena, and would then reimburse them by paying off phony bills. "They'd call up and say [which politician] they want you to make a check out to," one subcontractor told the *Rocky Mountain News.* "You'd make a check out on Friday and on Monday you'd invoice them." Meanwhile, revealed *Time* magazine, "as Denver secretly negotiated with neighboring Adams County for a new site [for the airport], MDC and Silverado quietly began buying up farmland that would eventually be selected as part of the development corridor leading to the airport."

Another way that the Silverado crowd cuddled up to the politically powerful was by wooing Neil Bush, a son of George

Bush. Silverado's chairman, Michael Wise, was thinking of running for the U.S. Senate, reports a former associate, and "the acquisition of Neil Bush was a logical part of his plan."

Soon after his dad was elected vice president, business opportunities always just seemed to present themselves to young Neil. In 1983, developers Kenneth Good and Bill Walters gave Bush's oil drilling venture, JNB, its start-up money. Walters put up $150,000 and got a 6.25 stake in the company; Bush himself put in $100 and got a 32.8 percent stake, plus a $75,000-a-year salary. Good eventually lent JNB $3 million, and came to own 38.57 percent stake in the company.

Walters's Cherry Creek Bank gave JNB a line of credit for at least $1 million. Bush's company defaulted on the line of credit, and repaid only $225,000. Apparently, that failed to put a dent in Neil's credit rating; in 1988, he received a $400,000 loan for a new house in the ritzy Cherry Hills section of Denver.

In 1985, at age thirty, Bush was asked to join the board of Silverado. He admittedly had no knowledge of the banking industry. While Bush served as a Silverado director, the board approved millions of dollars in loans to Good and Walters. Directors of an S&L have a "fiduciary" duty to see to it that a thrift's funds are carefully invested. As at any corporation, board members have to be very careful to avoid conflicts of interest—that is, putting the interest of oneself or a friend over that of the company and its shareholders. According to regulators, Bush engaged in "one of the worst kinds of conflict of interest" in his dealings with Silverado, Good, and Walters. Regulators make three charges:

- Bush didn't tell the Silverado board that Good had paid $3 million for a stake in JNB, at the very moment the developer was defaulting on $8 million of $11 million in loans from Silverado. Bush's explanation, before a congressional committee: He didn't have to tell the board, because he wasn't investing with Good—Good was investing with *him*.

- In 1986, Bush asked the Silverado board to provide a $900,000 line of credit from Silverado to a Kenneth Good–backed company that sought to begin oil and gas exploration in Argentina. Bush didn't vote on the request, and other board members knew of his ties to Good. But what he didn't tell them was that he himself was a partner in the Argentina project, and would benefit from its success. Two board members told regulators that they did not know of Bush's involvement in the Argentina venture; later, they changed their story and asserted that he had told them. Bush says that internal Silverado documents show that other directors knew of his involvement.
- Bush, like his fellow directors, voted to give gigantic loans to Walters, who took control of the holding company that owned Silverado at the same time he was sucking in millions of dollars in loans from the S&L. Bush says that nobody ever told him not to vote on loans to Walters. Maybe. But in a 1985 letter to shareholders, Silverado's chairman said that Neil would "abstain from any board considerations" regarding Good and Walters.

All told, Walters defaulted on about $91 million in loans from Silverado. Good, in turn, received a $34.5 million loan for a development project called C-Park . . . which was never built. The loan went into default. But instead of foreclosing on the property, Silverado accepted a $5 million cash payment.

As Silverado charged along, its success increasingly became dependent on spurious bookkeeping. Bush and the other directors routinely approved some startling transactions. Many involved what the thrift's executives called their "quid pro quo" plan: people who wanted to borrow from the S&L had to pump some of the money back into favors designed to improve Silverado's balance sheet. In sixteen cases discovered by regulators, borrowers used funds they had just been loaned to buy Silverado stock, take repossessed land off the thrift's hands (the old "cash for trash" ploy), or buy shares in failed loans.

Walters, for example, was given a loan on the condition that he use part of the money to buy Silverado's stock. That stock, in turn, counts as "capital" required by law to shore up a thrift's net worth.

"Desperado" gave away so much money in bad loans to insiders or cronies that its balance sheets began to show huge losses. In 1987, bank examiners wanted to begin disciplinary action, but were called off by the chief of the local Home Loan Bank, Kermit Mowbray. Silverado continued to pile up debt. Investigators realized that the S&L had to be shut down—and fast. In October 1988, the Colorado Banking Department asked federal regulators to seize the thrift. Federal regulators based in Denver agreed, and now Mowbray did too. But then a phone call came from Washington: *Don't seize Silverado just yet. Wait.* On November 8, 1988, George Bush was elected president of the United States. *The next day,* district chief Mowbray issued the order to take over Silverado. Regulators didn't actually move in until December 9.

Who ordered the delay? So far, answers have not been forth coming. Mowbray refused to appear voluntarily before the House Banking Committee. When he was subpoenaed, he testified that he couldn't remember who ordered the delay, or who on his staff took the phone call.

As the regulators pored over Silverado's books, they were shocked by the shoddiness of the deals and the acquiescence of the board. Inevitably, they edged closer to the politically explosive issue of Neil Bush's role. In January 1990, the president's son spent the night at the White House. Then, with secret service agents in tow, he walked across the street to the OTS, where he was questioned for five hours by enforcers. Regulators first tried to bar Bush from the banking industry, and then offered him a more lenient deal: he would sign a "cease and desist" order agreeing never to engage in unsafe banking practices again. But Bush refused, saying he had done nothing wrong. So the OTS brought "administrative" charges that would be decided by an "administrative law judge" within the agency. For the first time ever, the disciplinary hearing against Bush would be open to the public. The FDIC, on September 21, brought a lawsuit against the entire Silverado board for failing in its duties.

Congressional investigations began to unravel the goings on at Silverado. In June, Bill Walters, Bush's business partner, told the House Banking Committee that he was broke. "I have a negative net worth," he testified. We should all be so lucky: it turned out that Walters has three houses in California, worth at least $3 million, owned in his wife's name. Good, for his part, said, "I feel no shame."

The president's son fought back. In a flurry of interviews and press conferences, he defended his name. "I've been kind of like a little caged-in animal in an unsanitary zoo. Now my cage is open and I'm telling people . . . what my side of the story is," he told reporters. "And I feel good about it. I know I'm a better person for it. I am stronger. . . . I'm eating better, drinking fruit juice."

Neil Bush became a lightning rod for mounting public anger over the S&L scandal. At last, the arcane issue was encapsulated in terms every American could grasp. "No matter how complicated the rest of the story might be, this was something the dimmest couch potato could understand," joked columnist Russell Baker. "How come nobody ever offered him one of those $100,000 loans that don't have to be repaid?"

On Capitol Hill, Democrats wondered why the Justice Department had been so quick to renounce any possibility of criminal charges in the Silverado case. After all, how could prosecutors beholden to George Bush fairly assess a case involving his son? Also, how could a local U.S. attorney, who had received campaign contributions from the Silverado crowd during a previous run for office, lead an aggressive investigation? Representative Pat Schroeder launched a drive to have an independent special prosecutor appointed. Under the law, the attorney general must formally decide whether to appoint a special prosecutor if half the members of one party on the

House Judiciary Committee sign a request. Schroeder quickly rounded up the necessary twelve signatures for a letter to Attorney General Richard Thornburgh. But the House Democratic leadership, possibly fearful of a probe of Jim Wright and others, reportedly did not support such a call. Representative Edward Feighan (D–Ohio), who had signed the letter, abruptly reversed himself.

Bush says he is being made a "scapegoat" because of his political bloodlines. But at the time, notes *Denver Post* editorialist Penelope Purdy, "Denverites felt Neil Bush was lucky: he was made a director because he was George Bush's son." The reality of the situation was captured in a piercing editorial cartoon by Pat Oliphant. The caption reads: "Great S&L Moments: Neil Bush Abashedly Reveals to the Board of Silverado That He Is Indeed, None Other Than the Son of President George Bush." In it, a skinny, preppy Neil Bush is addressing a group of men who would look more at home at a crap game than a bank. "Well!! The kid put one over on us—I had no *idea*—why that rascal!" says one burly fellow. "Oh, I feel so naive!" says another.

The failure of Silverado is estimated to cost taxpayers up to $1 billion. And the S&L scandal of which it is a prominent part was a major reason George Bush broke his promise never to raise taxes. But Neil Bush, naive as ever, fails to see the magnitude of the controversy. In his mind, as he told the House Banking Committee, the failure of Silverado was "inconsequential."

EIGHT

NEVER AGAIN: AN AGENDA FOR ACTION

•

WE NOW KNOW that the $55 billion in U.S. Treasury funds allocated for the S&L bailout in 1989 simply wasn't enough. The Bush administration has asked for another installment—as much as $100 billion—or it won't be able to continue shutting down sick S&Ls. That makes it all the more critical that average citizens not get stuck with the bill again.

Fortunately, we can fight back.

Here is a five-point plan to cut the cost and shift the burden of paying for the bailout, restore law and order to the financial markets, *and ensure that this fiasco won't be repeated.*

SOLUTION ONE: MAKE THE PEOPLE WHO HAD THE PARTY PAY FOR THE PARTY

The first and most important task is to stop the S&L bailout from being the most expensive wealth transfer from the middle class to the rich in the country's history. Average citizens shouldn't have to pay for policies that they neither caused nor benefited from. That requires two things: taking away Uncle Sam's credit card—and handing the tab to the people who benefited the most from the go-go years of the Roaring Eighties.

One big reason the S&L bailout is so expensive is the elaborate effort by the Bush administration and Congress to mask its cost and magnitude. When they enacted the bailout in 1989, they funded it by selling bonds that stretched payment out over forty years. Instead of having the bonds sold by the government, quasi-governmental corporations were created, which have to pay higher interest rates to sell their securities. As a consequence, *the interest payments on bailout bonds amount to most of the cost for the rescue.*

Consider this calculation. Economists from Stanford University, using government data, estimated that the cost of the bailout over forty years could amount to $1.369 *trillion.* Of that mind-boggling sum, over $913 *billion* will be used to pay interest on borrowed funds. In the next decade alone, taxpayers will pay $216.5 billion in interest on the bailout. Our children will pay through the nose for mismanagement and criminality that transpired decades before they were born. This upsurge in federal borrowing has already helped cause rising interest rates. And when the federal government goes even further into debt to fund this expenditure, it can't spend money on needed projects—such as education, health care, and crime prevention. Moreover, it's not average citizens who can buy bailout bonds. Interest payments transfer funds from all taxpayers to a few bondholders.

There's a simple, good-government solution: pay for the bailout now, instead of stretching it out into the next century. This proposal has been advanced by one of the nation's leading financiers. Felix Rohatyn, an investment banker who led the effort to rescue New York City in the 1970s, said in a recent speech to the National Press Club, "Borrowing the money will turn a $130 billion problem into a $500 billion drain (or much more) over the next twenty to thirty years, leaving it to our children to pay off our own stupidity, as well as keeping a drag on the economy by the continued drain on the capital markets. This is an irresponsible approach." Instead, Rohatyn proposes a surcharge on all income tax to pay for the bailout.

If we're going to pay for the bailout now, that raises the obvious question: Who should foot the bill? There is an equally obvious answer: The people who caused and benefited from the policies that led to the S&L collapse.

From brokered deposits and sky-high interest rates, to rising stock prices inflated by junk bond–backed takeovers, the financial deregulation of the 1980s benefited the wealthy. Remember that only net creditors—people with more money in investments or on deposit than they owe in loans—benefit from high interest rates. Small businesses, farmers, and working families take it on the chin.

It is the wealthiest Americans who have most benefited from having their bank accounts backed up by deposit insurance. The average American has only $2,600 in the bank; yet an estimated 28 percent of the benefits of the bailout went to just 1 percent of the depositors at failed S&Ls. Even without the bailout costs, the tax system had become increasingly unfair. By 1990, the tax system was actually *regressive,* taxing the working middle class and poor more heavily on each new dollar than it taxed the rich. Multimillionaire David Rockefeller, for example, pays a federal tax rate of approximately 28 percent. On the other hand, a working couple each of whom earns $50,000 pays a total federal tax rate of about 40 percent, when Social Security payroll taxes are added to their income taxes.

Meanwhile, dropping tax rates on the very rich, combined with higher interest rates on their investments, caused the gap between the haves and the have-lesses to grow. From 1977 to 1987, average after-tax family income of the lowest 10 percent dropped 10.5 percent; average after-tax family income of the top 10 percent jumped 24.4 percent. But the income of the top 1 percent jumped *74.2 percent* over the decade. And according to Citizens for Tax Justice, a widely respected public interest group, from 1979 to 1989 personal interest income grew by 106 percent; personal dividend income grew by 49 percent; and capital gains income grew by 109 percent (all in inflation-adjusted dollars)—while wages grew by only 32 percent.

Taken together, these trends portray what conservative author Kevin Phillips calls the "triumph of Upper America": "Even adjusted for inflation, the number of millionaires had doubled between the late seventies and the late eighties," writes Phillips in his recent book, *The Politics of Rich and Poor.* "Meanwhile, the number of billionaires . . . went from a handful in 1981 to 26 in 1986 and 49 in 1987." At the same time, tax payments by the super-rich dropped as a percentage of their income.

In sum, the people who had the party were the beneficiaries of the money economy of the Roaring Eighties. They will be enriched disproportionately from the bailout, too. Instead, they should pay to clean it up. To pile it on to today's already unequal tax system is just unfair.

Representative Joe Kennedy has introduced a legislative plan that would place more of the burden on the wealthy. Kennedy's bill, entitled the "S&L Fair Financing and Anti-Fraud Enforcement Act of 1990" (H.R. 5499), would pay for the next installment of the bailout now, instead of extending the payments over decades. He would raise the funds through a variety of taxes on the economic upper bracket, instead of forcing most citizens to pay. Here's how the proposal would work:

- First, the plan includes a 7.5-percent surtax on *unearned* income (that is, interest, dividends, and capital gains) of individuals earning $100,000 or more, with an exemption for the first $7,500 of such income. Right now, these funds are exempt from the Social Security tax most of us pay on our wages. So a bailout surtax on these upper-bracket benefits "would be about the same as the 7.65-percent employee Social Security tax that already applies to wages up to $51,300," notes Bob McIntyre of Citizens for Tax Justice. This would bring in $15.6 billion per year.

- Second, a 5-percent surtax on the income tax of *corporations earning over $75,000 per year.* Corporate income taxes have dropped from their peak rate of 52 percent in 1953; they now are at an effective rate of 26 percent. This was even less than tax experts had expected, because so many firms have used tax loopholes to evade taxes (such as raising funds through junk bonds). This would bring in $3.6 billion annually.

- Finally, closing the "angel of death" loophole that forgives accumulated *capital gains* at death. Now, if a person buys stock in 1985 at $10 per share, and dies in 1990 when the stock is worth $15 per share, an heir who sells the stock pays no capital gains tax. This change in the capital gains law would bring in $2 billion each year.

All told, this bailout surcharge would bring in $21.2 billion in revenues per year. Over five years, this surcharge would pay for the new installment of the S&L bailout. After that, these extra taxes would end. If other similar upper-bracket taxes were used, the plan could pay for the *entire* bailout.

Under this plan, if you earn $60,000 in taxable income per year, and your spouse earns $30,000 per year, you would not have to pay a dime for the rising cost of the S&L bailout. If you even earn $90,000, and your spouse earns $40,000, you would pay only if your unearned income—interest payments, dividend checks from stock, capital gains—exceeds $7,500 per year. All told, very few Americans would have to pay for the next bailout; only those who benefited from financial deregulation would pay for its consequences.

In 1989, Representatives Kennedy and Bruce Morrison (D–Conn) had proposed a similar "pay as you go" scheme as an amendment to the S&L bailout. That amendment would have paid for the first installment of the bailout with a combination of taxes on corporations and the wealthy. The measure died when the House Rules Committee, which decides what provisions will be voted on by the full House, refused to allow a vote. As Congress prepares to allocate new funds for the bailout, Kennedy's sandlot irregulars are joined by some legislative sluggers: the bill is supported by senior members of both the House Rules Committee and the House Ways and Means Committee, which writes tax law. Democratic party leaders are alarmed by the fair financing plan; Speaker Thomas Foley reportedly persuaded some legislators to skip the press conference announcing the bill.

Politics in Washington has not yet caught up with rising

disquiet over the raw deal given average taxpayers in recent years. As for Republicans, President Bush in his first year in office proposed yet another tax cut for the rich, this one for capital gains income. And most Democrats seem incapable of grasping even the most fundamental populist precepts. Recently, Senator Daniel Patrick Moynihan (D–NY) caused a stir when he proposed cutting the regressive payroll tax, since Social Security receipts are being used to mask the true size of the federal budget deficit. The proposal had obvious middle-class allure, and its thrust was endorsed by New York governor Mario Cuomo and Democratic party chairman Ron Brown. But congressional leaders quickly squelched the plan.

So unless citizens let Congress know in no uncertain terms that they won't pay for another bailout, lawmakers will rush through yet another regressive bailout funding scheme.

SOLUTION TWO: RESTORE EFFECTIVE REGULATION THROUGH CITIZEN ACCOUNTABILITY

In the words of former Federal Communications Commissioner Nicholas Johnson, "The only way to keep the government upright is to lean on it from all sides." But the regulators and legislators in charge of the financial industry are leaned on by only one side—the bankers who can afford to pay campaign contributions, honoraria, and lobbying fees, sponsor think-tank studies, and buy full-page newspaper advertisements. To prevent another taxpayer-subsidized fiasco, we need to empower consumers and taxpayers to represent themselves in the regulatory process.

Washington is clogged with trade associations that speak for businesses of every variety. In the capital, at least 100,000 people work directly or indirectly for the business lobbies. The financial industry is represented by the American Bankers Association (banks), the U.S. League of Savings Institutions, the

Securities Industry Association (stockbrokers and investment banks), the Independent Bankers Association (small banks), and four separate insurance industry trade groups—not to mention all the individual firms that hire lobbyists. These mouthpieces testify before Congress, petition regulatory agencies, draft position papers, and release studies. Preferential industry access extends to within the agencies themselves. The S&Ls, after all, own and dominate the boards of the Home Loan Banks, and the commercial banks appoint most board members of the regional Federal Reserve Banks.

Who represents the consumer? Unfortunately, consumer and taxpayer interests are woefully underrepresented in financial policy decisions. In early 1989, at the beginning of the S&L bailout, consumer groups in Washington, D.C., employed a total of *six* lobbyists to work on all banking issues, none of whom had focused before on policies toward thrifts. It is simply too difficult to amass needed resources and expertise to effectively weigh in on fundamental banking policy issues.

This vacuum is particularly apparent at the state level, where few consumer experts participate in banking matters, and where regulators and legislators are deluged with bank and S&L lobbying. A survey of legislative staff in Connecticut, Florida, Michigan, and Illinois, conducted by Public Citizen's Congress Watch, showed that consumer representation in state financial services matters was slim or nonexistent, while industry was heavily represented. "The lobbying that was done on the interstate banking issue [whether banks could expand across state lines] came from Chemical Bank on one side and the Florida Bankers' Association on the other. Otherwise, there was no consumer input," commented the staff director of the Commerce Committee in the Florida legislation on one issue. "I wouldn't be opposed to consumer input, but the average consumer doesn't really care, or understand, issues of interstate banking." Of course, such arcane regulatory debates are exactly what led to the S&L bailout.

Banking issues present a classic political paradox: the loudest voices are those that have the most to gain, not necessarily those of the often-unorganized majority. Right now, if a policy change transfers a million dollars to a banker, costing a million consumers one dollar each, guess who has the incentive to hire a lobbyist. How can widely scattered and apathetic citizens be organized to help themselves?

One answer has emerged from a model developed by consumer advocate Ralph Nader: a voluntary, citizen-run Financial Consumers Association (FCA). In a policy innovation reminiscent of the union-dues checkoff, Nader proposed the creation of a consumer organization that would seek members through an insert in the monthly statements of federally insured banks and S&Ls. The insert from the FCA would ask the depositor to join the group and contribute $5 or $10.

For the first time, average citizens would be able to unite to represent and educate themselves. This citizen organization would be democratically accountable, with directors and an assembly elected by, and responsible to, members. In exchange for taxpayer-backed deposit insurance, financial insti tutions would be required to include the FCA insert in monthly mailings. FCA would have the authority to organize consumers, publish marketplace studies, file lawsuits, intervene with regulators, and lobby the legislature. "If Congress and the regulators had heard from consumers in such a powerfully organized fashion, and not just from the bankers, there wouldn't be an S&L crisis," Nader argues.

The concept is borrowed from state Citizen Utility Boards (CUBs), which exist in Wisconsin and Illinois, and are in planning stages in other states. The first CUB was formed in Wisconsin in 1979, working on electric, gas, and telephone issues. CUBs were created by the legislature in Illinois and by a referendum in Oregon. By 1984, several hundred thousand citizens were state CUB members. That year, however, the rapid development of CUBs was halted by a Supreme Court decision. In *PG&E* v. *California,* the court ruled that forcing utilities to include an enclosure from a consumer group violated the corporation's free-speech rights. (Banks, which would take the insert voluntarily as part of deposit insurance, would probably be viewed differently by the court. Alternately, a neutrally worded insert notice from the *government* would probably be found constitutional.) In different ways, the CUBs coped; Illinois CUB, for example, persuaded the legislature to include its material in state mailings.

Politically, the FCA concept is beginning to gain support. Legislation proposing the creation of state FCAs was first introduced in the one hundredth Congress. The Senate actually passed a small chunk of that plan in 1988, enabling states to create FCAs, as part of a larger banking bill. Senator William Proxmire held his last hearings as chairman of the Banking Committee on the need for FCAs. Subsequently, during the S&L bailout, consumer advocates sought the creation of state FCAs. An amendment to the bill, proposed by Representative Charles Schumer, would have authorized states to create FCAs when a minimum number of citizens petitioned for the action, but it lost by voice vote in the House Banking Committee.

Imagine the difference a federally chartered Financial Consumers Association would make. It's 1992, and the FDIC is holding a hearing on a complex regulatory change that would impose billions of dollars in costs on taxpayers. As usual, the S&Ls are represented; three thrifts have hired top-flight law firms to make presentations. The securities industry trade group is there, too, lugging thick legal briefs. But this time, the consumers are represented as well. An economist hired by FCA makes a presentation; a lawyer pounds home the unfairness of the proposed rule. The press is out in full force, too. In the face of public pressure, the FDIC decides to withdraw its plan and start again. That's the kind of difference an FCA can make.

SOLUTION THREE: TAKE BACK CONGRESS THROUGH PUBLIC FUNDING

On August 3, 1989, Representative Jim Leach (R–Iowa) stood on the floor of the House of Representatives, explaining why he would vote against the final version of the S&L bailout bill. "The first title of this bill should be about campaign reform," he said, "and the last title should be about ethics in government. Each is missing. So is my vote."

Leach was right. The underlying cause for the S&L crisis is a crisis in government. Representatives and senators are supposed to represent the people who elected them. Instead, they are increasingly beholden to the economic elite who funds their campaigns. Until Congress completely overhauls campaign finance laws, private interests—such as the bankers and S&Ls—will dominate policy. And there is only one surefire way to get the tainted special-interest money out of politics: replace it with voluntary public funds.

The campaign-finance arms race

It's hardly news that big money dominates politics. But in the past decade the campaign finance system has spun out of control, with ballooning campaign contributions leading to special-interest dominance of a Congress of permanent incumbents. We have reached the state Robert Kennedy warned about some twenty-five years ago: "We are in danger of creating a situation in which our candidates must be chosen from among the rich [like the Kennedys] . . . or those willing to be beholden to others."

The money spent waging a successful campaign for Congress has risen fivefold since 1976, far higher than the rate of inflation. In 1976, winning candidates spent over $58 million on congressional campaigns; by 1988, the amount rose to $294 million. Members of Congress must spend more and more time fund-raising. Indeed, lawmakers are themselves trapped by the system. Forced by a political "arms race" to raise huge sums to stay in office, they see little choice but to turn for funds to the lobbyists and corporations that daily ply Congress for favors and policies.

Explicit special-interest money has come to dominate our elections. When campaign law changes were enacted in 1974, political action committees formed by corporate, trade, or labor groups played a relatively minor role in campaign financing. The 608 PACs then in existence gave only $12.5 million to congressional candidates that year. The 1974 campaign amendments changed all this by allowing all trade associations and corporations, even those with government contracts, to form PACs. In the 1988 elections, over 4,000 PACs contributed $148 million to congressional campaigns. At present, nearly half the members of the House of Representatives receive the majority of their campaign funds from PACs—by definition the tools of Washington lobbyists. Representative Al Swift (D–Wash), the chairman of the House Subcommittee on Elections, who manages the campaign finance issue for the Democratic leadership, received fully 75 percent of his funds from PACs in 1988. That year, PACs gave Speaker Tom Foley 70.9 percent of *his* funds.

But PACs are hardly the only problem. In 1988, large individual political contributions (donations of $200 or more) accounted for $168 million, more than was given by PACs to congressional candidates. Much of the money contributed by individuals is also given with the goal of influencing legislation, whether by realtors supporting a capital gains tax cut, investment bankers opposing curbs on takeovers, or S&L operators such as Charles Keating seeking to evade federal regulation of their institutions. (This is especially true when the contributions are "bundled," that is, collected from individuals by a lobbying group and handed to a lawmaker at one time.) The number of these individual gifts is growing, too. In the 1980 election, donors to House races gave 27,560 campaign gifts of $500 or over; by the 1988 election, that figure had jumped to 69,286 gifts of $500 or over.

Nowadays, campaign contributions don't even need a contested election. A Public Citizen study showed that 59 House members who had no major-party opponent in 1988 nonetheless received over $14.7 million in campaign contributions, $7.5 million of it from PACs—gifts clearly designed to win access and influence, not to support compatible candidates. Early fund-raising disclosure suggests that even more incumbents are running unopposed in 1990, and raising even greater sums from PACs and individuals.

This avalanche of big money guarantees that incumbents rarely lose. In 1986 and 1988, about 98 percent of incumbents who were seeking reelection won, a far lower turnover rate than the Supreme Soviet in the Leonid Brezhnev era. A number of factors combine to produce this astounding incumbency effect, including the perquisites of office (such as free postage for members of Congress) and artfully drawn congressional districts. But by far the biggest incumbency advantage is fund-raising prowess from private interests. Nearly three out of every four PAC dollars contributed in 1988 went to incumbents. Even these numbers are misleading. More significant than the ratio of gifts to incumbents and challengers is the fact that the amount given to challengers is so low—often, too insignificant to allow them to get their message across to voters.

Like mountain snow, campaign cash gathers at the peaks—going more heavily to the legislative leaders and committee chairs who control policy. Read a politician's campaign disclosure statement, and you can tell what committee he or she sits on. Bennett Johnston (D–La) is chairman of the Senate Energy Committee. During one fifteen-month period in 1989 to 1990, Johnston received $236,500 from oil, gas, utility, and other energy industry PACs, more than anyone else in Congress. Part of that kitty was raised at a fund-raiser in Phoenix at a meeting of the Edison Electric Institute, a power company trade association. (Johnston was attending the meeting to give a speech, for a $2,000 fee.) Walker Nolan, head lobbyist for the utility group, explained the reasoning to the *Washington Post:* "He's chairman of the Energy Committee. That's why you hold fund-raisers and have PACs, not because we expect any *quid pro quo* or immediate thing. But if you're going to do fund-raisers, you're doing it for people who have jurisdiction over your issues." Between PAC checks and gifts from individuals, the one event raised $43,000.

Not surprisingly, campaign contributions often tip the balance in a legislative fight. To be sure, no amount of campaign cash would persuade Representative Henry Hyde (R–Ill) to come out *for* abortion rights, or Pat Schroeder *against* them. But most issues aren't black and white; they're a shade of gray. And on complicated regulatory or tax policies that generate little constituent outcry, the "access" that campaign gifts bring can be decisive. As Representative Barney Frank (D–Mass) aptly noted, "We are the only human beings in the world who are expected to take thousands of dollars from perfect strangers on important matters and not be affected by it." Echoes Representative Tom Downey (D–NY): "You can't buy a congressman for $5,000. But you can buy his vote."

Few donors are as explicit as Charles Keating. But few need to be. Does anyone really think that the $8 million in PAC contributions donated to 1988 House and Senate candidates by the electric utility, coal, oil, chemical, auto, and other PACs seeking to weaken the Clean Air Act reauthorization had nothing to do with that legislation's tortuous progress?

The elements of reform

Only comprehensive reform will keep the S&L scandal from recurring—if not in banking, than in other cash-rich industries that seek to sway Congress. Real reform has four elements: campaign spending limits, substantial public funding for elections, restrictions on PACs, and plugging the "soft money" loophole.

Ceilings on campaign spending are an essen-

tial component of any real reform plan. Such caps on spending would prevent candidates from engaging in an "arms race" of ever-escalating fund-raising and would reassure them that they will not be buried by free-spending or millionaire opponents. The 1974 campaign finance reforms originally included spending limits in congressional races. But the U.S. Supreme Court, in a logically convoluted opinion in the 1976 case of *Buckley* v. *Valeo,* ruled that mandatory caps on spending violated the free-speech rights of candidates and contributors. As a result, reform plans rely on voluntary spending ceilings, which need inducements to get candidates to comply.

Voluntary public funding of congressional elections would be the simplest and most effective way to reform the role of money in politics. Public funds would replace private, legislatively interested money, and provide the best incentive to limit candidates' spending. If we want lawmakers to be responsive to taxpayers and S&L depositors, instead of S&L owners, then *we* have to fund their elections. Period. That is the only truly effective way to end politicians' dependence on special-interest funds.

Here's how public funding would work. Instead of seeking thousands of dollars from private sources, candidates who raise a threshold of small contributions from their home state would qualify to receive public funds. The public money would come from the voluntary taxpayer checkoff, which now appears on federal tax forms for the publicly funded presidential election. Currently, citizens have the option of directing one dollar of their tax money to help pay for the presidential public funding system. If the checkoff were raised, say, up to six dollars, funds could be made available to congressional candidates as well as presidential contenders. (Today, about 24 percent of taxpayers now use the checkoff. If the government provided more information about the purpose of the checkoff at tax time—or at any other time—that number would undoubtedly go up.)

Since the checkoff is voluntary, the money comes only

from people who want their money to be used to fund campaigns. (Of course, taxpayers don't have the option of saying they don't want their money used for the S&L bailout.) It's voluntary for candidates, too, who are under no obligation to take the money. What it does do is offer a "floor" for candidates who want to run with no strings attached.

The amounts of public funding vary from plan to plan. For the Senate, the most comprehensive public funding proposal has been introduced by Senators John Kerry (D–Mass), Bill Bradley (D–NJ) and Joseph Biden (D–Del). Under this plan, general election candidates who agree to a limit on aggregate campaign spending would become eligible for public funds. This funding would cover nearly all the costs of the general election campaign for major-party nominees (and would include partial public funding for independents and minor-party candidates who demonstrate a threshold of support). Depending on the size of the state, the public funding could range from between about $900,000 to $5 million.

In the House of Representatives, where intraparty battles often decide who sits in Congress, most public funding proposals would provide "matching funds," available in both primaries and general elections. Under this system, candidates would raise small contributions from within their state or district; those private gifts would then be "matched" by public money. A matching fund proposal introduced by Representatives Mike Synar (D–Okla) and Jim Leach would provide up to half a candidate's resources through matching money.

One idea proposed by Public Citizen that has recently gained support is to provide candidates "communications vouchers," instead of cash. These vouchers could be used to buy television, radio, or newspaper ads, erect billboards, send mailings, or otherwise get a message out to voters. This plan would guarantee that funds wouldn't be misused for non-campaign purposes.

Public funding is far from a new, untested idea. It was first proposed for federal campaigns by President Theodore Roosevelt in a message to Congress in 1907, and has been revived periodically since then. Today, public funding is in place and working—on the presidential level, in states and localities around the country, and in other nations.

Public funding would be one of the best bargains taxpayers could obtain. At a small cost, compared to many other government expenditures, taxpayers would save huge sums now spent on weapons cost overruns, tax loopholes for wealthy contributors, and subsidies for powerful industries. If all costs for House and Senate elections were publicly funded, the total would amount to approximately $600 million per election cycle—roughly the cost of a single B-2 Stealth bomber, and a tiny fraction of the $1 trillion total federal budget. And the projected total cost for the Lincoln S&L bailout alone is four times the annual cost of full public financing. Put another way, four congressional election cycles could be publicly funded with the money now being used to rescue just Lincoln. And the $16.7-billion projected annual cost of the S&L bailout as a whole is thirty-three times the annual cost of public financing. In short, *private* campaign funding is far more expensive for taxpayers than *public* funding.

Representative Al Swift flatly says, "There are only three groups against [public funding]—incumbents, challengers, and the public." Incumbents, certainly. But the voters are a different story. Like dew after the dawn, public demand for institutional reform naturally follows scandal. Not surprisingly, support for public financing is at its peak since Watergate. The most comprehensive study of public attitudes on this subject was conducted in 1990 by pollsters Stanley Greenberg and Celinda Lake, and released by Public Citizen, the Advocacy Institute, People for the American Way, and the Arca Foundation. According to the survey, full public funding of congressional elections—accompanied by a total ban on private contributions—was supported by 58 percent of the public —the same percent that supported it in June 1973.

Support rose even higher when respondents were asked if

they supported providing candidates with a fixed amount of free television time and reduced mailing rates: 69 percent in support, and only 25 percent opposed. In addition, other elements of comprehensive reform won wide support. For example, 77 percent are in favor of spending limits of $500,000; and 57 percent rejected PACs, even when read a pro-PAC question drafted by the American Medical Association PAC.

Of all the competing reform proposals, why is public funding so necessary? For several reasons. First, only public funding would end lawmakers' dependence on special-interest campaign contributions, by replacing private money with "clean" public resources. Simply limiting PACs, or even eliminating them, will lead to a boom in individual contributions from the same vested interests. Second, only public funding will genuinely guarantee competitiveness by giving challengers a "floor" from which to launch their campaigns. Today, the first test of whether candidates for office are "credible" is whether they can raise large sums of money. A public funding plan would ensure that every bona fide candidate would be "credible." Third, public funding would end the need for perpetual fund-raising by elected officials. Reform that steers fund-raising away from PACs and toward individual gifts could mean more time for lawmakers at cocktail parties, not less. Fourth, public funding could be used to restrict the amount of shrill, substanceless, or "negative" campaigning that so alienates voters. "Communications vouchers" could be restricted to buying ads of two minutes or more in length, on the theory that candidates would be hard pressed to sustain a smear for longer than thirty seconds. Finally, public funding or some other benefit to candidates is needed to make the spending ceiling truly "voluntary," hence constitutional.

Comprehensive reform should also include greater limits on the role of PACs. Many reform plans limit PAC gifts to a percentage of the total amount that can be spent. Under full public funding, PACs should not be permitted to contribute to congressional candidates. PACs would still be permitted to participate in the electoral process through voter education and truly independent expenditures. Proposals to ban PACs altogether would probably be ruled unconstitutional by the courts, under the theory that PAC contributions are "speech." (We always knew money talked, but we thought that was the *problem.*) In any case, limits on PAC gifts can reduce their pernicious role without smacking into constitutional barriers.

Contributors are increasingly able to evade existing federal campaign spending laws by giving "soft money." A deceptively pleasant phrase, "soft money" refers to funds that, because of the indirect route they travel, remain unrestricted by federal law, despite the help they give federal candidates. Political parties are allowed to accept large contributions—as much as $100,000—that often exceed federal limits for individual candidates so long as the funds are channeled into soft money accounts. These funds are used for activities ranging from voter registration efforts and "get out the vote" drives to constructing party headquarters buildings.

Many critics call the underground funds "sewer money." Savings and loan owners and executives gave some of their biggest contributions as soft money. Charles Keating gave roughly $850,000 to three voter registration groups associated with Senator Alan Cranston's reelection campaign. Six S&L industry contributors alone gave $600,000 in soft money to George Bush's 1988 presidential race.

Any reform should be careful not to impinge on legitimate voter registration drives, or on private groups' constitutional right to communicate with their members. But reform should ensure that federal candidates can't raise huge sums and launder it through state parties, as is currently done.

Congress' response: Phony reform

In 1990, the public is finally letting Congress know that it is fed up with the role of PACs and fat cats in the political system. After two years of tumult—including the pay raise, the S&L scandal, Jim Wright, Tony Coelho, the Keating Five, Neil Bush, the HUD scandal, and a dozen lesser fiascos—citizens are rapidly losing faith in Congress. According to a national public-opinion survey conducted by pollsters Stanley Greenberg and Celinda Lake, the percentage of respondents expressing a positive opinion of congressional ethics dropped 10 points in one year, from 61 to 51 percent. The S&L debacle is a prime cause of that decline, the pollsters report.

The reaction to the 51-percent congressional pay raise proposal was the first evidence of the growing gulf between the citizenry and Congress. Lawmakers, who already earned $89,500—plus substantial perks, benefits, and pensions—insisted on a huge raise, which would go into effect without a vote. The amount of the raise itself was double the median income for average citizens. Yet members of Congress see their peers as the affluent lobbyists and PAC managers who give them money and with whom they socialize. Many of them couldn't fathom why voters didn't understand their need for a raise. In early 1989, a huge public outcry defeated the "salary grab," led by a curious coalition of Ralph Nader and Public Citizen, conservative groups, and radio talk-show hosts. Later that year, House leaders didn't make the same mistake again. They introduced a 40-percent raise two days before it was voted on. This time, the pay hike passed the House.

Now, some members of Congress have begun to treat their S&L money as if it were radioactive. For one thing, they're giving away campaign funds. Senate Banking Committee chairman Don Riegle, for example, announced on July 19, 1990, that he would give to the U.S. Treasury the $120,000 he had received in campaign gifts from the S&L industry since 1983. "The magnitude of the problems in the S&L industry—stemming from multiple causes over a fifteen-year period—leaves a shadow across the industry and across any campaign contributions from that industry," he said delicately. He also announced he would never again accept campaign money from companies under his committee's jurisdiction, or their executives. The next day, Senator Tim Wirth of Colorado announced he would also reject S&L contributions.

Piecemeal abstinence from special interest money is nice, but essentially meaningless. Only comprehensive reform will change politics for the better. And here Congress has been much less forthcoming. The Senate, with 7 percent of its members under ethics investigation, was the first to act. In the 1987–88 Congress, Democrats had put forward a comprehensive reform bill that included public funding up to 40 percent of spending ceilings. That year, reform was killed by a Republican filibuster, led by Senators Mitch McConnell (R–Ky) and Robert Dole (R–Kans). (While *Senator* Bob Dole was bitterly denouncing public funding, *presidential candidate* Bob Dole was quietly accepting it for his campaign.) President Bush continues to vow that he will veto any proposal that includes spending ceilings.

In late July 1990, Democrats David Boren (D–Okla) and George Mitchell (D–Maine) brought to the floor a package that included several worthy reforms, including spending limits, tight soft-money restrictions, and a modest amount of communications vouchers. The plan also *banned* PAC contributions. (This might be unconstitutional.) During debate on the measure, Senator Chris Dodd (D–Conn) risked the ire of his colleagues by offering an amendment to ban honoraria; it passed, 77–23.

However, in the weeks before the bill was debated, the bill's sponsors deleted a provision to provide nearly full public funding for general elections. Senator John Kerry, who refuses all PAC contributions for his campaigns, offered an amendment to restore public funding. "It would allow us to do what we are supposed to do in our system, which is run for office on the basis of what we believe in, on our records, and not on the size of our bank accounts and our ability to fund campaigns," he told his colleagues. But in the key vote on genuine campaign finance reform in the One hundred and First Congress, the amendment lost, 38–60 (see Appendix A for votes.) In the end, the Republicans dropped their filibuster threat, and the Boren-Mitchell bill passed, 59–40 on August 1.

If the Senate vote was tragedy, the House vote was a farce. House Democrats, afraid of giving up their advantage in PAC funds, put forward a plan that codified the status quo and was immediately denounced as "phony" by citizen groups. Representatives Mike Synar (D–Ok) and David Obey (D–Wis) offered an amendment that included some public funding, as well as a reduction in the size of individual contributions and a lower aggregate PAC limit. Democratic leaders said they supported the Synar-Obey proposal, but quietly hoped it would die. (Some wanted to pass a reform bill, even an inadequate one, but thought that southern Democrats would join with Republicans to kill real reform; others didn't want reform themselves.)

On August 3, 1990, only two days after the proposals were revealed to the public, the House met in a stormy session to debate campaign finance reform, the first time it had even voted on the issue in more than a decade. First up for debate was the public funding amendment. The chair called for a voice vote. "The amendments are agreed to," he said, and then turned to the Republicans, expecting them to insist on a roll call (where the proposal would likely lose). Instead, the Republicans stood silent, grinning: they had tricked the Democrats into adopting *their own* campaign finance reform plan! Now they expected the full House would vote to defeat the measure.

Over the next hour, as the cheers and boos of raucous debate echoed through the House chamber, panicked Democratic leaders huddled and devised a way to use the parliamentary process to strip the public funding provision from the bill. Representative Marty Frost of Texas stood at the microphone, and moved to reverse the earlier vote. This time there was a roll call; members stick a plastic card in an electronic monitoring device that records their vote. Only seconds into the new vote, the tally board registered that nearly every Republican had voted *present,* therefore abstaining. The GOP had tricked the Democrats again. Now, the Democrats would be forced to round up the votes to kill reform! For fifteen minutes, chaos ensued, as Republicans shouted "Trapped!" and "Hypocrites!" across the aisle at anguished Democrats, who were milling in confusion. In the end, there were 122 votes for public funding, 128 votes against, and 158 abstaining! Commented one longtime lobbyist, "In twenty-five years of working the Congress, I've never seen anything like that."

SOLUTION FOUR: GET TOUGH ON CRIME IN THE SUITES

If we're going to have any chance of recovering our money, we need vigorous enforcement against the pinstriped racketeers who looted the S&Ls. Lately, it seems everyone wants to be tough on S&L crime. Congress has gone to great lengths to enact legislation that purports to stiffen penalties against S&L fraud. But incredibly, at the very same moment, powerful financial industries are pushing hard to weaken the strongest law now used against S&L crooks. And they are working hand-in-hand with the Justice Department—which has done everything it can to prevent citizens from joining the fight against fraud.

This can't continue. Instead, we need a full-scale crackdown on corporate crime. In 1986, even before the S&L scam became public, the Justice Department estimated that white-collar crime cost the economy $200 billion per year—about the size of the budget deficit. Congress recently has voted for measures that impose harsher sentences on S&L swindlers (including a "life sentence" for S&L kingpins, whatever that means), and that give law enforcers expanded authority. But despite these measures, overburdened public prosecutors won't begin to catch up with the wave of fraud that has engulfed the financial industry. It's time to expand the enforcement team, by letting whistleblowers and fraud victims themselves fight S&L fraud.

Save the civil racketeering laws

Visitors to the nation's capital are often astounded by the funhouse mirror set of values frequently in evidence there. This was never so clear as during Senate Judiciary Committee deliberations on a measure that would eviscerate the civil racketeering laws. A group of high school students, jammed into the back of the committee hearing room, were wide-eyed at the heavy turnout of lobbyists. "Are there always so many people here?" one of the students asked. "No, but this is a bill that a lot of business groups support," came the response. "What would it do?" "Well, it would weaken the white-collar crime laws. It would make it harder for victims to sue." The high school student wrinkled her nose. "Gross! Why would anyone want to do that?"

Why? Because these laws are starting to bite. The big accounting firms, banks and S&Ls, and Wall Street investment houses are pushing to gut the civil provisions of the Racketeer Influenced and Corrupt Organizations Act (RICO), the statute being used against Charles Keating. Leading the charge is none other than Arizona Senator Dennis DeConcini, a ringleader of the Keating Five senators. And until outraged Lincoln bondholders brought the story to the press, the legislation would have applied *retroactively,* slashing possible damages for defendants in pending lawsuits (such as Keating). If this legislation passes, it would be the first time in history that the remedies in a federal criminal law were weakened at the behest of the defendants.

Enacted in 1970, RICO gives prosecutors and crime victims strengthened penalties if it can be proved that a pattern of criminal acts—including mail fraud, bank fraud, or securities fraud—was conducted through an "enterprise." RICO was originally designed to be used against traditional organized crime, such as money launderers or the Mafia. But in recent years it has also been used as a tool against white-collar perpetrators. In the most prominent criminal case, junk bond impresario Michael Milken pleaded guilty to securities fraud following a ninety-eight-count racketeering indictment.

RICO has criminal provisions, which can be used by federal prosecutors to win convictions. But it also includes civil provisions, which let victims of crime (as well as prosecutors) sue the criminals for money damages. If a crime victim wins his or her case, he or she recovers three times her damages *plus* her attorneys' fees. This triple-damage remedy is critically important, for two reasons. First, hefty damages are necessary to deter *future* crime. Without triple damages, would-be scam artists know that—in the slim chance they are caught and punished—all they have to do is give the money back. Second, civil RICO's triple damages are necessary to enable *today's* victims to recoup their losses. Most valid lawsuits result in a settlement before a trial begins. Since the amount a court is likely to award will determine how much the defendant is willing to pay beforehand, the triple-damage provision enables crime victims to get closer to recovering their actual losses.

The most celebrated use of civil RICO has been against Charles Keating, his colleagues at Lincoln Savings and Loan, and his accountants and attorneys. The government has sued Keating under the RICO statute, asking for $1.1 billion in damages for the taxpayers, and also for the creditors of Lincoln and Keating's other companies. (More than 25,000 creditors are owed more than $2.7 billion by Keating's empire.)

And 23,000 consumers—mostly senior citizens or poor—who bought bonds from Lincoln in the false belief that they were insured by the government have filed a civil RICO case, too. This lawsuit represents the bondholders' only chance of recovering any of their money. Already, the suit is beginning to recover some of the money for the bondholders. Kaye Scholer, one of Keating's law firms, agreed in June, 1990 to pay the victims $20 million as settlement of the litigation.

The Keatings of the banking world, as well as their allies, are petrified at the thought of a powerful legal weapon aimed at confiscating their unjust enrichment. Fearful of losing in court, they have gone to Congress to dismember the law.

For several years, a powerful grouping of industries enmeshed in white-collar crime scandals has lobbied for legislation to eviscerate civil RICO. The Big Six accounting firms (through their trade association, the American Institute of Certified Public Accountants) have been the driving force behind this coalition. The accountants have hired some of Washington's big-gun lawyer-lobbyists, including Richard Moe, former top aide to Walter Mondale. The securities, commodities, and banking industries, as well as other business groups, have weighed in, too. The U.S. League of Savings Institutions was originally a visible member of the coalition, but it dropped from view once the S&L scandal became public. All told, these financial industries gave members of the Senate Judiciary Committee $1.46 million in PAC money, plus many more individual contributions, during the time RICO legislation has been considered.

These corporations say that they are being deluged with a "flood" of civil RICO cases. In fact, it is less a flood than a trickle. Because of the narrowness of the statute, few civil RICO cases are filed, and even fewer brought to trial. According to the administrative office of the U.S. Courts in 1988, less than one half of one percent of federal lawsuits were racketeering cases. The lobbyists also point out that the law is too vague. It's true that RICO's language is imprecise, thus allowing some improper suits; but these suits are almost always tossed out by the courts. The defendants' coalition isn't really worried about imprecise law or invalid suits. Their motive is much simpler: they don't want to pay.

In 1989, after several years of pushing, it looked as if business had finally found a way to defang RICO. The defendants' coalition was pushing a bill that would have slashed the available damages by two thirds in nearly all civil RICO cases. In a

highly unusual twist, it would have done this *retroactively.*
Most laws passed by Congress apply only to future litigation,
but this bill would have bailed out defendants in pending
cases to the tune of hundreds of millions of dollars. The measure's lead sponsor in the Senate, Dennis DeConcini, joined
forces with Representative Rick Boucher of Virginia, a former
Wall Street lawyer who represents a poor coal-mining district,
but who has devoted much of his congressional career to
weakening the white-collar crime laws.

At first, it looked as if the proposal would be ramrodded
through Congress. In June 1989, DeConcini held a few hours
of hearings; Washington's power centers testified for the bill,
including the bankers' association and a lawyer from Kaye
Scholer, Keating's law firm, as well as the ACLU and the AFL-
CIO. A week later, the Lincoln bondholders filed their lawsuit,
and wrote to DeConcini and judiciary Chairman Joseph Biden,
asking to testify. The senators refused.

Then the government filed its racketeering suit against
Keating, part of which alleged that he had diverted depositors'
funds for campaign contributions. DECONCINI BILL MAY OFFER
KEATING HELP, screamed the lead headline in the *Arizona Republic.* A political cartoon in the rival *Phoenix Gazette*
showed DeConcini, money bulging from his pocket, back-to-
back with Keating, with a piece of paper marked RICO REFORM
jutting out of his pocket. An embarrassed DeConcini quickly
announced he would drop the retroactivity provision from his
bill.

After a top lobbyist for the defendants' coalition let slip to a
reporter that the business groups' goal was to reinsert retroactivity later in the legislative process, three bondholders came
to Washington, hoping to persuade the judiciary committee to
vote against the RICO bill. One of them, Rae Luft, is ninety-
two years old, legally blind, and in a wheelchair. "Who would
have dreamed I'd be here?" she asked. Only one member of
the committee—Senator Paul Simon (D–Ill)—would meet
with them. DeConcini refused point-blank to see them, saying

he didn't like their lawyer. Responded Ramona Miller-Jacobs, one of the bondholders, "The man is a coward, and if he had nothing to hide, he would meet with all three of us. He doesn't have the guts to stand up to three women." But their passion was no match for industry's power. Committee chairman Joseph Biden said that the powerful RICO shouldn't be used in a "garden-variety fraud case." And Senator Orrin Hatch said the attacks on DeConcini were "pathetic and criminal." With the Lincoln bondholders watching from the back row of a crowded committee room, the committee voted 12–2 to gut RICO on February 1, 1990.

In the House of Representatives, a different proposal was crafted. Instead of reducing damages wholesale, Judiciary Committee members wrote a plan that would give judges greater discretion to dismiss inappropriate RICO suits. So far, so good. But the proposal includes an "accountants' exemption," which stipulates that the powerful statute can only be used against the kingpin in a white-collar crime scheme. That means it could be used against Keating—but not so easily against the professionals who allegedly aided his schemes. As the 1990 congressional session drew to a close, it was still not clear whether the accountants' lobby would prevail.

The battle line remains drawn on RICO. Fortunately, a growing chorus of editorial writers and law enforcers is calling for Congress to keep the law intact. Representative John Conyers, chairman of the House Government Operations Committee, has led the efforts to preserve strong civil RICO. "When the public becomes aware of this blatant favoritism, it will not stand for it," he asserts hopefully. The FDIC has weighed in, expressing worry that the proposed changes would put obstacles in the path of recovery for taxpayers. State attorneys general, securities law enforcers, and insurance commissioners, as well as consumer groups and a new plaintiffs attorneys' association, are actively lobbying as well. But the Justice Department has actively supported gutting this vital white-collar crime law, shedding further doubt on the Bush administration's commitment to cracking down on S&L fraud.

Citizen prosecutors: Whistle-blower provisions

The financial fraud wave is so massive, so complex, that under the best of circumstances federal enforcement officials could not hope to cope with it. As we know, these are *not* the best of circumstances: the Justice Department has been feeble in its efforts against S&L crooks. One answer is an innovative law enforcement proposal that lets whistle-blowers bring lawsuits against financial fraud on behalf of the government. But the Justice Department, seeking a monopoly on enforcement, has so far smothered the proposal.

Under a traditional procedure known as *qui tam,* a private citizen can bring a lawsuit on behalf of the taxpayers when the government has been defrauded. *(Qui tam* is part of a Latin phrase for "on behalf of the King.") If the lawsuit wins, the government gets the money, and the citizen gets a cut (between 15 and 25 percent). This has been part of American law since the Civil War, but was made easier to use in 1986 as part of amendments to the False Claims Act. *Qui tam* has mostly been used by whistle-blowers to combat defense contractor fraud. Since 1986, reports the *National Journal,* 274 *qui tam* suits have been filed, resulting in recovery of $70 million for the government. Under the statute, whistle-blowers must first bring the information to the Justice Department. The government can choose to bring suit itself, join a whistleblower's suit, or let the private citizen proceed on his or her own. These suits represent a free-market remedy for overburdened prosecutors, by giving victims or whistle-blowers the incentive to bring suit for the government.

Some members of Congress have proposed expanding *qui tam* suits to explicitly include bank fraud. In one stroke, the ranks of S&L prosecutors would expand to include the private bar. Representative Joe Kennedy included such a provision in his S&L financing and enforcement bill. "If the federal government is unable or unwilling to enforce the law against thrift bandits, the least we can do is strengthen the hand of private citizens who want to do so," he says. Originally, the Senate version of a recent crime bill included language similar to Kennedy's proposal. But intense lobbying by the Justice Department persuaded the bill's sponsors to drop the *qui tam* proposal and replace it with a watered-down "bounty hunter" provision that would provide cash rewards for some whistleblowers if they give their information to the Justice Department. Unfortunately, few S&L employees or others with explosive information will risk their jobs by adding their criminal allegations to the pile of complaints that is gathering dust at the department.

The federal law enforcement bureaucracy so far has proven inadequate to the task of grappling with the avalanche of S&L fraud. At this rate, the assets will have been frittered away by the time prosecutors bring enough fraud actions. Citizens should insist that they be given the tools to enforce the law themselves. Senator Charles Grassley is a conservative Republican who is an enthusiastic backer of *qui tam*. As Grassley told the House Judiciary Committee in April 1990, "Just as somebody said war is too important to leave to the generals, so, too, with the antifraud efforts. They are too important to leave to the Justice Department."

FOIA: Ending government secrecy

Corruption flourishes in secret. In Justice Louis Brandeis' memorable aphorism, "Sunlight is the best disinfectant." Nowhere is that proven more conclusively than in the S&L nightmare, in which special provisions allow enforcers to hide facts from the public.

For more than twenty years the Freedom of Information Act (FOIA) has enabled American citizens to inform themselves about government activities. FOIA creates a legally enforceable right of access to government information. Countless journalists and public-interest groups have used FOIA to reveal major scandals in areas ranging from defense fraud to nuclear power plant mishaps.

But not banking, which is the only industry that has a *blanket* exemption from FOIA. Not coincidentally, it is also the only industry that has required a multibillion dollar taxpayer bailout.

This banking exemption allows regulators to withhold from the press and public any and all information that relates to financial regulation. Bankers argue that this exemption is necessary, because otherwise regulators would be forced to give out data that might cause runs on financially troubled banks. But this exemption goes far beyond such safety and soundness concerns—it allows regulators to avoid dispensing information on white-collar crime, racial discrimination in lending patterns, industry solvency, and political pressure on enforcement agencies. There is no possible rationale for this kind of secrecy.

Legislation to restrict this exemption was introduced during the S&L bailout legislation by John Conyers, chairman of the House Government Operations Committee. Congressional leadership would not allow a vote of the full House of Representatives, but the reform is still long overdue.

SOLUTION FIVE: NO MORE DESTRUCTIVE DEREGULATION

The S&Ls perished because their investments were deregulated. As a consequence, rampant speculation led to a huge taxpayer bailout. Therefore, the next appropriate policy step is . . . deregulate the commercial banks?

By the pretzel logic of Washington, that's exactly right. Even as taxpayers are dazed from the sucker punch of the S&L bailout, banking lobbyists and Bush administration officials are working to prepare the public for another round of financial deregulation. This time, it's the commercial banks' turn.

The White House lobbying effort will probably begin in early 1991, when the Bush administration announces its plan to "restructure" (translation: "deregulate") the banks. Many people expect this proposal to be included in a package with a tax increase to pay for the S&Ls, the *last* failed experiment in financial deregulation.

Ironically, this comes at a time when the banking system is already nursing a hangover from the debt binge of the 1980s—not only because of the S&L fiasco, but also because many commercial banks are failing as well. Indeed, commercial banks may need a government bailout in the near future. The FDIC bank insurance fund has lost money for two years in a row. At present, it only has $13 billion to insure $3 trillion in deposits. As the real estate market in the northeast plunges, some of the banks in that region will face insolvency. Already, bank regulators are reenacting the doomed strategy of "forbearance," which allows a broke bank to stay open, thereby accumulating bad loans that eventually are paid for by exposing taxpayers to even greater losses.

When will we learn? Citizens should heed the lesson of the last debacle, and demand that there be no more deregulation of the federally insured financial institutions on which we rely. Effectively, our banking system has privatized profits, and socialized risks. That trade-off seemed appealing when banks limited that risk and made certain to serve the broad public. Now there needs to be a renewed social contract between those who control capital and those who subsidize it. Consumers and taxpayers have every right to demand that the banking system be made more democratically accountable, that it include small institutions as well as financial giants, and that it once again serve the credit and banking needs of the poor and middle class.

Keep the commercial banks safe

In the wake of the 1929 stock market crash and subsequent bank panic, lawmakers resolved to limit the ability of banks to gamble with "other people's money." As discussed in chapter 2, the 1933 Glass-Steagall Act prohibited commercial banks from buying and selling stock on the stock market in return for the new system of federal deposit insurance. The rationale was simple: taxpayers should not insure gambling.

Lately, however, big banks have mounted an intense drive to repeal Glass-Steagall and win expanded investment powers for themselves. A new breed of aggressive banks—typified by Citibank—is eager to reap better returns through investments on the stock market, ownership of corporations, real estate investments, and insurance sales. The attitude of these banks should be familiar to the parents of any ten-year-old: "Ma! Why do I have to stay inside and do my homework while all the other kids get to have fun and play outside on Wall Street?" Similarly, banks are yearning to plunge into high-technology, high-risk, high-reward investments. The money would be theirs to gain, and ours to lose.

These "expanded powers" would threaten the security of the banking system. First, banks would risk economic instability if they could play the stock market. Assume that banks had taken huge losses on October 19, 1987, when the New York Stock Exchange plummeted more than 500 points. Can anyone doubt that a banking panic would have ensued? Second, letting banks "underwrite" securities (that is, provide the start-up money when corporations issue new stock or bonds) creates likely conflicts of interest. Banks will be greatly tempted to invest their depositors' money in an investment that benefits their stockbroker arm, no matter what protections are in place to prevent this.

Finally, if banks could buy securities firms and industrial corporations they would become megacorporations more powerful than any in this country's history. If Citibank owned American Express and Exxon, what government agency—or citizen—could stand up to that behemoth, let alone try to regulate it? And if Chase Manhattan owned Manville Corporation when it declared bankruptcy due to asbestos liability, how large would the taxpayer bailout have been?

Someone has to shake some sense into the heads of policymakers who think the cure for the ills of deregulation is more deregulation. Cutting loose the S&Ls led to massive fraud, reckless gambling with depositors' money, and, ultimately, a huge taxpayer bailout. For all the protestations of the banking lobby, there is simply no reason to expect anything different from commercial bank deregulation. It's time to say it plain: *No more taxpayer-subsidized deregulation.*

Deposit insurance

Some people blame deposit insurance for the S&L collapse. They would like to see the current system drastically overhauled; proposals vary, but all of them call for a change in the current $100,000 per account system.

Deposit insurance, after all, was originally created to protect the life savings of the poor and middle class. Thanks to brokered deposits, it has been twisted beyond all recognition, so that the S&L bailout now is a subsidy from those citizens with less money to those with more money. So it might make sense to limit deposit insurance to $100,000 per *consumer,* rather than per bank.

But even this reasonable restriction on deposit insurance might have adverse consequences. Small banks worry that people would move their deposits to big banks, which are thought to be candidates for a federal rescue no matter how expensive the bailout. Restricting deposit insurance also might limit capital to low-income communities even further, by forcing lenders to restrict their activities in the face of reduced consumer deposits. And, of course, the less deposit insurance, the more bank panics.

No, tinkering with deposit insurance simply won't fix our banking system. The social contract created in the 1930s with the establishment of deposit insurance is vital to a stable economy. In return for the government protections they receive, thrifts and commercial banks should live up to their public obligations. Under deregulation, these obligations withered while the government exempted financial firms from the normal risks of doing business. The key to reforming the financial system is not to revoke the social contract, but instead to make sure the financial industry lives up to its part of the bargain.

Banking for the people

Instead of encouraging banks to act more like Charles Keating or Ivan Boesky, we should encourage banking institutions to invest in communities and people, and make them accountable to the communities they serve.

Taxpayer subsidies, taxpayer representation. When taxpayers spend millions of dollars resuscitating a thrift, we should at least make sure that the revived institution serves the public interest. But today, S&Ls are spun off into the private sector, free to invest unwisely, discriminate against minorities, or evade regulators. Instead, every thrift or bank that is rescued by the taxpayers should have at least one taxpayer representative on its board of directors. This ombudsperson would ensure that at least one voice in the S&L boardroom speaks up for the people who ultimately foot the bill.

Community banking. Why should the RTC only sell defunct S&Ls to major commercial banks? There are hundreds of credit unions, nonprofit groups, and local development agencies that could put thrift deposits to good use—if they were given the financial assistance necessary to purchase the S&L. In recent years, these locally-oriented "points of light" have pioneered the development of low-income housing in cities across the country. Federal regulators should encourage the development of "community banking" by providing financial assistance to these community-oriented groups, on a pilot basis, to try and recover some of the thrifts' original function: providing capital for affordable housing.

Democratize the Federal Reserve. In many ways, the Federal Reserve laid the groundwork for the thrift crisis when it raised interest rates to record levels in 1979 in a tunnel-vision strategy to halt inflation. That kind of basic economic policy decision ought to be made by a democratically accountable branch of government.

The Fed controls monetary policy: it decides whether interest rates rise or fall, whether money is easy or tight, and whether the economy expands or contracts. These basic policy decisions can have a seismic impact on our economy and society, and should logically be made by politically accountable branches of government. But the Fed is an exception to American democracy. It is elaborately structured to evade such accountability, and to give big banks and other financial institutions a preferential say in how monetary policy is determined. (For example, the Fed's committee, which meets secretly to set the level of interest rates, is partly comprised of representatives elected by the local federal reserve banks, in turn elected by private banks.)

Defenders of the Fed argue that this insulation from accountability is precisely the point—that grubby politicians would pump money into the economy through low interest rates, leading to an unending spiral of inflation. In the words of former Fed Chairman William McChesney Martin, the Fed's job is "taking the punch bowl away just when the party is getting merry." But when did the American people abdicate responsibility for economic policy to a bevy of bankers and "experts" ? The political system is too biased toward low unemployment, warn Fed supporters. But that is a political choice, not an economic imperative, and it should be made by a democratically self-governing people. The S&L collapse is one consequence of the pursuit of theoretical perfection in policy. Instead, the Federal Reserve should be democratized to prevent future S&L or bank crises. At the very least, each new president should get to pick his or her own head of the Federal Reserve. And the president should get to pick, and the Senate confirm, the members of the committee that secretly meets to set monetary policy.

EPILOGUE: WHAT YOU CAN DO

"I am really outraged by the savings and loan thing. . . . How can this occur in our savings and loan institutions. . . . What I don't understand is how our officials could have allowed this to occur."

On a Seattle talk show late August 1990, the airwaves were crackling with anger. The topic: the S&L bailout. On call-in shows, in political campaigns, in taverns and editorial pages, America is fed up with the antics of the thrift robbers.

"I am just mad as hell. I am absolutely sick about the terrible thing that our government has allowed to happen to the American people."

Reported the *New York Times*, "Citizens are starting to shout over savings and loan costs." While in the past, resentment was vague and lacked direction, people are beginning to band together to try and hold the big boys accountable:

· In Arizona, the group that organized the recall drive against Governor Evan Mecham turned its attention to two of the Keating Five senators, Dennis DeConcini and John McCain. "Arizona has two fifths of the Keating Five, and Arizona has Charles Keating," says organizer Ed Buck. "So Arizona should take the lead for the country in cleaning up this mess." During the Fiesta Bowl in 1990, the group plastered thousands of cars in the parking lot with mock ten-dollar bills festooned with the senators' pictures and signed by

"Charles Cheating." USE THIS NOTE TO BUY INFLUENCE IN ARIZONA, it said. "Beyond Recall," as the group was known, gave up its drive when it won pledges from the two senators to support campaign finance reform.

- In California, citizens outraged about corruption in state government collected several hundred thousand signatures, enough to put a reform initiative on the ballot. The measure, which was scheduled for a vote in November 1990, would institute public funding for state legislative elections, limit the terms of members of the state legislature, and impose strict ethics rules. One of the reformers' main arguments for changing the system: the state legislature's role in bringing on the S&L scandal through lax laws for thrifts.

- In Seattle, KING-AM radio talk show host Mike Siegel called a meeting of his listeners to discuss what they could do about the S&L debacle. Conveners expected 250 attendees; instead, 750 people showed up, and a citizen uprising began. Starting a brown paper bag brigade—"We won't be their bagmen," Siegel told his listeners—the talk-show crusaded for campaign reform and strong white-collar crime laws. The listeners invited every member of the Seattle congressional delegation to attend a public meeting; only one had the courage to show up. "We've only begun," vowed Siegel.

- In Massachusetts in August 1990, the Pioneer Valley Pro-Democracy Campaign held a public forum on the S&L crisis. Speakers focused on the S&L bailout's impact on education, housing, and health care. Now, the group is organizing meetings with local members of Congress to push support for Representative Joseph Kennedy's S&L Fair Financing and Anti-Fraud Enforcement Act of 1990 (H.R. 5499).

- A coalition of 200 citizen groups, church groups, labor unions and housing groups have come together as the Financial Democracy Campaign. One of these groups, ACORN, has organized pickets at the U.S. League of Savings Institutions in Chicago, at the RTC offices in Washington, D.C., outside a hotel where Treasury Secretary Nicholas Brady was speaking (because of the crowd he was forced to use the kitchen entrance), and at mansions of S&L moguls throughout the country.

You can join the drive to tell Washington you don't want any more unfair bailouts. It's a cliché, but it's true—every citizen can make a difference. If enough people band together, you can fight city hall. For years, the people in power have only heard about banking issues from the bankers and developers. If they now start hearing from taxpayers, the dynamic of the issue will change entirely.

CITIZEN LOBBYING

For all their responsiveness to big money-givers, members of Congress still listen to their constituents. As often as not, the voice of the citizenry is not heard because it is not organized.

- Write to your member of Congress. Letters should be short, legible, and individually addressed to your senator or representative. Ask them to *cosponsor* H.R. 5499. You can write to your lawmakers at this address:

Senator _____   Representative _____
U.S. Senate   U.S. House of Representatives
Washington, D.C. 20510   Washington, D.C. 20515

  Be sure to ask for a response from the lawmaker. If you don't receive a response, call the representative or senator's office and ask why not. After all, a major campaign contributor would have gotten a prompt reply.
- Ask for a meeting with your representative, or with a member of his or her staff. All members of Congress have offices

in the district, and you should ask to have the meeting there.

- Convene a town meeting, and invite your representative to attend. If he or she refuses, then the meeting can be a forum to discuss how to hold the legislator accountable.
- Organize your friends, neighbors, and community groups to do the same.

LETTERS TO THE EDITOR

Believe it or not, the best-read section of the newspaper is the letters to the editor. By writing such a letter, you can tell your neighbors about the Kennedy bill and the position of your representatives, as well as communicate with the editors of your newspaper and the policymakers who read it.

If you write a letter to the editor on the S&L scandal and it is published, be sure to send a copy to your member of Congress.

CANDIDATES

Taxpayers will begin to get justice only if the S&L scandal becomes an issue in election campaigns throughout the country. Incumbent officeholders will often become more responsive when facing the electorate. Ask the candidates in your hometown to pledge to support the Agenda for Action in this book.

CALL-IN SHOWS

Radio call-in shows are today's town meetings, and are becoming a growing political force as well. Following the fight over the congressional pay raise, 180 talk-show hosts met in

Boston in June 1989 to exchange information. Now, they are trading facts and plans on the S&L bailout. *Encourage your local talk-show hosts to join the National Association of Radio Talk Show Hosts so they can share information with other stations around the country.* They can write to the organization care of

Mike Siegel
KING radio
333 Dexter Avenue North
Seattle WA 98109.

DO YOUR OWN RESEARCH AND INVESTIGATION

Even though all of the federal agencies that regulate financial institutions are exempt from the Freedom of Information Act (FOIA), the RTC is not. Thus, to do some watchdogging on your own you can request government information from the agency in charge of the bailout. Here's how to make a request from the RTC (801 17th St. NW, Washington, D.C. 20434):

You must first determine what you want, since the law requires that your request must "reasonably describe" the records you seek. This means that you may not simply ask questions but must request records describing or pertaining to a particular subject. You must provide a reasonable enough description to allow a government employee to locate the records you seek. Your request should state that it is being made pursuant to the Freedom of Information Act. You should write "Freedom of Information Request" on the envelope and on the letter. You do not have to explain the reasons for your request.

The RTC has ten days to reply to your request. Nevertheless, delay is common and agencies often extend the deadline. However, if the RTC fails to respond, you may appeal or go to court. Also, following up written requests with phone calls can speed up your request.

Note: Even though the other regulatory agencies for banks

and S&Ls are exempt from the FOIA, it is within their discretion to release records. Thus, sometimes it is worth requesting information from the Federal Reserve (which regulates banks), the OTS, or the FDIC.

•

The first S&L calamity took place in a vacuum—the void created by the silence of the American people. Now, we have no excuse. This book has attempted to spell out the root causes of the S&L collapse, has described the sorry state of the bailout, and has put forward a program to prevent this fiasco from recurring. If citizens allow policy and politics to continue as they have, with out-of-control financial institutions imposing enormous costs on the public, we will have only ourselves to blame.

THE S&L SCANDAL: A Timeline

APPENDIX 1

1933 Banking Act establishes Federal Deposit Insurance Corporation (FDIC) to guarantee bank deposits and regulate the banking industry.

1934 National Housing Act establishes Federal Savings and Loan Insurance Corporation (FSLIC) to guarantee S&L deposits.

1966 Interest Rate Control Act imposes interest rate caps on both S&Ls and banks, but allows S&Ls to offer a slightly higher interest rate for savings accounts.

1974 Bank Board begins authorizing S&Ls to switch from mutual to stock form.

1979 Federal Reserve adopts tight monetary policy, raising interest rates.

1980 Depository Institutions Deregulation and Monetary Control Act lifts interest rate caps and raises deposit insurance from $40,000 to $100,000 per account.

1981 Ronald Reagan sworn in as president. Imposes hiring freeze on S&L regulators, and appoints pro-deregulation Federal Home Loan Bank Board chief.

1982 Garn–St Germain Depository Institutions Act authorizes S&Ls to directly invest in real estate and other risky ventures, and lifts restrictions on converting to stock form. Federal thrift regulators loosen accounting standards, so that failing S&Ls can project false image of prosperity. States pass radical deregulation bills to keep up with federal government. California's Nolan Act goes farthest.

1983 Edwin Gray appointed as chairman of Bank Board.

1984 Bank Board tries to crack down on brokered deposits; blocked by courts.

1986 Bank Board asks Congress for $15 billion to rescue failing thrifts.

1987 Financial Institutions Competitive Equality Act allows Bank Board to raise $10.8 billion to rescue failing S&Ls. Congress rejects regulators' request for $15 billion. Bank Board chairman Edwin Gray retires, and is replaced by M. Danny Wall, former staff director of Senate Banking Committee. Vernon Savings and Loan fails.

1988 On November 8, George Bush is elected president. On November 9, thrift regulators issue order to seize Silverado Banking, Savings and Loan. In December, Bank Board secretly sells off seventy-five failing S&Ls in Southwest Plan.

1989 George Bush sworn in as president. Two weeks later, the new administration proposes a bailout for the savings & loan industry. Lincoln Savings and Loan fails. In June, Speaker of the House James Wright and Democratic Whip Tony Coelho resign in ethics controversies. In August, Congress enacts the Financial Institutions Regulatory Reform and Enforcement Act (FIRREA). FIRREA authorizes $50 billion to bail out S&L industry, and establishes the Resolution Trust Corporation (RTC) to handle failed thrifts. Beginning in September, House Banking Committee chair Henry B. Gonzalez launches series of hearings on Lincoln S&L. M. Danny Wall resigns shortly after. Senate Ethics Committee begins formal investigation of Keating Five senators.

1990 In April, Treasury Secretary Nicholas Brady, in testimony before Senate Banking Committee, doubles cost estimate of S&L bailout to between $90 and 130 billion.

In July and August, the House and Senate reject substantial public funding for congressional elections.

Office of Thrift Supervision schedules public hearings on failure of Silverado for September 25.

TAKING NAMES AND KICKING BEHINDS:

Holding Congress Accountable

Members of Congress should be held accountable for the mistakes and misdeeds that led to the savings and loan collapse. Citizens have a right to know basic facts about the role their elected officials played. How much money do they receive from the financial industry? Did they vote with the S&Ls? Are they in favor of eliminating the influence peddling of the campaign finance system?

This chart provides tools for answering those questions. First, for each current member of the House and Senate, the chart reveals how much money in campaign contributions the incumbent has received from PACs representing S&Ls, commercial banks, the securities industry, and credit unions. Second, it spells out where your representative stood on key S&L-related issues over the past eleven years. Third, the final columns tell how your senators and representatives voted on the most important campaign finance reform decisions in 1990.

Keep in mind: there are many reasons why a legislator might have voted for or against a particular bill. This chart will help you ask the right questions to determine what role your members of Congress played.

The following abbreviations tell you how your representatives and senators voted: Y = yes; N = no; P = present (abstaining); A = absent; NA = not applicable (not elected at time of vote).

SENATE S&L VOTING RECORD

Vote 1. Remove caps on interest rates: November 1, 1979. H.R. 4986, the Depository Institution Deregulation and Monetary Control Act. This was a vote to abolish interest rate ceilings on savings accounts, thus allowing S&Ls to offer whatever interest rates they choose on savings accounts. The bill was adopted on a vote of 76 to 9.

Vote 2. Provide partial funding for S&L regulators: March 27, 1987. S. 790, the Competitive Equality Banking Act. This bill proposed to rescue FSLIC with only $7.5 billion, instead of $15 billion, as requested by thrift regulators. The bill was adopted on a vote of 79 to 11.

Vote 3. Exempt M. Danny Wall from confirmation hearings: April 19, 1989. S. 774, the Financial Institutions Reform, Recovery and Enforcement Act. Senator Donald Riegle of Michigan offered a procedural motion that would allow M. Danny Wall to keep his job as chief thrift regulator without being renominated by the president and confirmed by the Senate. The amendment was adopted on a vote of 61–38.

Vote 4. S&L bailout: April 19, 1989. S. 774, the Financial Institutions Reform, Recovery and Enforcement Act. This bill proposed to appropriate $50 billion to bail out the S&L industry.

Vote 5. Full public funding of elections: July 31, 1990. S. 137, the Senate Election Campaign Ethics Act of 1990. Senator John Kerry of Massachusetts offered an amendment to make comprehensive reforms in Senate election campaign law. The amendment would have provided substantial public funding to general election candidates who comply with a spending cap. The amendment was defeated by a vote of 38 to 60.

SENATE

Senator	Financial industry PAC money	VOTE 1 Remove caps on interest rates (1979)	VOTE 2 Provide partial funding for regulators (1987)	VOTE 3 Keep Danny Wall on job (1989)	VOTE 4 S&L bailout (1989)	VOTE 5 Public funding of elections (1990)
ALABAMA						
Howell Heflin	$74,598	Y	Y	Y	Y	N
Richard Shelby	$181,113	NA	Y	Y	Y	N
ALASKA						
Frank Murkowski	$45,025	NA	Y	Y	Y	N
Ted Stevens	$41,000	Y	A	Y	Y	N
ARIZONA						
Dennis DeConcini	$115,650	Y	Y	Y	Y	Y
John McCain	$65,290	NA	Y	Y	Y	N
ARKANSAS						
Dale Bumpers	$40,350	Y	Y	N	Y	Y
David Pryor	$60,700	Y	Y	N	N	N
CALIFORNIA						
Alan Cranston	$248,700	Y	Y	Y	Y	Y

Senator	Financial industry PAC money	VOTE 1 Remove caps on interest rates (1979)	VOTE 2 Provide partial funding for regulators (1987)	VOTE 3 Keep Danny Wall on job (1989)	VOTE 4 S&L bailout (1989)	VOTE 5 Public funding of elections (1990)
Pete Wilson	$230,372	NA	Y	Y	Y	N
COLORADO						
William Armstrong	$2,500	N	N	Y	Y	A
Timothy Wirth	$172,550	NA	Y	N	Y	Y
CONNECTICUT						
Christopher Dodd	$152,294	NA	Y	Y	Y	Y
Joe Lieberman	$32,510	NA	NA	N	Y	Y
DELAWARE						
William Roth	$145,200	Y	N	Y	Y	N
Joseph Biden	$53,500	Y	A	N	Y	Y
FLORIDA						
Bob Graham	$194,369	NA	Y	N	Y	N
Connie Mack	$140,700	NA	NA	Y	Y	N
GEORGIA						
Sam Nunn	$63,050	N	Y	N	Y	N
Wyche Fowler	$110,085	NA	Y	N	Y	Y

HAWAII						
Daniel Inouye	$62,500	Y	Y	Y	Y	Y
Daniel Akaka	$11,030	NA	NA	NA	NA	N
IDAHO						
James McClure	$9,500	N	N	Y	Y	N
Steve Symms	$138,800	NA	N	Y	Y	N
ILLINOIS						
Alan Dixon	$235,089	NA	Y	Y	Y	N
Paul Simon	$68,785	NA	Y	N	Y	Y
INDIANA						
Richard Lugar	$97,236	Y	Y	Y	Y	N
Dan Coats	$94,540	NA	NA	Y	Y	N
IOWA						
Charles Grassley	$108,674	NA	Y	Y	Y	N
Tom Harkin	$47,161	NA	A	N	Y	Y
KANSAS						
Robert Dole	$166,820	Y	Y	Y	Y	N
Nancy L. Kassebaum	$10,700	Y	Y	Y	Y	N
KENTUCKY						
Wendell Ford	$49,740	Y	Y	Y	Y	Y
Mitch McConnell	$45,727	NA	Y	Y	Y	N

Senator	Financial industry PAC money	VOTE 1 Remove caps on interest rates (1979)	VOTE 2 Provide partial funding for regulators (1987)	VOTE 3 Keep Danny Wall on job (1989)	VOTE 4 S&L bailout (1989)	VOTE 5 Public funding of elections (1990)
LOUISIANA						
J. Bennett Johnston	$36,210	Y	A	N	Y	N
John Breaux	$78,210	NA	Y	N	Y	N
MAINE						
George Mitchell	$89,500	NA	Y	N	Y	Y
William Cohen	$23,000	Y	A	Y	Y	N
MARYLAND						
Paul Sarbanes	$66,250	Y	Y	N	Y	Y
Barbara Mikulski	$54,450	NA	Y	N	Y	Y
MASSACHUSETTS						
Edward Kennedy	$14,300	Y	A	N	Y	Y
John Kerry	$0	NA	Y	N	Y	Y
MICHIGAN						
Donald Riegle	$366,634	Y	Y	Y	Y	Y
Carl Levin	$40,305	Y	Y	N	Y	N

MINNESOTA						
Dave Durenberger	$168,563	Y	Y	Y	Y	N
Rudy Boschwitz	$70,566	Y	Y	Y	Y	N
MISSISSIPPI						
Thad Cochran	$36,400	Y	Y	Y	Y	N
Trent Lott	$113,900	NA	NA	Y	Y	A
MISSOURI						
John Danforth	$141,832	Y	Y	Y	Y	N
Christopher Bond	$211,883	NA	Y	Y	Y	N
MONTANA						
Max Baucus	$150,000	Y	Y	N	N	Y
Conrad Burns	$24,249	NA	NA	Y	Y	N
NEBRASKA						
J. James Exon	$43,250	Y	Y	N	N	N
Bob Kerrey	$42,416	A	NA	N	N	N
NEVADA						
Harry Reid	$26,000	NA	Y	N	Y	Y
Richard Bryan	$54,152	NA	NA	N	Y	N
NEW HAMPSHIRE						
Gordon Humphrey	$8,500	Y	N	Y	Y	N
Warren Rudman	$6,800	NA	N	Y	Y	N

Senator	Financial industry PAC money	VOTE 1 Remove caps on interest rates (1979)	VOTE 2 Provide partial funding for regulators (1987)	VOTE 3 Keep Danny Wall on job (1989)	VOTE 4 S&L bailout (1989)	VOTE 5 Public funding of elections (1990)
NEW JERSEY						
Bill Bradley	$205,112	Y	Y	N	N	Y
Frank Lautenberg	$165,822	NA	Y	N	Y	Y
NEW MEXICO						
Pete Domenici	$67,450	Y	Y	Y	Y	N
Jeff Bingaman	$58,687	NA	Y	N	Y	Y
NEW YORK						
Daniel P. Moynihan	$289,621	Y	Y	Y	Y	Y
Alfonse D'Amato	$307,968	NA	Y	Y	Y	N
NORTH CAROLINA						
Jesse Helms	$43,515	Y	N	Y	Y	N
Terry Sanford	$329,900	NA	Y	N	Y	Y
NORTH DAKOTA						
Quentin Burdick	$58,000	Y	Y	N	Y	Y
Kent Conrad	$39,500	NA	Y	N	N	Y

OHIO						
John Glenn	$40,750	A	Y	Y	Y	Y
Howard Metzenbaum	$34,050	Y	Y	N	N	Y
OKLAHOMA						
David Boren	$0	Y	Y	N	Y	Y
Don Nickles	$62,419	NA	Y	Y	Y	N
OREGON						
Mark Hatfield	$28,750	Y	A	Y	Y	N
Bob Packwood	$130,860	Y	Y	Y	Y	N
PENNSYLVANIA						
John Heinz	$223,631	A	Y	Y	Y	N
Arlen Specter	$161,688	NA	Y	Y	Y	N
RHODE ISLAND						
Claiborne Pell	$36,999	Y	Y	Y	Y	Y
John Chafee	$223,742	Y	Y	Y	Y	N
SOUTH CAROLINA						
Strom Thurmond	$59,950	N	Y	Y	Y	N
Ernest Hollings	$121,100	N	Y	N	N	N
SOUTH DAKOTA						
Larry Pressler	$78,500	A	Y	Y	Y	N
Thomas Daschle	$111,190	NA	Y	N	Y	Y

Senator	Financial industry PAC money	VOTE 1 Remove caps on interest rates (1979)	VOTE 2 Provide partial funding for regulators (1987)	VOTE 3 Keep Danny Wall on job (1989)	VOTE 4 S&L bailout (1989)	VOTE 5 Public funding of elections (1990)
TENNESSEE						
Albert Gore	$48,700	NA	Y	A	Y	Y
Jim Sasser	$244,190	Y	Y	Y	Y	Y
TEXAS						
Lloyd Bentsen	$404,372	Y	A	Y	Y	Y
Phil Gramm	$233,100	NA	Y	Y	Y	N
UTAH						
Jake Garn	$239,675	Y	N	Y	Y	N
Orrin Hatch	$85,412	Y	N	Y	Y	N
VERMONT						
Patrick Leahy	$57,150	Y	Y	N	Y	Y
James Jeffords	$51,600	NA	NA	Y	Y	N
VIRGINIA						
John Warner	$47,600	Y	Y	Y	Y	N
Charles Robb	$84,950	NA	NA	N	Y	N

WASHINGTON						
Brock Adams	$48,050	NA	Y	N	Y	Y
Slade Gorton	$297,623	NA	NA	Y	Y	N
WEST VIRGINIA						
Robert Byrd	$85,600	Y	Y	N	Y	Y
Jay Rockefeller	$98,785	NA	Y	N	Y	N
WISCONSIN						
Robert Kasten	$114,023	NA	Y	Y	Y	N
Herbert Kohl	$0	NA	NA	Y	Y	N
WYOMING						
Malcolm Wallop	$91,500	Y	N	Y	Y	N
Alan Simpson	$45,250	Y	A	Y	Y	N

Note: Information for financial industry political action committee (PAC) contributions came from reports filed by PACs at the Federal Election Commission. Contributions from financial industry PACs include PACs from the following categories: commercial banks, bank holding companies, savings banks, savings and loans, credit unions, credit agencies, finance companies, investment banking, mortgage bankers and brokers, security brokers and investment companies. Figures cover period from January 1, 1985 through May 1990. For Senators who also served in the House of Representatives during this period, figures include PAC funds received as House Members. Senator Slade Gorton (R-WA) was defeated for reelection in 1986 and reelected in an open seat race in 1988—his figures include PAC money from both elections. Senator David Boren (D-OK), John Kerry (D-MA), and Herbert Kohl (D-WI) do not accept PAC contributions. Senator Bob Packwood (R-OR), as of February 1986, no longer accepts PAC contributions.

Sources: Campaign Research Center, Federal Election Commission, Congressional Quarterly and the 1990 U.S. Congress Handbook.

HOUSE S&L VOTING RECORD

Vote 1. Remove cap on interest rates: March 27, 1980. H.R. 4986, the Depository Institution Deregulation and Monetary Control Act. This was a vote to abolish interest rate caps on savings accounts, thus allowing S&Ls to offer whatever interest rate they choose on savings accounts. The bill was adopted by a vote of 380 to 13.

Vote 2. Deregulate S&L investments: May 20, 1982. H.R. 6267, the Garn–St Germain Depository Institutions Act. This bill allowed federally-chartered S&Ls to make loans on speculative real estate ventures, and gave insolvent thrifts a variety of accounting devices to stay in business. The bill was adopted by a vote of 272 to 91.

Vote 3. Provide full funding for FSLIC regulators: May 5, 1987. H.R. 27, the Federal Savings and Loan Insurance Corporation Recapitalization Act. Rep. Fernand St Germain of Rhode Island offered an amendment to restore the amount authorized to rescue FSLIC from $5 billion—the amount lobbied for by the U.S. League of Savings Institutions —to $15 billion, the amount requested by S&L regulators. The amendment was defeated by a vote of 153 to 258.

Vote 4. Restrict risky S&L investments: May 5, 1987. H.R. 27, the Federal Savings and Loan Insurance Corporation Recapitalization Act. Rep. Jim Leach of Iowa offered an amendment to restrict risky investments by S&Ls. The amendment was defeated by a vote of 17 to 391.

Vote 5. Weaken capital standards for S&Ls: June 15, 1989. H.R. 1278, the Financial Institutions Reform, Recovery and Enforcement Act. Rep. Henry Hyde of Illinois offered an amendment to continue allowing S&Ls to count "goodwill" toward their capital requirements, which allows S&L owners to operate without putting up any of their own money. The amendment was defeated by a vote of 94 to 326.

Vote 6. Count S&L bailout as part of federal

budget: June 15, 1989. H.R. 1278, the Financial Institutions Reform, Recovery and Enforcement Act. Rep. John LaFalce of New York proposed an amendment to directly allocate $50 billion over the next three years for the S&L bailout. Under this amendment the $50 billion bailout would be included in the federal deficit, thereby forcing Congress to deal honestly with the issue of how to pay for the S&L bailout. The amendment was defeated by a vote of 171 to 259.

Vote 7. Disclose information on discriminatory lending practices: June 15, 1989. H.R. 1278, the Financial Institutions Reform, Recovery and Enforcement Act. Reps. Joseph Kennedy of Massachusetts and Henry Gonzalez of Texas offered an amendment to require regulatory agencies to disclose the ratings and evaluations they give to banks and S&Ls regarding lending to the communities. The amendment also required lenders to disclose the number of mortgage applications they receive by categories of race, income, and gender, and the number of applications they approve by the same categories. The amendment was adopted by a vote of 214 to 200.

Vote 8. Bail out S&Ls: June 15, 1989. H.R. 1278, the Financial Institutions Reform, Recovery and Enforcement Act. This bill proposed to appropriate $50 billion to bail out the S&L industry.

Vote 9. Public financing of elections: August 3, 1990. H.R. 5400, the Campaign Cost Reduction and Reform Act of 1990. Reps. Michael Synar of Oklahoma and David Obey of Wisconsin offered an amendment to make comprehensive reforms in the House campaign finance law. The amendment would have set voluntary limits on campaign spending, limited individual contributions to $500, and provided up to $100,000 in federal matching funds for small, in-state contributions. The amendment was defeated by a vote of 122 to 128, with 158 members voting "present."

HOUSE OF REPRESENTATIVES

Representative	District	Financial industry PAC money	VOTE 1 Remove caps on interest rates (1980)	VOTE 2 Deregulate S&L investments (1982)	VOTE 3 Provide full funding for S&L regulators (1987)	VOTE 4 Restrict risky S&L investments (1987)	VOTE 5 Weaken capital standards (1989)	VOTE 6 Put bailout on budget (1989)	VOTE 7 Disclose discriminatory lending (1989)	VOTE 8 S&L bailout (1989)	VOTE 9 Public funding of House elections (1990)
ALABAMA											
H. L. Callahan	1	$33,950	NA	NA	N	N	N	N	N	Y	P
William Dickinson	2	$20,000	Y	Y	Y	N	N	N	N	Y	P
Glen Browder	3	$17,750	NA	NA	NA	NA	N	N	N	Y	N
Tom Bevill	4	$12,800	Y	Y	N	N	N	N	Y	N	A
Ronnie Flippo	5	$156,741	Y	Y	N	N	N	N	Y	Y	N
Ben Erdreich	6	$155,306	NA	NA	N	N	N	N	Y	Y	N
Claude Harris	7	$31,250	NA	NA	N	N	N	N	Y	Y	N
ALASKA											
Don Young	1	$11,200	Y	Y	Y	N	Y	Y	N	Y	P
ARIZONA											
John Rhodes III	1	$38,900	Y	N	Y	N	N	N	N	Y	P
Morris Udall	2	$8,505	Y	Y	A	A	N	Y	Y	Y	Y
Bob Stump	3	$24,100	Y	N	N	N	Y	Y	N	N	P
Jon Kyl	4	$64,225	NA	NA	N	N	Y	Y	N	Y	P
Jim Kolbe	5	$67,175	NA	NA	N	N	N	Y	N	Y	P

State / Representative	District	Amount									
ARKANSAS											
Bill Alexander	1	$35,150	A	Y	N	N	N	Y	N	Y	N
Tommy Robinson	2	$14,100	NA	NA	N	N	Y	Y	N	Y	A
John Hammerschmidt	3	$6,300	Y	Y	N	N	Y	N	N	Y	P
Beryl Anthony, Jr.	4	$85,825	Y	A	N	N	N	N	N	Y	N
CALIFORNIA											
Douglas Bosco	1	$8,322	NA	NA	N	N	N	Y	N	Y	A
Wally Herger	2	$23,400	NA	NA	N	N	N	Y	N	Y	N
Robert Matsui	3	$129,149	Y	Y	Y	N	N	Y	Y	Y	Y
Victor Fazio	4	$44,275	Y	Y	N	N	N	N	Y	Y	Y
Nancy Pelosi	5	$77,500	NA	NA	NA	NA	N	N	Y	Y	Y
Barbara Boxer	6	$12,050	NA	NA	N	N	N	Y	Y	Y	Y
George Miller	7	$10,400	Y	Y	N	Y	N	Y	Y	N	Y
Ronald Dellums	8	$1,450	Y	Y	Y	N	Y	Y	Y	N	Y
Fortney Stark	9	$72,250	A	A	Y	A	A	N	Y	N	Y
Don Edwards	10	$6,950	Y	Y	N	N	N	N	Y	Y	Y
Tom Lantos	11	$6,500	NA	NA	N	N	N	Y	Y	Y	N
Tom Campbell	12	$22,150	NA	Y	NA	NA	N	Y	Y	Y	Y
Norman Mineta	13	$22,400	Y	N	N	N	N	N	N	Y	P
Norman Shumway	14	$157,124	N	NA	NA	NA	Y	NA	NA	NA	N
Gary Condit	15	$10,500	NA	NA	N	N	NA	N	NA	NA	Y
Leon Panetta	16	$15,600	Y	Y	Y	N	N	Y	Y	Y	Y
Charles Pashayan, Jr.	17	$13,050	N	N	N	N	N	N	Y	Y	P
Richard Lehman	18	$122,530	NA	Y	Y	N	N	N	Y	Y	Y
Robert Lagomarsino	19	$31,910	N	NA	Y	N	N	Y	Y	N	P
William Thomas	20	$50,050	A	A	N	N	N	N	Y	Y	P
Elton Gallegly	21	$30,915	NA	NA	N	N	Y	Y	N	N	P
Carlos Moorhead	22	$46,930	Y	N	Y	N	N	Y	N	N	P
Anthony Beilenson	23	$0	Y	Y	N	N	N	Y	Y	Y	Y

Representative	District	Financial industry PAC money	VOTE 1 Remove caps on interest rates (1980)	VOTE 2 Deregulate S&L investments (1982)	VOTE 3 Provide full funding for S&L regulators (1987)	VOTE 4 Restrict risky S&L investments (1987)	VOTE 5 Weaken capital standards (1989)	VOTE 6 Put bailout on budget (1989)	VOTE 7 Disclose discriminatory lending (1989)	VOTE 8 S&L bailout (1989)	VOTE 9 Public funding of House elections (1990)
Henry Waxman	24	$29,900	A	Y	Y	N	N	N	Y	Y	Y
Edward Roybal	25	$2,300	Y	Y	N	N	N	N	Y	Y	Y
Howard Berman	26	$44,200	NA	NA	Y	N	N	N	Y	Y	Y
Mel Levine	27	$56,600	NA	NA	A	A	N	N	Y	Y	Y
Julian Dixon	28	$8,000	Y	A	N	N	N	Y	Y	Y	Y
Augustus Hawkins	29	$3,700	Y	A	N	N	N	N	Y	Y	A
Matthew Martinez	30	$3,650	NA	NA	N	N	N	N	Y	Y	N
Mervyn Dymally	31	$9,100	NA	Y	N	N	N	N	Y	Y	Y
Glenn Anderson	32	$21,352	Y	Y	N	N	N	Y	Y	Y	Y
David Dreier	33	$119,750	NA	A	N	N	Y	Y	N	Y	P
Esteban Torres	34	$74,275	NA	NA	N	N	N	Y	Y	Y	N
Jerry Lewis	35	$23,050	Y	A	Y	N	N	N	N	N	P
George Brown, Jr.	36	$5,000	Y	Y	N	A	N	N	Y	Y	Y
Al McCandless	37	$43,850	NA	NA	Y	N	Y	N	N	Y	P
Robert Dornan	38	$10,950	NA	N	N	N	Y	N	N	Y	P
William Dannemeyer	39	$13,550	Y	N	N	N	Y	Y	Y	N	P
C. Christopher Cox	40	$14,800	NA	NA	NA	NA	N	Y	N	N	P
Bill Lowery	41	$51,875	NA	Y	N	N	Y	N	N	Y	P
Dana Rohrabacher	42	$11,400	NA	NA	NA	NA	N	Y	N	N	P
Ron Packard	43	$12,100	NA	NA	N	N	Y	N	N	Y	P
Jim Bates	44	$14,725	NA	NA	Y	N	N	Y	Y	N	N
Duncan Hunter	45	$23,960	NA	N	Y	N	N	N	N	Y	P

	#	Amount								
COLORADO										
Patricia Schroeder	1	$3,750	Y	N	N	N	Y	Y	Y	Y
David Skaggs	2	$12,000	NA	Y	N	N	N	N	Y	Y
Ben Campbell	3	$3,050	NA	N	N	N	Y	Y	N	Y
Hank Brown	4	$21,650	N	N	N	N	Y	Y	N	N
Joel Hefley	5	$15,000	NA	N	N	Y	Y	N	N	P
Daniel Schaefer	6	$23,750	NA	N	N	N	Y	N	N	P
CONNECTICUT										
Barbara Kennelly	1	$64,620	Y	N	N	N	N	N	A	Y
Sam Gejdenson	2	$10,295	Y	N	N	N	Y	Y	N	Y
Bruce Morrison	3	$62,700	NA	Y	Y	N	Y	Y	Y	Y
Christopher Shays	4	$21,854	NA	NA	NA	N	Y	Y	Y	Y
John Rowland	5	$21,230	NA	N	N	N	N	N	Y	P
Nancy Johnson	6	$20,121	NA	N	N	N	N	N	Y	P
DELAWARE										
Thomas Carper	1	$145,233	NA	Y	N	N	Y	Y	Y	Y
FLORIDA										
Earl Hutto	1	$19,450	Y	N	N	N	N	N	N	N
Bill Grant	2	$36,250	NA	N	N	N	N	N	Y	P
Charles Bennett	3	$10,950	Y	N	N	N	Y	Y	N	N
Craig James	4	$11,250	NA	NA	NA	Y	Y	Y	Y	P
Bill McCollum	5	$75,100	NA	N	N	N	N	N	Y	P
Cliff Stearns	6	$37,200	NA	NA	NA	N	N	N	Y	P
Sam Gibbons	7	$136,050	Y	N	N	N	N	N	Y	N
C. W. Young	8	$13,925	Y	Y	N	N	Y	Y	Y	P
Michael Bilirakis	9	$37,833	NA	Y	N	N	N	N	N	A
Andy Ireland	10	$57,175	Y	N	N	N	N	N	Y	P

Representative	District	Financial industry PAC money	VOTE 1 Remove caps on interest rates (1980)	VOTE 2 Deregulate S&L investments (1982)	VOTE 3 Provide full funding for S&L regulators (1987)	VOTE 4 Restrict risky S&L investments (1987)	VOTE 5 Weaken capital standards (1989)	VOTE 6 Put bailout on budget (1989)	VOTE 7 Disclose discriminatory lending (1989)	VOTE 8 S&L bailout (1989)	VOTE 9 Public funding of House elections (1990)
Bill Nelson	11	$75,575	Y	Y	N	N	N	N	N	Y	Y
Tom Lewis	12	$16,440	NA	NA	N	N	N	Y	N	N	P
Porter Goss	13	$28,750	NA	NA	NA	NA	N	Y	N	Y	P
Harry Johnston	14	$31,650	NA	NA	NA	NA	N	N	N	Y	Y
E. Clay Shaw, Jr.	15	$32,200	NA	Y	N	N	N	N	N	Y	P
Lawrence Smith	16	$47,550	NA	NA	N	N	N	N	Y	Y	Y
William Lehman	17	$29,950	Y	Y	N	N	A	N	Y	Y	Y
Ilena Ros-Lehtinen	18	$24,050	NA	NA	NA	NA	NA	NA	NA	NA	P
Dante Fascell	19	$32,600	Y	Y	N	N	N	Y	N	Y	Y
GEORGIA											
Robert Thomas	1	$29,320	NA	NA	N	N	N	N	N	Y	N
Charles Hatcher	2	$32,350	NA	A	N	N	N	Y	N	Y	N
Richard Ray	3	$29,250	NA	NA	N	N	N	Y	N	N	A
Ben Jones	4	$11,980	NA	NA	NA	NA	N	N	N	Y	N
John Lewis	5	$28,300	NA	NA	N	N	N	N	Y	Y	Y
Newt Gingrich	6	$59,650	Y	Y	N	N	N	N	N	Y	P
George Darden	7	$38,900	NA	NA	N	N	N	N	N	Y	N
J. Rowland	8	$19,800	NA	NA	N	N	N	N	N	Y	N
Ed Jenkins	9	$59,650	N	N	N	N	N	N	Y	Y	N
Doug Barnard, Jr.	10	$246,789	Y	Y	Y	N	N	Y	N	Y	N

State / Member	District	Amount	V1	V2	V3	V4	V5	V6	V7	V8	V9
HAWAII											
Patricia Saiki	1	$84,350	NA	NA	Y	N	Y	N	N	Y	P
Vacant	2	$0	NA	NA	NA	NA	NA	NA	NA	NA	NA
IDAHO											
Larry Craig	1	$13,400	NA	N	N	N	Y	Y	N	Y	P
Richard Stallings	2	$27,850	NA	NA	N	N	N	N	N	Y	N
ILLINOIS											
Charles Hayes	1	$1,050	NA	NA	N	N	N	N	Y	Y	N
Gus Savage	2	$3,800	NA	A	N	N	N	Y	Y	N	Y
Marty Russo	3	$98,042	Y	Y	N	N	Y	N	Y	N	N
George Sangmeister	4	$4,300	NA	NA	NA	NA	N	N	N	N	N
William Lipinski	5	$2,250	NA	A	N	N	Y	N	A	A	N
Henry Hyde	6	$38,565	Y	Y	N	N	Y	A	N	Y	Y
Cardiss Collins	7	$33,950	Y	Y	N	N	A	N	A	A	N
Dan Rostenkowski	8	$93,200	Y	Y	N	N	N	Y	Y	Y	N
Sidney Yates	9	$3,500	Y	Y	Y	N	N	Y	Y	Y	Y
John Porter	10	$14,635	Y	N	N	N	Y	N	N	Y	P
Frank Annunzio	11	$164,100	N	Y	A	A	Y	N	Y	Y	N
Philip Crane	12	$0	Y	N	N	N	Y	N	N	N	A
Harris Fawell	13	$18,250	NA	NA	N	N	Y	Y	N	Y	P
J. Hastert	14	$19,936	NA	NA	N	N	Y	N	N	Y	P
Edward Madigan	15	$42,875	Y	N	N	N	A	N	A	A	P
Lynn Martin	16	$44,300	NA	Y	N	N	Y	Y	Y	Y	P
Lane Evans	17	$19,200	Y	NA	Y	N	N	Y	Y	N	Y
Robert Michel	18	$152,450	Y	N	N	N	N	N	Y	Y	P
Terry Bruce	19	$37,100	NA	NA	Y	N	Y	Y	N	N	N
Richard Durbin	20	$22,560	NA	NA	Y	N	Y	Y	N	N	N
Jerry Costello	21	$17,625	NA	NA	NA	NA	N	Y	Y	N	N

Representative	District	Financial industry PAC money	VOTE 1 Remove caps on interest rates (1980)	VOTE 2 Deregulate S&L investments (1982)	VOTE 3 Provide full funding for S&L regulators (1987)	VOTE 4 Restrict risky S&L investments (1987)	VOTE 5 Weaken capital standards (1989)	VOTE 6 Put bailout on budget (1989)	VOTE 7 Disclose discriminatory lending (1989)	VOTE 8 S&L bailout (1989)	VOTE 9 Public funding of House elections (1990)
Glenn Poshard	22	$4,450	NA	NA	NA	NA	N	Y	Y	N	N
INDIANA											
Peter Visclosky	1	$10,545	NA	NA	N	Y	N	Y	Y	Y	N
Philip Sharp	2	$58,450	Y	Y	N	N	N	Y	Y	Y	Y
John Hiler	3	$206,720	NA	N	Y	N	Y	Y	N	Y	P
Jill Long	4	$2,100	NA	NA	NA	NA	N	Y	Y	N	N
Jim Jontz	5	$12,255	NA	NA	N	N	N	Y	Y	N	N
Dan Burton	6	$28,540	NA	NA	A	A	Y	Y	N	Y	P
John Myers	7	$13,083	N	N	N	N	N	N	N	Y	A
Frank McCloskey	8	$13,225	NA	NA	N	N	N	N	Y	Y	Y
Lee Hamilton	9	$20,900	Y	Y	N	N	N	Y	N	Y	Y
Andrew Jacobs, Jr.	10	$0	Y	A	N	N	Y	Y	Y	N	Y
IOWA											
Jim Leach	1	$0	Y	A	Y	Y	N	N	Y	Y	Y
Thomas Tauke	2	$52,750	Y	Y	Y	Y	N	Y	Y	Y	P
Dave Nagle	3	$40,730	NA	NA	Y	N	N	N	Y	Y	N
Neal Smith	4	$24,750	Y	Y	Y	Y	Y	N	Y	Y	N
Jim Lightfoot	5	$20,900	NA	NA	Y	N	N	Y	N	N	P
Fred Grandy	6	$43,850	NA	NA	Y	Y	N	Y	N	Y	P

KANSAS											
Pat Roberts	1	$14,750	NA	Y	N	N	Y	N	Y	N	P
Jim Slattery	2	$63,800	NA	NA	N	N	Y	Y	Y	N	N
Jan Meyers	3	$13,000	NA	NA	Y	N	N	N	Y	N	P
Dan Glickman	4	$41,800	Y	Y	N	N	N	Y	Y	N	Y
Robert Whittaker	5	$17,100	Y	Y	N	N	Y	N	Y	N	P
KENTUCKY											
Carroll Hubbard, Jr.	1	$197,652	Y	Y	Y	N	N	N	N	Y	N
William Natcher	2	$0	Y	Y	N	N	N	N	Y	Y	N
Romano Mazzoli	3	$13,700	Y	Y	Y	N	N	Y	N	Y	Y
Jim Bunning	4	$107,550	NA	NA	Y	N	N	N	Y	N	P
Harold Rogers	5	$3,950	A	A	N	N	N	N	Y	N	P
Larry Hopkins	6	$12,650	Y	N	N	N	N	Y	N	Y	P
Carl Perkins	7	$6,550	NA	NA	Y	N	N	N	N	Y	N
LOUISIANA											
Bob Livingston	1	$5,980	Y	N	N	N	Y	N	Y	N	P
Lindy Boggs	2	$29,000	A	A	Y	N	Y	N	Y	Y	N
W. J. Tauzin	3	$67,867	NA	N	A	A	Y	Y	Y	N	N
Jim McCrery	4	$8,250	NA	NA	NA	NA	N	N	Y	N	A
Jerry Huckaby	5	$4,550	Y	Y	Y	N	N	N	Y	N	N
Richard Baker	6	$27,050	NA	NA	Y	N	Y	N	N	N	P
Jimmy Hayes	7	$9,750	NA	NA	N	N	A	A	A	A	N
Clyde Holloway	8	$8,360	NA	NA	N	N	Y	Y	Y	N	P
MAINE											
Joseph Brennan	1	$14,650	NA	NA	N	N	N	N	Y	Y	Y
Olympia Snowe	2	$12,700	Y	Y	Y	N	N	N	Y	Y	P

Representative	District	Financial industry PAC money	VOTE 1 Remove caps on interest rates (1980)	VOTE 2 Deregulate S&L investments (1982)	VOTE 3 Provide full funding for S&L regulators (1987)	VOTE 4 Restrict risky S&L investments (1987)	VOTE 5 Weaken capital standards (1989)	VOTE 6 Put bailout on budget (1989)	VOTE 7 Disclose discriminatory lending (1989)	VOTE 8 S&L bailout (1989)	VOTE 9 Public funding of House elections (1990)
MARYLAND											
Roy Dyson	1	$18,850	NA	Y	Y	N	N	N	Y	N	N
Helen Bentley	2	$43,825	NA	NA	Y	N	N	Y	N	N	P
Benjamin Cardin	3	$54,716	NA	NA	Y	N	N	N	Y	Y	Y
Thomas McMillen	4	$117,325	NA	NA	N	N	N	N	N	Y	Y
Steny Hoyer	5	$50,730	NA	Y	Y	N	N	N	Y	Y	P
Beverly Byron	6	$17,795	Y	Y	N	N	Y	N	N	N	N
Kweisi Mfume	7	$28,410	NA	NA	N	N	N	N	Y	Y	Y
Constance Morella	8	$27,000	NA	NA	Y	N	N	Y	Y	Y	Y
MASSACHUSETTS											
Silvio Conte	1	$6,400	Y	Y	Y	N	N	N	Y	Y	Y
Richard Neal	2	$11,850	NA	NA	NA	NA	N	N	Y	Y	Y
Joseph Early	3	$17,700	Y	Y	Y	N	Y	Y	Y	Y	N
Barney Frank	4	$132,400	NA	Y	Y	A	N	N	A	Y	N
Chester Atkins	5	$0	NA	NA	Y	A	N	N	Y	Y	N
Nicholas Mavroules	6	$15,950	Y	Y	Y	N	N	Y	Y	Y	Y
Edward Markey	7	$0	Y	Y	Y	N	N	N	Y	Y	Y
Joseph Kennedy, II	8	$43,820	NA	NA	Y	N	N	Y	Y	Y	Y
Joe Moakley	9	$97,750	Y	Y	Y	N	N	N	Y	Y	N
Gerry Studds	10	$1,500	Y	Y	A	N	N	Y	Y	Y	Y
Brian Donnelly	11	$45,000	Y	Y	Y	N	N	N	Y	N	Y

MICHIGAN										
John Conyers	1	$12,040	Y	Y	N	N	N	Y	Y	Y
Carl Pursell	2	$28,400	Y	Y	N	N	Y	Y	Y	A
Howard Wolpe	3	$9,300	Y	Y	N	N	Y	Y	N	Y
Fred Upton	4	$12,750	NA	NA	N	N	Y	Y	N	P
Paul Henry	5	$18,925	NA	NA	N	N	Y	Y	N	P
Bob Carr	6	$24,425	Y	Y	Y	Y	Y	Y	N	N
Dale Kildee	7	$11,600	Y	Y	Y	N	N	Y	Y	Y
Bob Traxler	8	$19,705	Y	Y	Y	N	N	Y	Y	A
Guy Vander Jagt	9	$43,980	Y	Y	N	N	N	N	Y	P
Bill Schuette	10	$46,550	NA	NA	N	N	N	Y	A	A
Robert Davis	11	$19,400	Y	Y	N	Y	N	A	Y	N
David Bonior	12	$63,050	Y	Y	Y	N	N	Y	Y	Y
George Crockett, Jr.	13	$4,700	NA	A	N	N	Y	Y	N	A
Dennis Hertel	14	$18,160	NA	Y	Y	N	N	Y	Y	Y
William Ford	15	$25,815	Y	Y	N	N	N	Y	Y	A
John Dingell	16	$141,555	A	A	A	N	N	N	Y	N
Sander Levin	17	$69,500	NA	NA	Y	N	N	Y	Y	P
William Broomfield	18	$11,625	Y	Y	N	N	Y	Y	Y	P
MINNESOTA										
Timothy Penny	1	$22,000	NA	NA	N	N	Y	N	Y	P
Vin Weber	2	$33,650	NA	N	N	N	N	N	Y	P
Bill Frenzel	3	$93,638	Y	A	Y	N	N	N	Y	P
Bruce Vento	4	$73,200	Y	Y	N	Y	Y	Y	Y	Y
Martin Sabo	5	$25,275	Y	A	N	Y	N	Y	Y	P
Gerry Sikorski	6	$43,550	NA	NA	N	N	Y	Y	Y	P
Arlan Stangeland	7	$26,435	Y	N	N	N	Y	N	N	P
James Oberstar	8	$8,400	Y	Y	N	N	N	Y	Y	Y

Representative	District	Financial industry PAC money	VOTE 1 Remove caps on interest rates (1980)	VOTE 2 Deregulate S&L investments (1982)	VOTE 3 Provide full funding for S&L regulators (1987)	VOTE 4 Restrict risky S&L investments (1987)	VOTE 5 Weaken capital standards (1989)	VOTE 6 Put bailout on budget (1989)	VOTE 7 Disclose discriminatory lending (1989)	VOTE 8 S&L bailout (1989)	VOTE 9 Public funding of House elections (1990)
MISSISSIPPI											
Jamie Whitten	1	$19,850	Y	Y	N	N	A	N	N	Y	N
Mike Espy	2	$29,525	NA	NA	N	N	Y	N	Y	Y	N
G. Montgomery	3	$8,250	Y	Y	N	N	N	N	N	Y	N
Mike Parker	4	$13,460	NA	NA	NA	NA	NA	NA	Y	Y	N
Gene Taylor	5	$12,300	NA	NA	NA	NA	NA	NA	NA	NA	N
MISSOURI											
William Clay	1	$9,600	Y	A	Y	N	N	N	Y	Y	Y
Jack Buechner	2	$27,450	NA	NA	N	N	Y	A	N	A	P
Richard Gephardt	3	$146,606	Y	Y	A	A	N	N	Y	Y	Y
Ike Skelton	4	$21,114	A	Y	N	N	N	N	N	A	N
Alan Wheat	5	$35,650	NA	NA	N	N	N	Y	Y	Y	Y
E. Coleman	6	$27,859	Y	Y	N	N	Y	N	A	A	P
Mel Hancock	7	$6,600	NA	NA	NA	NA	N	Y	N	N	P
Bill Emerson	8	$25,100	NA	Y	N	N	Y	N	N	Y	P
Harold Volkmer	9	$22,730	Y	Y	N	N	N	N	N	Y	N
MONTANA											
Pat Williams	1	$17,800	Y	Y	N	N	N	N	N	N	Y
Ron Marlenee	2	$13,235	Y	Y	N	N	Y	N	N	N	P

State / Representative	District	Amount									
NEBRASKA											
Doug Bereuter	1	$68,745	Y	Y	Y	N	N	Y	N	Y	P
Peter Hoagland	2	$69,850	NA	NA	NA	NA	N	Y	N	Y	Y
Virginia Smith	3	$25,526	Y	N	Y	N	N	N	N	Y	P
NEVADA											
James Bilbray	1	$11,025	NA	NA	N	N	N	Y	N	Y	N
Barbara Vucanovich	2	$12,350	NA	NA	Y	Y	Y	N	N	Y	P
NEW HAMPSHIRE											
Robert Smith	1	$16,450	NA	NA	Y	N	N	Y	N	N	P
Chuck Douglas	2	$22,300	NA	NA	NA	NA	Y	N	N	N	P
NEW JERSEY											
Vacant	1	$0	NA	NA	NA	NA	NA	NA	NA	NA	
William Hughes	2	$18,690	Y	Y	Y	N	N	Y	Y	Y	N
Frank Pallone	3	$9,850	NA	NA	NA	NA	Y	N	Y	N	Y
Christopher Smith	4	$11,329	NA	Y	N	N	N	N	Y	Y	P
Marge Roukema	5	$147,180	NA	Y	Y	N	N	N	N	Y	A
Bernard Dwyer	6	$17,950	NA	Y	N	N	N	N	Y	Y	Y
Matthew Rinaldo	7	$114,510	Y	Y	N	N	N	N	Y	Y	Y
Robert Roe	8	$21,650	Y	Y	A	A	N	N	Y	Y	N
Robert Torricelli	9	$27,115	NA	NA	N	N	N	N	Y	Y	N
Donald Payne	10	$18,450	NA	NA	NA	NA	N	Y	Y	N	N
Dean Gallo	11	$58,825	NA	NA	Y	N	N	N	N	Y	P
James Courter	12	$53,350	NA	Y	Y	N	A	A	Y	Y	P
Jim Saxton	13	$60,975	NA	NA	Y	N	N	N	N	Y	P
Frank Guarini	14	$78,700	Y	Y	Y	N	N	Y	Y	Y	Y

Representative	District	Financial industry PAC money	VOTE 1 Remove caps on interest rates (1980)	VOTE 2 Deregulate S&L investments (1982)	VOTE 3 Provide full funding for S&L regulators (1987)	VOTE 4 Restrict risky S&L investments (1987)	VOTE 5 Weaken capital standards (1989)	VOTE 6 Put bailout on budget (1989)	VOTE 7 Disclose discriminatory lending (1989)	VOTE 8 S&L bailout (1989)	VOTE 9 Public funding of House elections (1990)
NEW MEXICO											
Steven Schiff	1	$10,950	NA	NA	NA	NA	N	Y	N	N	P
Joe Skeen	2	$7,550	NA	N	N	N	N	N	N	Y	P
Bill Richardson	3	$34,650	NA	NA	N	N	N	N	Y	Y	Y
NEW YORK											
George Hochbrueckner	1	$8,700	NA	NA	Y	N	Y	N	Y	Y	P
Thomas Downey	2	$87,490	Y	Y	Y	N	N	N	Y	Y	P
Robert Mrazek	3	$6,480	NA	NA	Y	N	N	N	Y	Y	N
Norman Lent	4	$85,725	Y	Y	Y	N	N	N	N	Y	P
Raymond McGrath	5	$118,904	NA	Y	Y	N	Y	N	N	N	N
Floyd Flake	6	$64,197	NA	NA	N	A	Y	Y	Y	Y	A
Gary Ackerman	7	$19,800	NA	NA	Y	N	Y	N	Y	Y	Y
James Scheuer	8	$6,450	Y	Y	Y	N	N	Y	Y	Y	Y
Thomas Manton	9	$159,750	NA	NA	N	N	Y	N	N	Y	N
Charles Schumer	10	$107,025	NA	Y	Y	Y	N	N	Y	Y	Y
Edolphus Towns	11	$16,945	NA	NA	Y	N	N	Y	Y	Y	Y
Major Owens	12	$1,550	NA	NA	N	N	N	Y	Y	N	Y
Stephen Solarz	13	$3,250	Y	Y	Y	N	N	N	Y	N	Y
Susan Molinari	14	$0	NA	NA	NA	NA	NA	NA	NA	NA	P
Bill Green	15	$79,892	Y	Y	Y	N	N	N	Y	Y	P
Charles Rangel	16	$149,425	Y	Y	Y	A	N	A	Y	A	Y

Name	District	Amount	1	2	3	4	5	6	7	8	9
Ted Weiss	17	$3,600	Y	Y	Y	N	N	Y	Y	Y	Y
Jose Serrano	18	$6,750	NA	NA	NA	NA	NA	NA	NA	NA	Y
Eliot Engel	19	$4,550	NA	NA	NA	NA	N	N	Y	Y	Y
Nita Lowey	20	$8,700	NA	NA	NA	N	Y	N	Y	Y	Y
Hamilton Fish, Jr.	21	$67,830	Y	A	Y	N	N	N	Y	Y	P
Benjamin Gilman	22	$18,555	Y	Y	N	NA	N	Y	Y	Y	Y
Michael McNulty	23	$13,725	NA	NA	NA	N	Y	Y	Y	Y	Y
Gerald Solomon	24	$14,150	Y	Y	N	N	N	N	N	N	P
Sherwood Boehlert	25	$18,151	NA	NA	A	N	A	N	Y	Y	Y
David Martin	26	$9,720	NA	Y	N	NA	N	N	A	A	P
James T. Walsh	27	$31,475	NA	NA	NA	N	N	N	Y	Y	P
Matthew McHugh	28	$16,715	Y	Y	Y	A	Y	Y	A	Y	Y
Frank Horton	29	$7,425	Y	Y	A	N	N	N	Y	N	P
Louise Slaughter	30	$17,225	NA	NA	N	NA	Y	N	Y	Y	P
Bill Paxon	31	$75,733	NA	NA	NA	N	Y	Y	N	Y	P
John LaFalce	32	$136,600	Y	Y	Y	N	Y	Y	Y	Y	Y
Henry Nowak	33	$10,075	Y	Y	Y	N	Y	Y	N	N	Y
Amory Houghton	34	$48,300	NA	NA	Y	N	N	N	N	Y	P
NORTH CAROLINA											
Walter Jones	1	$7,600	Y	A	N	N	N	N	N	Y	N
Tim Valentine	2	$10,650	NA	NA	N	N	N	N	N	Y	N
Martin Lancaster	3	$15,900	NA	NA	N	N	N	N	N	Y	N
David Price	4	$153,900	NA	NA	N	N	N	Y	N	Y	P
Stephen Neal	5	$334,800	Y	Y	N	N	N	N	N	Y	N
Howard Coble	6	$38,082	NA	NA	N	N	N	N	Y	Y	P
Charles Rose	7	$24,074	Y	A	N	N	N	N	N	Y	N
W. Hefner	8	$29,100	Y	Y	N	N	N	N	N	Y	N
J. McMillan	9	$165,778	NA	NA	Y	N	N	N	N	Y	P
Cass Ballenger	10	$14,200	NA	NA	Y	N	N	N	N	Y	P

Representative	District	Financial industry PAC money	VOTE 1 Remove caps on interest rates (1980)	VOTE 2 Deregulate S&L investments (1982)	VOTE 3 Provide full funding for S&L regulators (1987)	VOTE 4 Restrict risky S&L investments (1987)	VOTE 5 Weaken capital standards (1989)	VOTE 6 Put bailout on budget (1989)	VOTE 7 Disclose discriminatory lending (1989)	VOTE 8 S&L bailout (1989)	VOTE 9 Public funding of House elections (1990)
James Clarke	11	$2,900	NA	NA	N	N	N	N	N	Y	N
NORTH DAKOTA											
Byron Dorgan		$100,225	NA	Y	N	N	N	Y	Y	N	Y
OHIO											
Thomas Luken	1	$53,152	Y	Y	N	N	Y	Y	Y	Y	A
Willis Gradison	2	$0	Y	A	Y	N	N	N	Y	N	P
Tony Hall	3	$29,674	Y	N	N	N	Y	Y	Y	N	Y
Michael Oxley	4	$39,100	NA	A	NA	NA	N	N	N	Y	P
Paul Gillmor	5	$43,250	NA	NA	NA	NA	N	N	N	Y	P
Bob McEwen	6	$17,500	NA	Y	N	N	Y	N	N	Y	P
Michael DeWine	7	$13,075	NA	NA	N	N	Y	Y	N	Y	P
Donald Lukens	8	$13,450	NA	NA	N	N	Y	Y	N	Y	P
Marcy Kaptur	9	$46,700	NA	NA	N	N	N	Y	Y	N	Y
Clarence Miller	10	$4,600	Y	N	N	N	N	Y	Y	N	A
Dennis Eckart	11	$79,900	NA	A	N	N	N	N	Y	Y	Y
John Kasich	12	$18,090	NA	NA	N	N	N	Y	Y	Y	P
Donald Pease	13	$44,300	Y	Y	Y	N	N	Y	Y	Y	N
Thomas Sawyer	14	$15,155	NA	NA	N	N	N	N	Y	Y	P
Chalmers Wylie	15	$159,828	Y	N	Y	Y	N	N	N	Y	A
Ralph Regula	16	$0	Y	N	Y	N	N	Y	N	N	N

James Traficant, Jr.	17	$250	NA	NA	N	N	N	N	Y	N
Douglas Applegate	18	$3,000	Y	N	N	N	N	Y	Y	N
Edward Feighan	19	$25,400	NA	NA	N	N	N	Y	Y	N
Mary Rose Oakar	20	$147,340	Y	Y	N	N	N	Y	Y	Y
Louis Stokes	21	$11,950	Y	A	Y	N	N	Y	Y	Y
OKLAHOMA										
James Inhofe	1	$23,100	NA	NA	N	Y	N	N	Y	P
Michael Synar	2	$0	Y	Y	Y	N	Y	Y	Y	Y
Wes Watkins	3	$16,630	Y	A	N	Y	Y	Y	Y	A
Dave McCurdy	4	$19,050	NA	Y	N	Y	N	Y	Y	N
Mickey Edwards	5	$17,925	Y	A	N	Y	N	N	N	P
Glenn English	6	$24,400	Y	Y	N	Y	Y	N	Y	N
OREGON										
Les AuCoin	1	$57,420	Y	A	N	Y	Y	Y	Y	Y
Robert F. Smith	2	$17,559	NA	NA	N	Y	Y	Y	N	P
Ron Wyden	3	$53,297	NA	Y	N	N	Y	Y	Y	N
Peter DeFazio	4	$7,750	NA	NA	N	Y	Y	Y	Y	Y
Denny Smith	5	$23,100	NA	N	N	Y	N	N	Y	P
PENNSYLVANIA										
Thomas Foglietta	1	$13,425	NA	A	N	N	N	Y	Y	P
William Gray III	2	$114,725	Y	Y	A	Y	Y	Y	Y	Y
Robert Borski	3	$7,000	NA	NA	N	N	N	Y	Y	P
Joseph Kolter	4	$9,220	NA	A	N	Y	N	Y	N	N
Richard Schulze	5	$57,031	Y	N	N	N	Y	Y	N	P
Gus Yatron	6	$3,450	Y	A	N	Y	Y	Y	Y	N
Curt Weldon	7	$32,125	NA	N	N	Y	N	Y	Y	P
Peter Kostmayer	8	$19,850	Y	N	N	N	Y	Y	N	Y

Representative	District	Financial industry PAC money	VOTE 1 Remove caps on interest rates (1980)	VOTE 2 Deregulate S&L investments (1982)	VOTE 3 Provide full funding for S&L regulators (1987)	VOTE 4 Restrict risky S&L investments (1987)	VOTE 5 Weaken capital standards (1989)	VOTE 6 Put bailout on budget (1989)	VOTE 7 Disclose discriminatory lending (1989)	VOTE 8 S&L bailout (1989)	VOTE 9 Public funding of House elections (1990)
Bud Shuster	9	$14,350	Y	A	N	N	N	Y	N	N	N
Joseph McDade	10	$30,350	A	Y	Y	N	N	N	Y	Y	P
Paul Kanjorski	11	$182,799	NA	NA	N	N	Y	Y	N	Y	Y
John Murtha	12	$33,720	Y	Y	N	N	Y	N	N	Y	N
Lawrence Coughlin	13	$22,925	Y	A	Y	N	N	N	Y	Y	P
William Coyne	14	$25,100	NA	Y	Y	N	N	N	Y	Y	Y
Don Ritter	15	$46,937	A	Y	Y	N	N	Y	Y	N	P
Robert Walker	16	$8,000	Y	N	Y	N	N	Y	Y	Y	P
George Gekas	17	$11,483	NA	N	N	N	Y	Y	Y	Y	P
Doug Walgren	18	$30,925	Y	Y	A	N	Y	Y	Y	Y	Y
William Goodling	19	$0	Y	N	N	N	Y	Y	N	Y	P
Joseph Gaydos	20	$18,900	Y	Y	N	N	Y	Y	N	N	N
Thomas Ridge	21	$173,300	NA	NA	Y	N	Y	Y	N	Y	P
Austin Murphy	22	$5,780	Y	A	N	N	Y	Y	N	Y	N
William F. Clinger	23	$35,650	Y	Y	N	Y	N	N	N	Y	P
RHODE ISLAND											
Ronald Machtley	1	$20,300	NA	NA	NA	NA	N	N	Y	N	P
Claudine Schneider	2	$15,400	NA	Y	N	N	N	N	Y	N	P
SOUTH CAROLINA											
Arthur Ravenel, Jr.	1	$22,975	NA	NA	Y	N	N	N	Y	Y	P

Name	Dist	Amount	V1	V2	V3	V4	V5	V6	V7	V8	V9
Floyd Spence	2	$21,080	P	Y	N	N	N	N	N	Y	Y
Butler Derrick	3	$140,100	N	Y	N	Y	N	N	N	Y	Y
Elizabeth Patterson	4	$151,749	N	Y	N	Y	N	N	N	NA	NA
John Spratt	5	$35,326	N	Y	Y	N	N	N	N	NA	NA
Robin Tallon	6	$37,155	N	N	Y	Y	N	N	N	NA	NA
SOUTH DAKOTA											
Tim Johnson		$20,300	Y	Y	N	N	N	N	N	NA	NA
TENNESSEE											
James Quillen	1	$104,850	A	N	N	N	Y	N	N	A	A
John Duncan	2	$7,050	N	Y	N	Y	N	N	N	Y	Y
Marilyn Lloyd	3	$25,850	N	N	N	N	N	N	N	NA	NA
Jim Cooper	4	$99,733	N	Y	Y	Y	N	N	A	NA	NA
Bob Clement	5	$32,400	N	N	N	N	N	NA	NA	NA	NA
Bart Gordon	6	$120,706	N	Y	Y	Y	N	N	N	NA	NA
Don Sundquist	7	$43,350	P	Y	N	N	N	N	N	NA	NA
John S. Tanner	8	$39,623	N	A	N	N	N	NA	NA	NA	NA
Harold Ford	9	$28,400	Y	Y	A	N	A	A	N	Y	Y
TEXAS											
Jim Chapman	1	$10,350	N	Y	N	N	N	N	Y	NA	NA
Charles Wilson	2	$18,750	Y	Y	N	Y	N	N	Y	Y	A
Steve Bartlett	3	$152,575	P	Y	N	N	Y	N	Y	NA	NA
Ralph Hall	4	$49,450	A	Y	N	Y	Y	N	N	Y	Y
John Bryant	5	$87,250	Y	Y	Y	Y	N	N	Y	NA	NA
Joe Barton	6	$53,960	P	Y	N	Y	N	N	Y	NA	NA
Bill Archer	7	$0	P	Y	N	N	N	N	Y	N	Y
Jack Fields	8	$68,200	P	Y	N	N	N	N	Y	N	NA
Jack Brooks	9	$73,200	N	A	A	A	A	A	N	Y	A

Representative	District	Financial industry PAC money	VOTE 1 Remove caps on interest rates (1980)	VOTE 2 Deregulate S&L investments (1982)	VOTE 3 Provide full funding for S&L regulators (1987)	VOTE 4 Restrict risky S&L investments (1987)	VOTE 5 Weaken capital standards (1989)	VOTE 6 Put bailout on budget (1989)	VOTE 7 Disclose discriminatory lending (1989)	VOTE 8 S&L bailout (1989)	VOTE 9 Public funding of House elections (1990)
J. J. Pickle	10	$59,396	N	Y	N	N	N	N	N	Y	N
Marvin Leath	11	$4,800	A	N	N	N	N	Y	N	N	A
Pete Geren	12	$24,300	NA	NA	NA	NA	NA	NA	NA	NA	N
Bill Sarpalius	13	$4,650	NA	NA	NA	NA	N	Y	N	Y	N
Greg Laughlin	14	$7,600	NA	NA	NA	NA	N	Y	N	Y	N
E. de la Garza	15	$14,000	Y	Y	N	N	N	N	Y	Y	N
Ronald Coleman	16	$19,650	NA	NA	Y	N	N	N	Y	Y	N
Charles Stenholm	17	$5,000	Y	N	Y	N	N	Y	Y	Y	N
Craig Washington	18	$6,600	NA	NA	NA	NA	NA	NA	NA	NA	Y
Larry Combest	19	$10,158	NA	NA	A	A	N	N	N	Y	P
Henry Gonzalez	20	$30,400	Y	Y	Y	N	N	N	Y	Y	Y
Lamar Smith	21	$13,977	NA	NA	Y	N	N	N	Y	Y	P
Thomas DeLay	22	$23,300	NA	NA	Y	N	Y	N	N	N	P
Albert Bustamante	23	$6,850	NA	NA	N	N	N	N	Y	Y	N
Martin Frost	24	$109,600	Y	Y	N	N	N	Y	Y	Y	N
Michael Andrews	25	$92,249	NA	NA	Y	N	N	Y	N	Y	N
Richard Armey	26	$26,550	NA	NA	Y	N	Y	N	N	Y	P
Solomon Ortiz	27	$8,100	NA	NA	Y	N	N	N	Y	Y	N
UTAH											
James Hansen	1	$16,850	NA	A	N	N	N	N	N	Y	P
Wayne Owens	2	$27,420	NA	NA	N	N	N	Y	Y	Y	Y

Name	Dist.	Amount	P	Y	N	Y	N	N	Y	NA	NA
Howard Nielson	3	$15,700	P	Y	A	Y	N	N	Y	NA	NA
VERMONT											
Peter Smith		$17,050	Y	Y	A	Y	N	NA	NA	NA	NA
VIRGINIA											
Herbert Bateman	1	$32,300	P	N	N	N	N	A	A	NA	NA
Owen Pickett	2	$17,350	N	Y	N	N	N	N	N	NA	NA
Thomas Bliley	3	$80,205	P	Y	N	Y	N	N	N	N	NA
Norman Sisisky	4	$11,500	N	A	A	N	A	N	N	NA	NA
Lewis Payne, Jr.	5	$19,750	N	Y	N	Y	N	NA	NA	NA	NA
James Olin	6	$15,650	N	Y	N	Y	N	N	N	NA	NA
D. Slaughter, Jr.	7	$13,450	P	Y	N	N	N	A	A	NA	NA
Stanford Parris	8	$105,493	P	Y	N	N	N	N	Y	Y	Y
Rick Boucher	9	$100,150	N	Y	N	N	Y	A	A	NA	NA
Frank Wolf	10	$39,700	P	Y	N	N	N	N	Y	Y	NA
WASHINGTON											
John Miller	1	$25,710	Y	Y	Y	N	N	N	N	NA	NA
Al Swift	2	$95,898	N	Y	Y	N	N	N	N	Y	Y
Jolene Unsoeld	3	$6,750	N	Y	Y	N	N	NA	NA	NA	NA
Sid Morrison	4	$15,200	P	Y	N	N	Y	N	N	Y	NA
Thomas Foley	5	$117,105	A	A	A	A	A	A	Y	Y	Y
Norman Dicks	6	$23,700	N	Y	Y	N	N	NA	N	Y	Y
James McDermott	7	$26,450	Y	Y	Y	N	N	NA	NA	NA	NA
Rod Chandler	8	$58,205	N	Y	N	Y	N	N	N	NA	NA
WEST VIRGINIA											
Alan Mollohan	1	$5,150	N	Y	N	N	Y	N	N	Y	Y
Harley Staggers, Jr.	2	$7,400	Y	Y	Y	Y	Y	N	N	NA	NA

Representative	District	Financial industry PAC money	VOTE 1 Remove caps on interest rates (1980)	VOTE 2 Deregulate S&L investments (1982)	VOTE 3 Provide full funding for S&L regulators (1987)	VOTE 4 Restrict risky S&L investments (1987)	VOTE 5 Weaken capital standards (1989)	VOTE 6 Put bailout on budget (1989)	VOTE 7 Disclose discriminatory lending (1989)	VOTE 8 S&L bailout (1989)	VOTE 9 Public funding of House elections (1990)
Robert Wise	3	$3,850	NA	NA	N	N	N	Y	Y	Y	Y
Nick Rahall	4	$6,300	Y	A	N	N	N	N	Y	Y	Y
WISCONSIN											
Les Aspin	1	$35,350	Y	Y	Y	N	N	N	Y	Y	N
Robert Kastenmeier	2	$16,050	Y	Y	N	N	N	Y	Y	Y	Y
Steven Gunderson	3	$29,850	NA	N	Y	N	N	N	Y	Y	P
Gerald Kleczka	4	$58,150	NA	NA	Y	Y	N	Y	Y	Y	Y
Jim Moody	5	$79,750	NA	NA	N	N	N	Y	Y	N	Y
Tom Petri	6	$12,620	Y	N	N	Y	N	N	Y	N	P
David Obey	7	$25,680	Y	Y	N	N	N	Y	Y	Y	Y
Toby Roth	8	$108,860	Y	N	Y	N	N	N	N	Y	P
James Sensenbrenner	9	$11,950	Y	N	N	N	N	Y	Y	N	P
WYOMING											
Craig Thomas		$10,500	NA	NA	NA	NA	N	Y	N	Y	P

Note: Information for financial industry political action committee (PAC) contributions came from reports filed by PACs at the Federal Election Commission. Contributions from financial industry PACs include PACs from the following categories: commercial banks, bank holding companies, savings banks, credit unions, credit agencies, finance companies, investment banking, mortgage bankers and brokers, security brokers and investment companies. Figures cover period from January 1, 1985 through May 1990. For Representatives who ran for Senate during this period, figures include PAC funds raised for those Senate races. Representatives Bill Archer (R-TX), Chet Atkins (D-MA), Anthony Beilenson (D-CA), Phil Crane (R-IL), Bill Goodling (R-PA), Willis Gradison (R-OH), Andy Jacobs (D-IN), Jim Leach (R-IA), Ed Markey

(D-MA), William Natcher (D-KY), Ralph Requla (R-OH) and Mike Synar (D-MA) do not accept PAC contributions. Representative Romano Mazzoli (D-KY), no longer accepts PAC contributions as of December 1989, and Representative Glenn Foshard (D-IL) does not accept PAC money as of August 1989.

Sources: Campaign Research Center, Federal Election Commission, Congressional Quarterly and the 1990 U.S. Congress Handbook.

APPENDIX 3

•

S & L FAILURES
STATE BY STATE

FACT SHEET

State	Number of institutions	Total assets (millions)	Total deposits (millions)
Alabama	1	$ 492	$ 531
Arizona	5	$12,213	$10,377
Arkansas	9	$ 2,588	$ 3,081
California	14	$23,368	$16,920
Colorado	5	$ 1,354	$ 1,072
Connecticut	3	$ 190	$ 158
Florida	12	$ 7,875	$ 6,213
Georgia	1	$ 71	$ 57
Illinois	22	$ 5,744	$ 4,850
Indiana	2	$ 253	$ 230
Iowa	3	$ 1,643	$ 1,431
Kansas	5	$10,293	$ 5,575
Kentucky	1	$ 50	$ 50
Louisiana	25	$ 3,409	$ 3,238
Maine	1	$ 52	$ 40
Maryland	4	$ 1,686	$ 1,270
Massachusetts	2	$ 3,860	$ 3,063
Minnesota	3	$ 2,373	$ 2,144
Missouri	2	$ 714	$ 647
Mississippi	10	$ 1,185	$ 941
North Carolina	3	$ 902	$ 703
North Dakota	2	$ 1,081	$ 678
Nebraska	2	$ 429	$ 347
New Jersey	11	$12,090	$ 9,322
New Mexico	4	$ 2,691	$ 2,520
New York	3	$ 8,884	$ 8,676
Ohio	5	$ 791	$ 720
Oklahoma	6	$ 2,705	$ 2,142
Oregon	1	$ 4,968	$ 3,214
Pennsylvania	4	$ 5,982	$ 4,287
Puerto Rico	1	$ 1,665	$ 1,273
South Carolina	1	$ 711	$ 639
Tennessee	2	$ 125	$ 102
Texas	65	$18,279	$18,358
Utah	2	$ 327	$ 269
Virginia	4	$ 1,573	$ 1,208
West Virginia	2	$ 117	$ 108

Total S&Ls enrolled in joint regulatory oversight program: 248 institutions in 37 states with
Total assets: $142,733 million
Total deposits: $116,454 million

Source: Resolution Trust Corporation, Thrift Financial Reports, 12/31/89

Alabama
CITY FEDERAL S&L ASSOCIATION, Birmingham—
03/30/89

Arizona
MERABANK FEDERAL SAVINGS BANK, Phoenix—
01/31/90
PIMA FEDERAL S&L ASSOCIATION, Tucson—03/02/89
SECURITY S&L ASSOCIATION, Scottsdale—02/17/89
SOUTHWEST S&L ASSOCIATION, FA, Phoenix—
02/17/89
SUN STATE S&L ASSOCIATION, FSA, Phoenix—
06/14/89

Arkansas
COMMONWEALTH S&L ASSOCIATION, Osceola—
03/02/89
FIRST AMERICA SAVINGS BANK, FSB, Fort Smith—
05/25/90
FIRST FEDERAL S&L ASSOCIATION, Fayetteville—
03/02/89
FIRST SAVINGS OF ARKANSAS, FA, Little Rock—
02/10/89
FIRST STATE SAVINGS BANK FSB, Mountain Home—
03/02/89
GRAND PRAIRIE FEDERAL S&L ASSOCIATION, Stuttgart
—01/26/90
INDEPENDENCE FEDERAL S&L ASSOCIATION, Batesville
—02/17/89
MADISON GUARANTY S&L ASSOCIATION, McCrory—
03/02/89
SAVERS SAVINGS ASSOCIATION, FS&LA, Little Rock—
02/10/89

California
BROOKSIDE FEDERAL S&L ASSOCIATION, Los Angeles—
11/30/89

CHARTER SAVINGS BANK, Newport Beach—06/15/90

FIRST NETWORK FEDERAL SAVINGS BANK, Los Angeles —04/20/90

FOUNDERS FEDERAL S&L ASSOCIATION, Los Angeles— 04/06/89

IMPERIAL FEDERAL SAVINGS ASSOCIATION, San Diego —02/23/90

INVESTMENT FEDERAL S&L ASSOCIATION, Woodland Hills—01/11/90

LINCOLN S&L ASSOCIATION, FA, Irvine—04/14/89

MERCURY FEDERAL S&L ASSOCIATION, Huntington Beach—02/23/90

PACIFIC COAST FSA OF AMERICA, San Francisco— 03/16/90

SANTA BARBARA FEDERAL S&L ASSOCIATION, Santa Barbara—04/27/90

SOUTHWEST FEDERAL SAVINGS ASSOCIATION, Los Angeles—04/27/89

TIME FEDERAL S&L ASSOCIATION, San Francisco— 06/01/90

WESTERN EMPIRE FEDERAL S&L ASSOCIATION, Yorba Linda—02/16/90

WESTWOOD S&L ASSOCIATION, Los Angeles—02/17/89

Colorado

CAPITOL FEDERAL S&L ASSOCIATION OF DENVER, Aurora—05/04/90

EQUITY FEDERAL SAVINGS BANK, Denver—04/06/89

FIRST AMERICA FEDERAL SAVINGS BANK, Longmont— 03/16/90

GREAT WEST, FSB, Craig—05/11/90

HERITAGE FEDERAL SAVINGS ASSOCIATION, Lamar— 04/20/90

Connecticut

CHARTER FEDERAL SAVINGS ASSOCIATION, Stamford— 06/29/90

COMMUNITY FEDERAL SAVINGS ASSOCIATION, Bridgeport—12/07/89

FINANCIAL OF HARTFORD, FSB, Hartford—08/17/90

Florida

AMERICAN PIONEER FEDERAL SAVINGS BANK, Orlando —05/25/90

CITIZENS & BUILDERS FEDERAL SAVINGS, FSB, Pensacola—07/27/90

COMMONWEALTH FEDERAL S&L ASSOCIATION, Fort Lauderdale—07/20/89

COMMUNITY FEDERAL S&L ASSOCIATION, Tampa— 03/16/89

DUVAL FEDERAL SAVINGS ASSOCIATION, Jacksonville— 01/18/90

ENTERPRISE FEDERAL, FSA, Clearwater—04/20/90

GENERAL FEDERAL SAVINGS BANK, Miami—11/16/89

GREAT LIFE FEDERAL SAVINGS ASSOCIATION, Sunrise— 06/01/90

HAVEN S&L ASSOCIATION, FA, Winter Haven—03/02/90

INVESTORS FEDERAL SAVINGS BANK, Deerfield Beach— 06/01/90

PIONEER FEDERAL SAVINGS BANK, Clearwater— 02/02/90

PROFESSIONAL FEDERAL SAVINGS BANK, Coral Gables— 07/27/90

Georgia

MOULTRIE SAVINGS BANK, FSB, Moultrie—06/15/90

Illinois

AMERICAN SA OF MT CARMEL, FA, Mt. Carmel— 08/10/90

ARLINGTON HEIGHTS SAVINGS ASSN, FA, Arlington Heights—12/07/89

BANK USA SAVINGS ASSOCIATION, Silvis—05/25/90

CHILLICOTHE FEDERAL S&L ASSOCIATION, Chillicothe —03/16/89

CLYDE FEDERAL SAVINGS ASSOCIATION, North
Riverside—02/02/90

COMMUNITY FEDERAL SAVINGS BANK, East Moline—
02/23/90

CREST FEDERAL S&L ASSOCIATION, Kankakee—
11/09/89

FIDELITY FEDERAL SAVINGS ASSOCIATION, Galesburg—
11/09/89

FIDELITY SAVINGS BANK, FSB, Danville—02/16/90

FIRST FEDERAL SAVINGS ASSOCIATION OF TUSCOLA,
Tuscola—08/17/90

FRONTIER FEDERAL SAVINGS BANK, Belleville—
01/18/90

GEM CITY FEDERAL S&L ASSOCIATION, Quincy—
01/18/90

GERMANIABANK, FSB, Alton—06/22/90

GREAT AMERICAN S&L ASSOCIATION, FA, Oak Park—
02/16/90

HERITAGE SAVINGS ASSN, FA, Jerseyville—08/24/89

HOME SAVINGS, FS&LA, Joliet—03/16/89

HOMETOWN FEDERAL SAVINGS ASSOCIATION,
Winfield—08/03/90

HORIZON SAVINGS BANK, FSB, Wilmette—01/11/90

MIDWEST HOME FSB, Belleville—03/16/89

NEW ATHENS FEDERAL S&L ASSOCIATION, New Athens
—03/02/90

ST. CHARLES FEDERAL SAVINGS ASSOCIATION, St.
Charles—01/11/90

SUMMIT FIRST S&L ASSOCIATION, FA, Summit—
07/31/90

Indiana

FIRST FEDERAL S&L ASSOCIATION OF CENTRAL
INDIANA, Anderson—11/16/89

HOMETOWN SAVINGS BANK, FSB, Delphi—06/08/90

Iowa

AMERICAN FEDERAL SAVINGS ASSOCIATION OF IOWA
—02/09/90

FIRST CENTRAL FEDERAL SAVINGS BANK, Chariton—
01/04/90

STATESMAN FEDERAL SAVINGS BANK, Waterloo—
07/27/90

Kansas

FIRST FSB OF KANSAS, Wellington—03/02/89

FRANKLIN SA, Ottawa—02/16/90

MID KANSAS S&L ASSOCIATION FA, Wichita—10/19/89

THE HIAWATHA FEDERAL SAVINGS ASSOCIATION,
Hiawatha—03/09/90

VALLEY SAVINGS, FS&LA, Hutchinson—03/02/89

Kentucky

HENDERSON HOME S&L ASSOCIATION, FA, Henderson
—02/02/90

Louisiana

CAPITAL-UNION FEDERAL SAVINGS ASSOCIATION,
Baton Rouge—07/13/90

CITIZENS HOMESTEAD FEDERAL SAVINGS
ASSOCIATION, New Orleans—08/07/89

COLUMBIA FEDERAL HOMESTEAD, Metairie—10/13/89

COMMERCIAL S&L ASSOCIATION, FA, Hammond—
07/27/89

COMMONWEALTH FEDERAL SAVINGS ASSOCIATION,
New Orleans—07/20/90

DELTA S&L ASSOCIATION, FA, Kenner—08/07/89

DEPOSIT TRUST FEDERAL SAVINGS BANK, Nomroe—
01/11/90

FIRST FEDERAL S&L ASSOCIATION, Baton Rouge—
03/16/89

FIRST FEDERAL S&L ASSOCIATION, New Iberia—
03/16/89

FIRST FEDERAL S&L ASSOCIATION, Shreveport—
03/16/89
FIRST FEDERAL SAVINGS ASSOCIATION OF BREAUX
BRIDGE, Breaux Bridge—05/11/90
FIRST LOUISIANA FEDERAL SAVINGS BANK, FA,
Lafayette—11/02/89
FIRST SB OF NEW ORLEANS, FSB, Metairie—06/15/90
FRENCH MARKET HOMESTEAD FEDERAL SAVINGS
ASSOCIATION, Metairie—02/17/89
JENNINGS FEDERAL SAVINGS ASSOCIATION, Jennings—
05/18/90
JONESBORO FEDERAL SAVINGS ASSOCIATION,
Jonesboro—05/18/90
LOUISIANA SA, Lake Charles—12/14/89
PARISH FEDERAL S&L ASSOCIATION, Denham Springs—
07/20/89
PEOPLE'S HOMESTEAD SAVINGS BANK, FSB, Monroe—
10/19/89
PROGRESSIVE SAVINGS BANK, FSB, Natchitoches—
07/13/90
RED RIVER S&L ASSOCIATION, Coushatta—12/14/89
SECURITY HOMESTEAD FEDERAL SAVINGS
ASSOCIATION, New Orleans—08/07/89
SOUTH S&L ASSOCIATION, FA, Slidell—08/07/89
TERREBONNE S&L ASSOCIATION, FA, Houma—08/07/89
UNITED FEDERAL SAVINGS, FA, New Orleans—03/16/90

Maine
AMERICAN FEDERAL SAVINGS BANK, Sanford—
01/11/90
FAIRMONT FEDERAL SAVINGS ASSOCIATION, Fairmont
—02/09/90
LAKELAND SAVINGS BANK, FSB, Detroit Lakes—
03/16/90
MIDWEST SAVINGS ASSOCIATION, FA, Minneapolis—
02/13/89

Maryland

FIRST FSB OF ANNAPOLIS, Annapolis—06/01/90
LIBERTY SAVINGS BANK, FSB, Randallstown—02/09/90
VERMONT SAVINGS ASSOCIATION, FA, Timonium—02/09/90
YORKRIDGE-CALVERT FEDERAL SAVINGS ASSOCIATION, Pikesville—12/14/89

Massachusetts

HOME FSB OF WORCESTER, Worcester—06/08/90
HOME OWNERS SAVINGS BANK FSB, Boston—04/27/90

Mississippi

BROOKHAVEN FEDERAL S&L ASSOCIATION, Brookhaven—01/18/89
CENTRAL S&L ASSOCIATION, Jackson—04/06/89
CHARTER SAVINGS BANK, FSB, Hattiesburg—07/20/90
FIRST JACKSON FSB, Jackson—06/29/90
FIRST GUARANTY FEDERAL S&L ASSOCIATION, Hattiesburg—01/04/90
GREAT AMERICAN S&L ASSOCIATION, FA, Corinth—03/16/90
GREENWOOD FEDERAL S&L ASSOCIATION, Greenwood—02/23/90
MISSISSIPPI SAVINGS BANK, FSB, Batesville—05/08/90
SOUTHEASTERN FEDERAL SAVINGS BANK, Laurel—04/20/90
SOUTHERN FEDERAL SAVINGS BANK, Gulfport—06/22/90

Missouri

COLONIAL S&L ASSOCIATION, FA, Cape Girardeau—01/26/90
MISSOURI SAVINGS ASSOCIATION, FA, Clayton—06/29/89

Nebraska
EQUITABLE FEDERAL SAVINGS BANK, Fremont—
02/17/89
HERITAGE FSB OF OMAHA, Omaha—02/16/90

New Jersey
CITY SAVINGS BANK, FSB, Bedminister—12/08/89
COLONIAL FEDERAL SAVINGS ASSOCIATION, Roselle
Park—11/09/89
FIRST ATLANTIC FEDERAL S&L ASSOCIATION, Plainfield
—02/23/90
MAINSTAY FEDERAL SAVINGS, FSB, Red Bank—07/20/90
METROPOLITAN FEDERAL S&L ASSOCIATION, Denville
—04/27/89
MUTUAL AIDE S&L, Manasquan—05/04/90
NASSAU FEDERAL S&L ASSOCIATION, Princeton—
03/09/90
NORTH JERSEY S&L ASSOCIATION, Passaic—02/17/89
UNITED S&L ASSOCIATION OF TRENTON, NJ, FA,
Trenton—06/15/90
YORKWOOD FEDERAL S&L ASSOCIATION, Maplewood—
03/09/90

New Mexico
ABQ FEDERAL SAVINGS BANK, Albuquerque—02/09/90
SANDIA FEDERAL SAVINGS ASSOCIATION, Albuquerque
—02/10/89
SECURITY FEDERAL SAVINGS BANK, Carlsbad—05/04/90
SILVER SAVINGS ASSOCIATION, FA, Silver City—
12/21/89

New York
EMPIRE OF AMERICA, FSB, Buffalo—01/24/90
NASSAU S&L ASSOCIATION, Brooklyn—03/16/90
WHITESTONE FEDERAL S&L ASSOCIATION, Whitestone
—03/16/90

North Carolina

GUARANTY SAVINGS BANK, FSB, Fayetteville—07/27/90
HERITAGE FEDERAL S&L ASSOCIATION, Monroe—
03/30/89
NORTH CAROLINA S&L ASSOCIATION, FA, Charlotte,
NC—03/02/90

North Dakota

FIRST SAVINGS ASSOCIATION, FA, Bismarck—01/26/90
MIDWEST FEDERAL SAVINGS BANK OF MINOT, Minot
—01/04/90

Ohio

CIVIC SAVINGS BANK, Portsmouth—06/08/89
FIRST SAVINGS & LOAN COMPANY, FA, Massillon—
04/20/90
FREEDOM SAVINGS ASSOCIATION, FA, Columbus—
02/16/90
MIDLAND-BUCKEYE SAVINGS, FS&LA, Alliance—
03/30/89
PIONEER FEDERAL S&L ASSOCIATION, Marietta—
06/29/90

Oklahoma

AMERICAN HOME S&L ASSOCIATION, FA, Edmond—
10/05/89
CONTINENTAL FEDERAL S&L ASSOCIATION, FA,
Oklahoma City—03/16/89
FIRST FEDERAL S&L ASSOCIATION OF SEMINOLE,
Seminole—03/16/89
PEOPLE'S FEDERAL SAVINGS ASSOCIATION, Bartesville—
03/09/90
SOONER FEDERAL SAVINGS ASSOCIATION, Tulsa—
11/16/89
STATE FEDERAL SAVINGS ASSOCIATION, Tulsa—
02/16/90

Oegon
THE BENJAMIN FRANKLIN FEDERAL S&L
ASSOCIATION, Portland—02/21/90

Pennsylvania
ATLANTIC FINANCIAL SAVINGS, FA, Bala Cynwyd—
01/11/90
COLONY FEDERAL SAVINGS BANK, Monaca—04/05/90
HERITAGE FEDERAL SAVINGS ASSOCIATION, Lancaster
—07/06/90
VANGUARD SAVINGS BANK, FSB, Vandergrift—02/23/90

Puerto Rico
CAGUAS–CENTRAL FEDERAL SAVINGS BANK OF PR,
Caguas—05/25/90

South Carolina
SECURITY FEDERAL SAVINGS, FSB, Columbia—11/30/89

Tennessee
INVESTOR SAVINGS BANK, FSB, Nashville—03/09/90
TENNESSEE FSB, Cookeville—08/03/90

Texas
ALAMO FEDERAL SAVINGS ASSOCIATION OF TEXAS,
San Antonio—03/02/89
AMERICAN S&L ASSOCIATION OF BRAZORIA, Lake
Jackson—03/09/89
AMIGO FEDERAL S&L ASSOCIATION, Brownsville—
08/03/90
AUSTIN FS&L ASSOCIATION, Austin—11/30/89
BANCPLUS SAVINGS ASSOCIATION, Pasadena—03/09/89
BANNERBANC FEDERAL S&L ASSOCIATION, Garland—
01/04/90
BAYSHORE SAVINGS ASSOCIATION, La Porte—03/09/89
BENJAMIN FRANKLIN FEDERAL SAVINGS
ASSOCIATION, Houston—03/09/89

CAPITOL CITY, FEDERAL SAVINGS ASSOCIATION, Austin—07/27/89

CAPROCK FEDERAL S&L ASSOCIATION, Lubbock—08/01/89

CENTRAL TEXAS S&L ASSOCIATION, Waco—04/06/89

CERTIFIED FEDERAL SAVINGS ASSOCIATION, Georgetown—01/11/90

CITY SAVINGS ASSOCIATION, League City—03/09/89

COLUMBIA FEDERAL S&L ASSOCIATION, Webster—12/21/89

COMMERCE SAVINGS ASSOCIATION, San Antonio—03/02/89

COMMONWEALTH FEDERAL SAVINGS ASSN, Houston—03/09/89

CONTINENTAL SAVINGS, FS&LA, Bellaire—03/09/89

DEEP EAST TEXAS SAVINGS ASSN, Jasper—03/16/89

EXCEL BANC SAVINGS ASSOCIATION, Laredo—04/06/89

FIDELITY FEDERAL SAVINGS ASSOCIATION, Port Arthur —03/16/89

FIRST BANKERS TRUST & SA, FA, Midland—06/08/90

FIRST FEDERAL SAVINGS ASSOCIATION OF CONROE, Conroe—05/18/90

FIRST FEDERAL SAVINGS ASSN, Borger—05/18/90

FIRST FEDERAL SAVINGS, FSA, New Braunfels—05/25/90

FIRST FEDERAL S&L ASSOC. OF WICHITA FALLS, Wichita Falls—03/16/90

FIRST SAVINGS ASSOCIATION OF SOUTHEAST TEXAS, Silsbee—03/16/89

FIRST SOUTH SAVINGS ASSOCIATION, Port Neches—03/16/89

FORTUNE FINANCIAL FEDERAL S&L ASSOCIATION, Copperas Cove—11/30/89

GOLDEN CIRCLE SA, FSB, Corsicana—04/06/89

GOLDEN TRIANGLE S&L ASSOCIATION, Bridge City—03/16/89

JASPER FEDERAL S&L ASSOCIATION, Jasper—03/16/89

JEFFERSON S&L ASSOCIATION, Beaumont—03/16/89

KARNES COUNTY FEDERAL S&L ASSOCIATION, Karnes City—01/18/90

LIBERTY COUNTY FEDERAL S&L ASSOCIATION, Liberty —03/09/89

MERITABANC SAVINGS ASSOCIATION, Houston— 03/16/89

MUTUAL S&L ASSOCIATION, FA, Weatherford—06/01/90

NORTH TEXAS FEDERAL SAVINGS ASSOCIATION, Wichita Falls—07/13/90

NOWLIN FEDERAL SAVINGS ASSOCIATION, North Richland—02/23/90

PADRE FEDERAL SAVINGS & LOAN, Corpus Christi— 03/02/89

PALO DURO FEDERAL S&L ASSOCIATION, Amarillo— 01/26/90

REMINGTON FEDERAL SAVINGS ASSOCIATION, Eglin— 05/25/90

RESOURCE SAVINGS ASSOCIATION, Denison—04/06/89

SABINE VALLEY S&L ASSOCIATION, Center—03/16/89

SAVINGS OF TEXAS, Jacksonville—03/16/89

SECURITY FEDERAL SAVINGS ASSOCIATION, Texarkana —03/16/89

SOUTHEAST TEXAS S&L ASSOCIATION, Woodville— 03/16/89

SOUTHEASTERN SAVINGS ASSOCIATION, Dayton— 03/09/89

SOUTHMOST S&L ASSOCIATION, Brownsville—03/02/89

SOUTHWEST SA, Dallas—05/18/90

SOUTHWESTERN FEDERAL SAVINGS ASSOCIATION, El Paso—11/30/89

SPRING BRANCH S&L ASSOCIATION, Houston— 03/09/89

STANDARD FEDERAL SAVINGS ASSOCIATION, Houston —01/18/90

SUBURBAN SAVINGS ASSOCIATION, San Antonio—
03/02/89
SUPERIOR SAVINGS BANK, FSB, Nacogdoches—08/10/90
SURETY FEDERAL SAVINGS ASSOCIATION, El Paso—
10/19/89
TEXAS FEDERAL SAVINGS ASSOCIATION, San Antonio—
04/20/90
TEXASBANC FSB, Conroe—02/23/90
THE FEDERAL SAVINGS BANC, FA, Arlington—05/11/90
TIMBERLAND SAVINGS ASSOCIATION, Nacodoches—
03/16/89
TRAVIS FEDERAL S&L ASSOCIATION, San Antonio—
06/29/90
UVALDE FEDERAL S&L ASSOCIATION, Uvalde—
01/26/90
VICTORIA SAVINGS ASSOCIATION, FSA, San Antonio—
06/29/89
VISION BANC SAVINGS ASSOCIATION, Kingsville—
03/02/89
WESTERN GULF S&L ASSOCIATION, Bay City—03/09/89
WINDSOR FEDERAL SAVINGS ASSOCIATION, Austin—
06/29/90

Utah
HOME SAVINGS BANK FSB, Salt Lake City—07/05/90
WILLIAMSBURG FEDERAL S&L ASSOCIATION, Salt Lake
City—01/26/90

Virginia
ATLANTIC PERMANENT FEDERAL SB, Norfolk—
12/08/89
SEASONS FEDERAL SAVINGS BANK, Richmond—
10/19/89
SECURITY FEDERAL SAVINGS ASSOCIATION, Richmond
—03/02/90
UNITED FEDERAL SAVINGS BANK, Vienna—07/31/90

West Virginia
FIRST FEDERAL SAVINGS ASSOCIATION OF BLUEFIELD,
Bluefield—02/23/90
FIRST STANDARD FEDERAL SAVINGS ASSOCIATION,
Fairmont—02/23/90

RESOURCES

These books, articles, and organizations will be of use if you are interested in learning more about the S&L scandal.

BOOKS

Stephen Pizzo, Mary Fricker and Paul Muolo, *Inside Job: The Looting of America's Savings and Loans* (McGraw Hill, 1989). The authors, reporters who have covered the crisis for years, trace a network of organized-crime linked swindlers who hopped from one S&L to another during the 1980s

James Ring Adams, *The Big Fix* (John Wiley and Sons, 1990). Adams, a *Wall Street Journal* reporter, covers the bank and thrift collapses of the 1980s, with an emphasis on the role of political corruption.

Brooks Jackson, *Honest Graft* (updated edition, Farragut Publishing Co., 1990). Jackson, now with the Cable News Network, is the reporter who uncovered many of the money and politics scandals of the 1980s. This book is largely drawn from the time Jackson was allowed to sit in on Tony Coelho's fund-raising operation at the Democratic Congressional Campaign Committee.

Phillip M. Stern, *The Best Congress Money Can Buy* (Pantheon, 1988). This book is the most complete account of how the well-funded special-interests purchase influence in Washington.

William Greider, *Secrets of the Temple* (William Morrow,

1988). Greider—the reporter whose interviews with David Stockman caused a furor when they were published in the *Atlantic Monthly*—explains the mysterious workings of the Federal Reserve Board and describes how high interest rates redistribute income to the rich.

MAGAZINE AND NEWSPAPER ARTICLES AND STUDIES

These are some of the best survey articles on the S&L mess. They should be understandable to the lay reader.

Alan Pusey and Lee Hancock, *Dallas Morning News* (series beginning December 4, 1988).

David Maraniss and Rick Atkinson, series beginning June 11, 1989, *Washington Post.*

James O'Shea, in the *Chicago Tribune* (series beginning September 25, 1989).

Ronnie Dugger, "Blitzing the American Dream," *Texas Observer* (December 15, 1989).

"Meltdown on Main Street" (special edition) *Southern Exposure* (December 1989).

Byron Harris, "The Party's Over," *Texas Monthly* (June 1987).

Thomas Moore, "The Bust of '89," *U.S. News and World Report* (January 23, 1989).

Larry Martz, "Bonfire of the S&Ls," and Steven Waldman and Rich Thomas, "How Did It Happen?" *Newsweek* (May 21, 1990).

Kathleen Day, "S&L Hell," *New Republic* (March 20, 1989).

Curtis Lang, "Licensed to Steal," *Village Voice* (July 10, 1990).

Rowland Evans and Robert Novak, "Who's to Blame for the Great S&L Scandal?" *Reader's Digest* (April 1990).

L. J. Davis, "Chronicle of a Debacle Foretold," *Harper's* (September 1990).

The following reports and journals are more technical, but are useful introductions for those interested in learning more about the subject.

Ralph Nader and Jonathan Brown, "Report to U.S. Taxpayers on the Savings and Loan Crisis" (*Bank Watch*, February 1989). Available from Bank Watch, P.O. Box 19367, Washington, D.C. 20036.

Stanford Law and Policy Review, "Savings and Loan Crisis: Lessons and a Look Ahead," S&L symposium, Spring 1990. This law journal features articles by a wide range of commentators, ranging from Representative Charles Schumer to Charles Keating (available from: Stanford Law & Policy Review, Stanford Law School, Stanford CA 94305-8610).

ORGANIZATIONS

In addition to Public Citizen's Congress Watch, other citizen groups are working to bring various aspects of the S&L scandal to light. Some of them include:

Financial Democracy Campaign. This coalition of 200 labor, community, low-income, and religious groups is actively working to make the bailout fairer. At the same address, the Institute for Southern Studies publishes *Southern Exposure* magazine, which regularly covers the RTC; and the Southern Finance Project conducts research on banking issues. 604 W. Chapel Hill St., Durham NC 27702 (919) 687-4004.

United States Public Interest Research Group (U.S. PIRG). This federation of public-interest research groups from twenty-six states works for greater consumer involvement in financial regulation. 215 Pennsylvania Ave. SE, Washington, D.C. 20003. (202) 546-9707.

ACORN. A national coalition of low-income and neighborhood groups, ACORN has been a leader in the effort to make banks and S&Ls more responsive to the concerns of the poor. 522 8th Street SE, 2d fl., Washington, D.C. 20003. (202) 547-9292.

Bank Watch. This research organization, founded by Ralph Nader, is digging deep into various aspects of the bailout, especially the subsidies and giveaways to acquirers of failed S&Ls. P.O. Box 19367, Washington, D.C. 20036. (202) 387-8034.

Consumers Union, 2001 S Street NW, Suite 520, Washington, D.C. 20009, and **Consumer Federation of America,** 1424 16th Street NW, Washington, D.C. 20036, are national organizations representing consumers in the marketplace and in Washington.

Common Cause. The good-government group is a leader in the fight for campaign finance reform. 2030 M Street NW, Washington, D.C. 20036.

Center for Responsive Politics. The Center is a research organization that studies the role of money in Congress. 1320 19th Street NW, Washington, D.C. 20036. (202) 857-0044.

Campaign Research Center. This new research organization conducts studies for journalists and citizen groups on special interest money in campaigns. 1010 Vermont Ave. NW, Suite 710, Washington, D.C. 20005. (202) 347-5400.

ACKNOWLEDGMENTS

Who Robbed America? was pulled together with necessary urgency, through the collaborative effort of many dedicated colleagues.

Staff members of Public Citizen's Congress Watch collaborated in the preparation of this book. *Sherry Ettleson*, Congress Watch's chief staff attorney working on banking issues, developed many of the policies embodied in this work, and closely monitors the (weak) pulse of the bailout. *Thomas Hilliard*, a staff researcher, energetically tracked down documents and information, and wrote first drafts of some sections. *Karen Hobert*, a field organizer who is a highly knowledgeable student of campaign finance issues, organized the charts at the back of the book. *Pamela Gilbert*, Congress Watch's legislative director, is the leader of efforts to preserve the white-collar crime laws against S&L crooks; her expertise, as well as friendship, was invaluable. Other Congress Watch staff members, including David Eppler, Nancy Watzman, Victor Lewton, Cindy Campbell, Bill Parsons, Betsy Broughton, and Rob Kaplan were helpful in different ways. Other Public Citizen and colleague organization staff, including David Vladeck and Seyoum Haregot, assisted in the preparation of this work.

This book was prepared under the wings of two leading citizen activists. Joan Claybrook, the president of Public Citizen, and the first director of Congress Watch, encouraged this project and provided useful editorial and policy suggestions. And Ralph Nader, who founded Public Citizen, serves as a constant source of inspiration—and goading—for younger col-

ACKNOWLEDGMENTS

leagues too easily worn down by Washington politics-as-usual. Their faith in democracy drove this project to completion.

Many colleagues and friends provided invaluable help. Jonathan Cuneo, who is general counsel of NASCAT, an organization of attorneys including those who represent the Lincoln S&L bondholders, was generous with his time and insight. Bart Naylor, former chief investigator for the Senate Banking Committee, provided valuable historical perspective. The Southern Finance Project, especially Tom Schlesinger and Marty Leary, was generous with its research material and product. The Campaign Research Center, founded by Phil Stern, calculated the campaign contributions from financial industry PACs. Steven Waldman, Roland Lewis and John Siegal made useful editorial suggestions. Mark Green, though busy as New York City's Commissioner of Consumer Affairs, had time to offer encouragement and advice.

At Random House, we were fortunate to find David Rosenthal, an editor who understood the need for a usable citizen's guide. His skill and enthusiasm, and that of Jennifer Ash, Linda Kaye and Mitchell Ivers, allowed this project to move rapidly from brainstorm to bookstore. Richard Emery, our agent, is an impassioned peoples' attorney in his own right, and was very helpful in his representation and his encouragement.

The book's most tireless editor, reader, supporter, and critic was my wife, Liz Fine. (I won't apologize, as too many authors do, for "missed dinners." I *never* miss a dinner.) I thought I knew all her wonderful qualities, but I was wrong: she is also an extremely talented editor. I am eternally grateful.

Michael Waldman
Washington, D.C.
September 1990

ABOUT THE AUTHOR

MICHAEL WALDMAN is the director of Public Citizen's Congress Watch, the legislative advocacy arm of the consumer group founded by Ralph Nader. An attorney, Waldman is the coauthor of *Who Runs Congress?* (fourth edition, Dell, 1984) and coeditor of *The Big Business Reader* (second edition, Pilgrim Press, 1983), both with Mark Green. He writes widely on business and government for publications including *The New York Times, USA Today, Newsday, The Boston Globe, The New Republic, The Nation* and *The Washington Monthly.* A graduate of Columbia College and New York University School of Law, he lives with his wife, Elizabeth Fine, in Washington, D.C.

PUBLIC CITIZEN

Who We Are and What We Do

Public Citizen, known to many as "Nader's Raiders," is a non-profit organization based in Washington, D.C., with 95,000 members nationwide. Public Citizen represents citizens' interests through lobbying, litigation, research, and publications. Since its founding by Ralph Nader in 1971, Public Citizen has fought for consumer rights and for corporate and govemment accountability.

Public Citizen is active in the Congress, the courts, government agencies, and the media. In addition to our work on white collar crime and the savings and loan scandal, Public Citizen fights for campaign finance reform, congressional ethics, and limits on congressional pay raises. To prevent injuries and illness, we push for installation of air bags and other safety devices in cars, and we helped pass legislation protecting consumers against toxic wastes and pesticides. We also publish directories on unsafe or ineffective drugs, questionable doctors, and ratings of state health programs. Our attorneys have won sixteen victories in the U.S. Supreme Court since 1975.

Public Citizen does not accept government or corporate grants. Support funding comes generously from individual contributions and from the sale of publications.

Public Citizen has five components:

Congress Watch monitors legislation on Capitol Hill, documents, campaign financing abuses, tracks House and Senate voting records, and lobbies for the public interest.

Health Research Group fights for protection against unsafe foods, drugs, and workplaces, and for greater consumer control over personal health decisions.

Litigation Group brings precedent-setting lawsuits on behalf of citizens against the government, large corporations, and labor unions to enforce rights and ensure justice under the law.

Critical Mass Energy Project works for safe, efficient, and affordable energy.

Buyers Up is a group-buying organization that enables individuals to become more knowledgeable consumers and to exercise their economic leverage in the marketplace.

JOINING PUBLIC CITIZEN

We encourage you to become a member of Public Citizen and to support our work. With your annual membership contribution of \$20 or more, you will receive *Public Citizen* magazine. This bimonthly publication will keep you posted on Public Citizen's many projects and other important issues affecting you and your famliy. With your membership contribution of \$35 or more, you will also receive an annual subscription to our monthly *Health Letter*. This informative monthly guide will show you how to lead a healthier and happier life.

Send your check or money order to:

Public Citizen Membership
2000 P Street N.W. - Suite 605
Washington, D.C. 20036

PUBLIC CITIZEN BOOKS FOR YOU AND YOUR FAMILY

Worst Pills, Best Plls This best-seller, which has sold almost one million copies in the past two years, exposes prescription drugs that are dangerous and sometimes deadly for older adults. This important reference book highlights 104 pills you should not use and 183 safer alternatives. Authored by Public Citizen physician Dr. Sidney M. Wolfe and the Public Citizen Health Research Group (1989, 532 pages). Price \$12.00, including postage.

Representing Yourself Do you need to spend hundreds, and maybe even thousands of dollars on an attorney? Or can you handle a routine legal matter yourself? This informative publication tells you how to solve routine legal problems without a lawyer, how to decide if you do need a lawyer, and make sure you are adequately represented. Chapters on buying and selling a house, defective products, marriage and divorce, employee rights, and many others. Authored by Kenneth Lasson and the Public Citizen Litigation Group staff (reprinted 1987, 270 pages). Price: \$12.95.

Send your check or money order for these books to:

Public Citizen Books
2000 P Street N.W. - Suite 605
Washington, D.C. 20036